Lionel Robbins on the Principles of Economic Analysis

Lionel Robbins (1898–1984) is best known to economists for his *Essay on the Nature and Significance of Economic Science* (1932 and 1935). To the wider public he is known for the 'Robbins Report' of the 1960s on Higher Education, which recommended a major expansion of university education in Britain. However, throughout his academic career – at Oxford and the London School of Economics in the 1920s, and as Professor of Economics at the School from 1929 to 1961 – he was renowned as an exceptionally gifted teacher. Generations of students remember his lectures for their clarity and comprehensiveness and for his infectious enthusiasm for his subject.

Besides his famous graduate seminar his most important and influential courses at the School were the Principles of Economic Analysis, which he gave in the 1930s and again in the late 1940s and 1950s, as well as the History of Economic Thought, from 1953 until long after his official retirement. This book publishes for the first time the manuscript notes Robbins used for his lectures on the Principles of Economic Analysis from 1929/30 to 1939/40. At the outset of his career he took the advice of a senior colleague to prepare his lectures by writing them out fully before he presented them; the full notes for most of his pre-war lectures survive and are eminently decipherable.

Since he made two major revisions of the lectures in the 1930s the Principles notes show both the development of his own thought and the way he incorporated the major theoretical innovations made by younger economists at LSE, such as John Hicks and Nicholas Kaldor, or elsewhere, notably Joan Robinson. He intended to turn his lecture notes into a book, abandoning the project only when he was asked to chair the Committee on Higher Education in 1960. This volume is not exactly the book he wanted to write, but it is a unique record of what was taught to senior undergraduate and graduate economists in those 'years of high theory.' It will be of interest to all economists interested in the development of economics in the twentieth century.

Susan Howson is Emeritus Professor of Economics at the University of Toronto and a Fellow of Trinity College Toronto, Canada. She is the author of the distinguished biography, *Lionel Robbins*, published in 2011. Having written many articles on the history of economic policy in Britain, on the life and work of Lionel Robbins and on James Meade, she is now working on a biography of James Meade.

Routledge Studies in the History of Economics

Lionel Robbins on the Principles of Economic Analysis

The 1930s Lectures

Authored by Lionel Robbins

Edited by Susan Howson

LONDON AND NEW YORK

First published 2018 by Routledge

2 Park Square, Milton Park, Abingdon, Oxfordshire OX14 4RN
52 Vanderbilt Avenue, New York, NY 10017

Routledge is an imprint of the Taylor & Francis Group, an informa business

First issued in paperback 2020

British Library Cataloguing-in-Publication Data
A catalogue record for this book is available from the British Library

Library of Congress Cataloging-in-Publication Data
A catalog record for this book has been requested

ISBN: 978-1-138-65419-8 (hbk)
ISBN: 978-0-367-66713-9 (pbk)

Typeset in Times New Roman
by Apex CoVantage, LLC

For Anne and Christopher

Contents

Comparative statics   303

Dynamics   325

Editor's introduction

Lionel Robbins (1898–1984) was Professor of Economics at the London School of Economics (LSE) from 1929 to 1961. He had been an undergraduate at the School in 1920–3, after seeing active service as an artillery officer on the Western Front in 1917–18 (and working for the labour movement in 1919–20). After graduating with first class honours in the BSc(Econ) (Bachelor of Science in Economics) degree he worked for six months as research assistant to the Director of LSE, William Beveridge, on the revision of Beveridge's *Unemployment* (1931) and for a year as a temporary lecturer at New College Oxford before being appointed an assistant lecturer at LSE in 1925 (and promoted to lecturer a year later); he returned to New College Oxford as Fellow and Lecturer in Economics in 1927, where he gave tutorials and lectured on economics to undergraduates reading for the new Philosophy, Politics and Economics degree. At Oxford he began to publish seriously in the academic journals but he had only a handful published, plus a short popular book on *Wages* (1926), when he was asked in April 1929 if he would consider leaving Oxford for a professorship at LSE.

Edwin Cannan, Professor of Political Economy at LSE from 1907, had retired in 1926; his successor was the American Allyn Abbot Young, who arrived in 1927 but died suddenly in the influenza epidemic of March 1929. Hugh Dalton, then Cassel Reader in Commerce at LSE, persuaded Beveridge that since Robbins was too young at age 30 to be offered Cannan's chair he might instead be offered a new junior chair of economics while the university continued to look for a senior professor. It was an offer Robbins could hardly refuse.

He was immediately faced with a heavy teaching load: his only colleague in economics was John Hicks, as Dalton was now on leave to serve as a junior minister in the second Labour government. Beveridge had no success in his attempts to appoint a successor to Cannan; he also failed to persuade the Cambridge economist Hubert Henderson to accept the revived Tooke Chair of Economic Science and Statistics. Robbins thus became and remained for the next thirty years the head of the Economics Department at the School; Cannan's chair was never filled and eventually abolished in 1961. During the Second World War Robbins served in the Economic Section of the Cabinet Offices (as director from 1941) from June 1940 to December 1945. He continued to teach at the School as a part-time lecturer after his official retirement in 1961.

In the first of those three decades Robbins's teaching load included Elements of Economics until 1935, General Principles of Economic Analysis and his famous graduate seminar every year, as well as numerous short courses mainly on economic policy or in the history of economic thought. The lecture course on Principles of Economic Analysis was the centrepiece of economics teaching at LSE, intended for undergraduates specializing in economics for the BSc(Econ). The idiosyncratic Cannan had offered it as a two-year course, one year on Production, the next on Value and Distribution. It was challenging, to say the least, for a second year student who arrived at the beginning of a Distribution year – as Robbins had in 1921: he overcame the challenge by borrowing the notes of a fellow student who had arrived a year earlier (Robbins 1971 page 84). Allyn Young gave the lectures in the conventional way as a single-year course. In the year (1926/27) between Cannan's retirement and Young's arrival Dalton had lectured on the Principles of Economics in the Michaelmas and Lent terms and Robbins had given a course in the Lent and Summer terms on Comparative Economic Theory which dealt 'historically and comparatively' with the same material. When Robbins took over the Principles course in 1929/30, he gave it only in the Lent and Summer terms of his first year; thereafter it was a full year course given twice a week (and again in the evenings for part-time students) in the Michaelmas and Lent terms and the first six weeks of the Summer term.

The syllabi and reading lists for Robbins's Principles course for every year from 1929/30 to 1939/40 survive in the published LSE *Calendars*. His manuscript lecture notes for the course also survive – as do those for most of his other courses at LSE and Oxford. He described in his autobiography how as a result of a chance meeting with Graham Wallas, the Professor of Political Science, at the beginning of his first year lecturing at LSE (1971 pp 104–5),

> I wrote out my lectures in full and spent much time conning them over. I hasten to say that, when they had to be delivered, I never read them. I used as a reminder only brief summaries inscribed in broad margins. But the process of marshalling my material and committing them more or less to memory gave me a confidence in free delivery which I should certainly not have had otherwise, and compelled me to pay attention to expositional form which I might easily have neglected.

He followed this practice for most of his teaching career, though when he had given a course several times and made revisions, the revised versions of the notes are much briefer. He wrote his notes in notebooks similar to those in which he had taken notes as a student.

Robbins had learned his economics from Hugh Dalton, Edwin Cannan and Theodore Gregory. In his first year at LSE he heard Dalton's and Gregory's introductory lectures; in his second and third years, although he had chosen to specialize in the history of political ideas under the socialist Harold Laski, he obtained Cannan's permission to attend his class in economic theory as well as his lectures and also attended many of Gregory's lectures by choice. Dalton was

Cambridge-trained and a Marshallian; he was also a superb lecturer with 'a splendid capacity for lucid exposition, with no undue fuss about inessentials and a strong perspective of salient relevant points' (Robbins quoted in Howson 2011 page 72). Cannan, who was a poor lecturer but whose interest in the history of economic thought Robbins inherited, was notoriously critical of Alfred Marshall's work.[1] Gregory, like Dalton a Cassel Reader, lectured on currency and banking and international trade; Robbins enjoyed his lectures and learned much from them. The teaching of Gregory, Dalton and Cannan is reflected in the content of Robbins's own early lecturing at LSE, when he gave the courses on the Elements of Currency and Banking and International Finance for first year undergraduate students in 1925/6 and 1926/7 and on Elements of Economics, also for first year students, in 1926/7, and in his Comparative Economic Theory course in 1926/7. At Oxford he utilized his Comparative Economic Theory notes for lectures on value, distribution, production and the history of economic thought. James Meade remembered the lectures (Meade quoted in Howson 2011 page 155):

> It was a memorable experience. The ebullient and exuberant purposefulness of his exposition was infectious. As an irreverent undergraduate I used to describe his performance as combining the qualities of a rowing coach with those of the conductor of a great orchestra . . . He was not interested in devising new elaborate theoretical constructions, but used his first-rate analytical mind to discover and teach us how the application of good economic theory . . . could make an important contribution to the formulation of wise and effective policy.

At Beveridge's request he also continued to give the Comparative Economic Theory course at LSE for a couple more years. The topics of his research at Oxford included Schumpeter and J.B. Clark on the stationary state, economies of scale, labour economics and population theory; his work led to several papers and articles (1927, 1928, 1929a, 1929b, 1930a) (Howson 2011 pp 154–9).

The Comparative Economic Theory lectures were the last time Robbins taught economic theory in the traditional format of production and value and distribution. In the summer of 1929, when he had at short notice to provide a description of the Principles course for the LSE *Calendar*, he submitted merely: 'The course will cover the ground which is sometimes indicated by the heading "Value and Distribution"'. The content of the course, however, corresponds to that indicated in the syllabus provided for the following year, 1930/31. The main topics covered were: the nature of economic analysis; exchange equilibrium; equilibrium of production first with factors given and then with factors flexible; and special topics in equilibrium analysis such as consumers' surplus, the law of diminishing returns, the theory of costs (where he was strongly critical of Marshallian partial equilibrium analysis), the theory of rent and the theory of profits.

---

1 For the substance of Cannan's lectures see *A Review of Economic Theory* (1929) which he prepared after his retirement.

xiv Editor's introduction

Nicholas Kaldor, as a final year undergraduate at LSE, heard the Principles lectures the first time that Robbins gave them. As he remembered (Kaldor 1986 pp 4–5),

> Lionel Robbins, young, flamboyant and enthusiastic . . . and extremely devoted both to teaching and to economics as a subject, . . . lavished his energies and vitality on his pupils . . . It was inevitable that those of us who were fortunate to have been among his first pupils . . . should fall completely under his spell. Robbins' economics (much influenced by his contacts with Viennese economists, mainly von Mises) was the general equilibrium theory of Walras and the Austrians, rather than of Marshall, and his lectures followed the method of presentation of Wicksell and of Knight, *Risk, Uncertainty and Profit* (a book which contains in its first half an admirably clear and concise account of neo-classical theory). Robbins as a young economist absorbed this theory – the keystone of which is the marginal productivity theory of distribution in its generalised form, as expounded by Wicksell and Wicksteed – with the fervency of a convert and propounded it with the zeal of a missionary.

Having learnt German as an undergraduate, Robbins had been able to read Wicksell's lectures on political economy in German. He had read Wicksteed's *The Common Sense of Political Economy* (1910) as an undergraduate and was deeply impressed:

> There are certain chapters in it from which I have learnt as much as from any other chapters in the whole of economic literature. I shall never forget the thrill with which as a student I first read the masterly chapter on the universal applicability of the rent analysis.
>
> (Robbins quoted in Howson 2011 page 98)

He had read Ludwig von Mises's *Die Gemeinwirtschaft* (1922) soon after he graduated; he worked on a translation of part of it in 1925/6, over which he corresponded with Mises in Vienna. He probably met Mises in London in 1927 or 1928 and certainly did so in 1931 (Howson 2011 pp 135, 147, 210; Hülsmann 2007 pp 479–83).[2]

Robbins's Principles lectures for these first two years were prepared as he was entering his most 'Austrian' phase, when he was discovering the new Austrian trade cycle theory. He read Hayek's work (1929a, 1929b) soon after it was published (Howson 2011 pp 176–8); he had not then met Hayek but he suggested to Beveridge that Hayek be invited to give the annual University Advanced Lectures in Economics for 1930/1, with the result that he first met Hayek at LSE when he came to give the lectures in January 1931. Hayek was subsequently offered

---

2 Robbins's translation was never published but it was used by Robbins's friend Jacques Kahane when he translated the second German edition (Mises 1936).

a visiting professorship for the academic year 1930/31 and, at the end of that appointment, the long vacant Tooke Chair, so that he became Robbins's closest colleague. Since Robbins made two major rewritings of his Principles lectures, in 1932 and 1934, the surviving lecture notes clearly show the waxing and waning of the Austrian influence.[3]

In those first two years Robbins was also writing his most important book, *An Essay on the Nature and Significance of Economic Science* (1932). He had already arrived at its most well-known contribution – the definition of economics as 'the science which studies human behaviour as a relationship between ends and scarce means which have alternative uses' (Robbins 1932 page 15) – when he was still in Oxford and he lectured on it in a short course entitled Unsettled Problems in Theoretical Economics in Hilary Term 1929 (Howson 2004). At LSE, he lectured on The Nature of Economics and its Significance in relation to the Kindred Social Sciences in the Summer term of 1930 and again in 1931 and 1932. The lectures on Exchange Equilibrium in the first part of the Principles course clearly reflect the standpoint of the book. The revisions he made in 1932 reflect the fact that the book was now published. The revisions of the lecture notes in and after 1934 are more extensive, as they increasingly incorporate the new ideas and insights of the most recent literature, especially that of his younger colleagues at LSE, such as John Hicks, Nicky Kaldor and Abba Lerner, but also of other young economists such as Joan Robinson at Cambridge.

The 1930s Principles lecture notes survive in three 8" x 9" loose-leaf note-books, the same type of notebook that Robbins used to take notes as a student. He labelled the three notebooks: 'Principles of Economics I Old Notes 1929–31'; 'Principles of Economics II (+ Transitional Notes 32–34)'; and 'Principles of Economics Notes 1939–40'. The first notebook contains lecture notes corresponding to the first three sections of the course syllabi for 1930/31 to 1934/35. The second notebook includes the notes for most of the special topics of the same years; the notes for two of the special topics, however, turn up in the third notebook as do those for two other subjects in the earlier sections. The topics of the notes in the third notebook generally match the course syllabi in the *Calendars* for 1935/36 to 1939/40. The notes on most topics are much briefer than those of earlier years: in 1935, before going to lecture at the Graduate Institute of International Studies in Geneva, Robbins told William Rappard that he would not read from his notes: 'I never prepare lectures that way nowadays. But I like to get the sort of skeleton which keeps me within certain limits' (quoted in Howson 2011 page 277). While the notes in the first and second notebooks (including the 'transitional notes') are filed in approximately the correct order, the third notebook is less well-ordered and contains more than one version of the 'skeletal' notes on some topics. Fortunately there also survive two sets of notes taken by students, one for each of the

---

3 Robbins's most Austrian work was his book, *The Great Depression* (1934), where he tried to explain both the initiating causes of the worldwide slump of 1929–30 and the reasons for its subsequent severity, using a monetary overinvestment theory for the former.

last two academic years of the decade, from which the order in which the lectures were given can be ascertained, as can the reason for the filing of the earlier notes on labour supply, rent and profits, namely, that Robbins was still using them to lecture on those subjects.

The student notes for 1938/39 were taken by Victor Urquidi, an undergraduate from Mexico, those for 1939/40 by Puey Ungphakorn, a graduate student from Thailand; both were in their second year at LSE when they attended Robbins's Principles lectures; both became distinguished economists and public servants. Victor Urquidi gave the editor a copy of his notes, which he had himself typed up at the time, on a Hermes Baby typewriter his mother had just given him. After graduating in 1940 he joined the economic studies department of the Banco de Mexico; he met Robbins again in July 1944 when they were both delegates to the UN Monetary and Financial Conference at Bretton Woods, New Hampshire.[4] He later worked for the World Bank in Washington and, in 1964, was a founder of the Centre for Economics and Demographic Studies at the Colegio de Mexico. Puey Ungphakorn also became a central banker and an academic but the Second World War interrupted his studies. In Cambridge, where LSE spent the war years, he had gained a first in the BSc (Econ) in 1941 and commenced doctoral studies at LSE on a Leverhulme Scholarship when Thailand declared itself an ally of Japan. Refusing repatriation he was one of a group of Thai students in Cambridge who created the Free Siamese movement and joined the British Army in August 1942. After training in India he was commissioned in October 1943, parachuted in northern Thailand in March 1944 and almost immediately captured, by Thai villagers, and imprisoned. In May 1945, now a major in the British Army, he was flown to England for two months to try to persuade the British government to recognize the Free Siamese as the legal government after the end of the war (Puey 1953). In December 1945 he returned to London to resume his studies and received his PhD (Robbins was his supervisor) in 1949. After four years in his country's Ministry of Finance, he was appointed Deputy Governor of the Bank of Thailand in 1953 and, after a spell as Economic and Financial Counsellor at the Royal Thai Embassy in London, Governor 1959-1971 (Ramon Magsaysay Award Foundation 1965). He became Dean of the Faculty of Economics at his alma mater, Thammasat University, and then Rector – resigning in protest against the massacre of student protesters on 6 October 1976 and going into exile in London. His notes of the Principles lectures that Robbins gave in 1939/40 survive because after Robbins left for wartime government service in June 1940 they were photographed and placed in the small library that LSE had in Grove Lodge in Cambridge. His handwritten notes are naturally less carefully written than Urquidi's. Robbins commented when he saw them after the war that 'The notes are excellent as notes go. But they are "written up" with interspersed references to the literature & I am not prepared to answer for the accuracy of the transcript'. They are, however, more extensive than Urquidi's and mention more references to the recommended reading. Both have been truly invaluable in preparing this edition.

---

4 Urquidi to Howson 11 October 1991, 15 May 1992 and 7 January 1993.

Many of Robbins's notes on the topics of the course ended with short reading lists, which I have included in this edition in preference to the lengthy reading lists Robbins produced for the LSE *Calendars*, many of whose items he made no mention of in his lecture notes. I have, however, used the *Calendar* lists to complete references and to help identify which edition of a work Robbins would have been recommending in the years the lectures were given. In the lists for the years 1931/2 to 1934/5 he placed double asterisks beside some items to indicate that they were 'indispensable to attainment of the minimum standard in the final examination': Marshall's *Principles of Economics*, A.C. Pigou's *Economics of Welfare*, Cannan's *Review of Economic Theory* and Wicksteed's *Common Sense of Political Economy* (in that order). From 1935/6 onwards he was more explicit:

> The ground covered by the course is roughly the same as that covered by Knight's *Risk, Uncertainty and Profit*. But to understand this work much preliminary reading is necessary and there are many matters on which its treatment needs supplementing. All students preparing for the final examination should read Marshall's *Principles of Economics*, Wicksell's *Lectures on Political Economy*, Vol. I, and Pigou's *Economics of Welfare*. The following works will also be found useful . . . Hicks, *The Theory of Wages*; Robinson, *The Economics of Imperfect Competition . . .* ; Mises, *The Theory of Money and Credit*; Robbins, *The Nature and Significance of Economic Science*; Schumpeter, *Epochen der Dogmen- und Methodengeschichte*.

In 1939/40 he mentioned only Knight, Marshall, Wicksell and Pigou before stating that the remainder of the list was 'in no sense a programme of obligatory reading. It is intended only to indicate books which may be found helpful in the study of branches of the subject presenting special difficulties'.

From 1935/36 on the course was divided into A. Introduction; B. Statics; C. Comparative Statics; D. Dynamics. B. included The Theory of Valuation and Exchange and The Theory of Production and Distribution, the latter divided into Acapitalistic Production and Capitalistic Production; C. 'Variations of demand and their effects on product and factor prices. Variations of factor supply: the conception of elasticity of demand and elasticity of substitution. Technical change. Accumulation and decumulation'; D. 'Foreseen and unforeseen change. The theory of risk and uncertainty. Profits. The short Period and the long. Quasi Rents. Money and Interest. Industrial Fluctuation'. But the surviving lecture notes for the second half of the decade do not include notes on the topics under D. except for those written earlier and used again, namely Profits and Quasi Rents.

Like all lecturers he often ran out of time at the end of a course and failed to complete his programme. In the Michaelmas term of 1935/36 he offered five additional lectures to the students who had taken the Principles course in 1934/35. In 1939/40 he explicitly told his students which subset of the Dynamics topics he would cover that year (see Final Editorial Note below). But the focus on general equilibrium theory also precluded serious consideration of monetary theory or trade cycle theory. At LSE, money and banking had, as elsewhere, been regarded as separate from economics and taught by different members of the academic staff. Theodore Gregory (who became the Professor of Banking and Currency in 1923) continued to do so until 1937 when he left LSE to become Economic Adviser to the Government on India. (In 1930/31 when Gregory was standing in for Henry Clay at the University of Manchester while Clay was an adviser to the Bank of England, Dennis Robertson came from Cambridge to give his main lectures.) As for trade cycle theory, after Hayek became the Tooke Professor he lectured on Industrial Fluctuations every year from 1932/33 on. (As a visiting professor in 1931/2, when Gregory was still in Manchester, he gave Gregory's money courses.) With respect to the new Keynesian macroeconomic developments, it was younger colleagues, notably Evan Durbin and Nicholas Kaldor who had been Hayekians and became Keynesians, who lectured on them. Robbins occasionally mentioned Keynes's *Treatise on Money* (1930) in his lecture notes; according to Ungphakorn he recommended Chapter 11 of the *General Theory* in the Lent term of 1940 in connection with interest theory. Although Robbins included Hicks's 'Mr Keynes and the Classics' (1937) at the end of his long *Calendar* reading list in 1938/39 he did not lecture on it.

In the first two sets of lecture notes there are relatively few diagrams; in the last set there are many, some very sketchy. Where these are obviously merely aids to memory like the marginal notes I have omitted them. Otherwise I have used the sources from which the diagrams derive (for instance Wicksteed (1910), Marshall (1920), Knight (1921) and Robinson (1933) or Victor Urquidi's notes to tidy them up and label the unlabelled axes. One undergraduate, who attended the lectures in 1936/37, remembered 'the loving care' with which he expounded the details of Joan Robinson's theory of monopoly (Howson 2011 page 315).

Robbins's lecture notes are printed here with only minor corrections to the text and with some elaboration of his references. (Complete references with publication details are listed in the bibliography.) Robbins often wrote his notes in paragraphs of only one or two sentences for ease of lecturing; where suitable I have put these together into longer paragraphs for ease of reading. I have also left out the scribbled marginal reminders.

When Robbins returned to LSE in 1946 after his wartime government service he did not expect to lecture on Principles again. Hayek had given the lectures during the war and Kaldor had taken them over at its end. In his first full year back at the School Robbins lectured on The Theory of Economic Policy, drawing, as he was also to do in the Marshall Lectures he gave in Cambridge in April and May 1947 (Robbins 1947), on his wartime experience of using economic theory for policymaking; he described the course as 'the application of economic principles to the main problems of public policy' and summarized its (rather Pigovian) content to his LSE colleagues as 'a simplified Economics of Welfare *plus* a little Theory of Public Finance *plus* J.M. Clark on the legal framework' (Howson 2011 pp 643, 659–60). He included employment policy, for as he told his audience in Cambridge (1947 pp 67–8), 'this is the point on which I am most conscious of a change of point of view, not, I think, to the war, but rather to the cumulative effect of reflections on pre-war controversies tested in relation to a somewhat new quantitative perspective', acknowledging the influence of both Keynes and Robertson.[5] But in the summer of 1947 Nicky Kaldor, enticed by Gunnar Myrdal to head the Planning and Research Division of the UN Economic Commission for Europe, resigned. Robbins felt obliged to step in to give the Principles course for 1947/48 rather than ask any of his colleagues to give it at such short notice.

He retained Kaldor's description of the course in the LSE *Calendar*, 'the general principles of the theory of value and distribution, money, employment and fluctuations', and most of his reading list, which included Marshall, Wicksell, Fisher and Keynes (*Treatise* and *General Theory*,) and thus lectured on macroeconomics as well as on microeconomics. As in the late 1930s he began with three lectures on the historical background and the nature of economics. Instead of his prewar division of price theory into statics, comparative statics and dynamics, he followed the example of Walter Eucken (whom he had first met in April 1947) in discussing first the centrally planned economy (without markets or money) and then the exchange economy.[6] The microeconomic *content* of the course was, however, similar to that of the later 1930s which included the innovations of Hicks and Allen, Lerner and Joan Robinson, but he could recommend, as had Kaldor, new textbooks such as Boulding (1941) and Stigler (1942). The macroeconomic content included the quantity theory of money, especially the Cambridge cash balance approach; the nature of savings and investment; classical and liquidity preference theories of interest; the consumption function and the multiplier; the IS-LM model; and (briefly) theories of the trade cycle (Howson 2011 pp 682–3).[7]

Robbins continued to give the Principles course for three years, until the course disappeared in a reform of the structure of the BSc(Econ) in 1950. In 1953/54 he took over the History of Economic Thought from Terence Hutchison who had himself taken it over from Hayek following Hayek's sudden departure for the United States in 1950; he gave this course most years until 1982. These lectures have been published from the transcript of the tape-recording made by his grandson Philip in 1979/80 (Robbins 1998).

In the Principles lecture notes of the later 1930s there are several comments such as 'Expand in book'; as he recalled in his autobiography (1971, page 273), he had long wanted to write a treatise on economic theory. When he found himself preparing Principles lectures again in the summer of 1947 he told his son he might turn them into a book. Ten years later he offered to teach a Principles-type course again: a Survey of Economic Analysis which had been taught by Helen Makower

---

5 During the war he had actively supported the development of national income estimates by James Meade and Richard Stone in 1940 and Keynesian ideas on employment policy in 1942–3, admitting his change of heart to Hayek in 1942 (see Howson 2011 especially pp. 368–70, 438–9, 483–92, 418–19).

6 Eucken's *Grundlagen der Nationalökonomie* had been published in German in 1939; it was published in English in 1950. Robbins also mentioned Eucken's ideas on method in the notes for the preliminary lectures but he soon discarded those notes.

7 Robbins's notes for his postwar Principles survive, as do those of one of the students, his daughter Anne.

since 1952. The reason was that he wanted to have a last shot at a treatise on the principles of economic theory; he started writing such a book in the summer of 1958. The drafts of the early chapters, on his favourite subject of the nature of economics, survive in his papers (Howson 2011 pp 672, 822–3 and 849). But although he was to lecture on Principles twice more, in 1964/65 and 1965/66, he abandoned the project of the book in 1960.

In December 1960 he was asked to call on the Home Secretary, R.A. Butler, who unexpectedly requested him to chair a committee on the present state and future prospects of university education in Britain. He demurred as he wanted to get on with his book. But when one of his wartime civil servant colleagues asked him 'if I thought that anything I had in mind to write was likely to be as important as trying to sort out the contemporary problems of the system of higher education in this country . . . I could not honestly deny it' (Robbins 1971 pp 272–3). His treatise was never written. He devoted most of the next three years to the 'Robbins Committee' and wrote its report (Committee on Higher Education 1963), which recommended a major expansion of university education in Britain, especially at the postgraduate level. He was also chairman of the board of the *Financial Times* newspaper from 1961 to 1971, an appointment which precipitated his retirement from his chair in 1961.

The idea of publishing Robbins's unpublished lecture notes was that of his son-in-law, the late economist and financial journalist Christopher Johnson, who initiated discussions with Routledge. I am deeply grateful to Anne Johnson for her encouragement of the project of an edition of the 1930s Principles lecture notes (as well as for permission to publish these notes and to utilize those for the post-war Principles lectures). James Johnson and Wilma Johnson gave me invaluable help. This edition of Lionel Robbins's lecture notes is not, of course, the book he wanted to write. It is offered in the hope that it will illuminate the development of economics, and the way it was taught, in the 'years of high theory'.

Part I 1929–31

Introduction

Editorial Note: The lecture notes in this section were written to be given first in the Lent and Summer Terms 1930 and the Michaelmas, Lent and Summer Terms of 1930/31. With the exception of the first part of Lecture 8 (Production: Factors Flexible: Labour Supply) the first 15 lectures come from the notebook labelled 'Principles of Economics I Old Notes 1929–31' and Lectures 16–20 come from the notebook labelled 'Principles of Economics II'. Lectures 8, 21 and 22, however, were filed in the notebook labelled '1939–40', as was lecture 15*. The lecture notes as a whole correspond to the description of the course in the LSE Calendars for 1930/31 and the next two years.

1 The framework of economic analysis

Today I want to discuss with you what you may call the analytical framework of Economics – questions of arrangement and division.

To some of you this may sound as if I am at once going back on my promise not to indulge in investigations of method. But this is not the case. I am not proposing to discuss *logical* method at all. What I want to do rather is simply to define a little the nature of our problem and sort out various ways in which we can approach it – to choose between tools – not to discuss the rationale of tool using.

For clearly there *is* a problem. We cannot do everything at once. Our business as I conceive it is to examine human behaviour as conditioned by the fact of scarcity – you may disagree with this if you like – and our subject matter is therefore the whole complex of human relations arising from this fact: Production, Exchange, Distribution, Localization, Trade and so on and so forth. Clearly if we are to do anything which takes us beyond the naive conclusions of experience and common sense we must attack the problem by stages. We must analyse. We must break up. And clearly if we are to do this, the way we are to do it is not a matter of indifference. There are some modes of approach which are better than others – better that is to say in that they lead to more significant results – in that they facilitate our understanding of the whole.

Now the traditional way of dividing the subject has been – or has pretended to be – division into sections on production and distribution.

> The . . . fundamental questions of economics are why all of us taken together are as well off . . . as we are and why some of us are much better off and others much worse off than the average, says Cannan
>
> (Wealth Int.)[1]

And this procedure – the procedure of dividing our enquiries so as to provide answers to these questions has been followed by perhaps a majority of English and Continental Economists. There are differences of content under these two headings and differences as regards supplementing divisions. But this division has been the main 'cut' – as it were – into the body of the subject.

---

1 [E. Cannan, *Wealth* 3rd edition (1928)]

And no doubt there are advantages to be gained from the use of this method.

I do not question Cannan's assertion that the two questions to which he makes the division correspond are the fundamental questions which we ask if we turn to Economics for guidance on matters of practical policy. What will be the effect on production What on Distribution Do the two effects work together or tend to cancel out – These are certainly the questions we ask when are considering the advisability of a tax or a bounty, or this form of control or that relaxation. We are out to better production and to better distribution. It is only natural that we should frame our analysis to assist these endeavours.

But in scientific investigation it does not always "pay" even in the most material sense of the word to have too exclusive an eye to the practical. Of course there is no guarantee that if we seek first accuracy and truth, if we seek light, fruit shall be added unto us. But it not infrequently happens that it is. We know that in the natural sciences enquiries which have seemed most recondite and abstract have ultimately proved to have the most important practical application. So that even if we regard the *raison d'etre* of economic study as amelioration of economic conditions rather than mere knowledge and understanding – and I am far from suggesting that this should be our attitude – even if you have practical ends in view, the fact that your analysis is framed with them in mind is not an infallible sign of its excellence. And as a matter of fact when we come to examine the production, distribution analysis not from the point of view of its suitability for providing broad answers to general questions but from the point of view of its suitability for affording a body of exact "laws" for generalizations we begin to be aware of certain deficiencies.

It is worth while to look at these closely.

Economic "laws" or generalizations must if they are to be exact relate to movements of quantities. They are concerned essentially with questions of more or less. They may not always be statistically verifiable. There may be profound difficulties in the way of experimental proof. But they should at any rate relate to quantities which are capable of more or less accurate definition. They need not have a numerical *content*. They should have a general quantitative form which is intelligible. This being so we should expect a law of production to conform to this general requirement. And no doubt there are laws of production – the law of diminishing returns in particular industries, e.g. which do succeed in doing so. But when we come answer the broad question what are the causes of increases or diminution of production quantitative exactitude is harder to conceive. It is easy enough to conceive broad qualitative generalizations such as that if men work harder or save more their power to produce will be greater. But it is when we come to give our generalizations more exact form that complications begin.

Let us examine the nature of these complications.

We want to discuss changes in the aggregate or average volume of production. How are we to conceive exactly of such changes[?]

It is easy enough to conceive of changes in the volume of any one kind of product. You simply measure in physical units.

But this plan is not available when you come to generalize about the movement of collections of commodities.

You might go some way if all the physical units moved in the same direction
100 A + 100 B + 100 C . . . becoming 200 A + 200 B + 200 C

Though here great precision would be difficult. For how could you say whether
one increase was *more* than another?

e.g. 150 A + 200 B + 250 C
than 250 A + 200 B + 150 C

But of course it is notorious that the production of heterogeneous aggregates
does not move in this simple way. It is a question of judging whether

100 A + 100 B is greater than, equal to or less than 50 A + 200 B

Some quantities move up, others move down. Obviously physical computations
are out of the question.

We therefore fall back upon comparing aggregates of *values*. We reduce our
products to a money denominator and add. Now I do not want to suggest that computations of this sort are useless. Clearly they do afford a more precise guide than
more guesses. Clearly if they are used simply as evidence of direction of change
they may be very helpful. But from the point of view of strict accuracy, they are
open to grave strictures.

(1) In the first place come the well-known technical difficulties of eliminating
     variations in the measured. The value of money changes and if corrections
     are not introduced the measurement is vitiated. (See Keynes & Haberler)[2]
     (If capital is being measured it is also necessary to take account of changes in
     the rate of interest.)
(2) Secondly if the elasticity of demand for a commodity is less than unity, the
     aggregate value moves inversely to the volume of supply.
(3) These are the elementary cautions of first year economics.

And it could be argued perhaps that they are not very important, that changes
in the value of money can be eliminated and that high inelasticity for important
products is the exception rather than the rule. I am not clear that these would be
valid replies. Still we may concede that they are respectable.

But there are yet more serious theoretical objections. In thinking of the validity
of these conceptions of aggregates we have to remember the fundamental rela-
tivity of the value concept. The whole system of valuations on which we base
our conception of an aggregate depends essentially upon a given distribution of
wealth. Alter the distribution of wealth and the whole system of values changes
also. You can see that quite clearly when you are thinking of calculations regarding the amount of the national income available for redistribution. You are all
acquainted with Professor Bowley's discussion of this matter in his Division of

---

2 [J.M. Keynes, *A Treatise on Money* (1930); G. Haberler, *Der Sinn des Indexzahlen* (1927)]

the Product of Industry.[3] No doubt, calculations of this sort do provide some sort of basis for discussion. But we shall be tempted to go too far on this basis if we neglect Professor Bowley's own caution that if great redistribution actually took place the basis of measurement would be gone.

This may sound abstract but it is really quite simple. it is common knowledge that the high incomes of some of the professional classes depend on the presence of other people in the community with high incomes who are willing to bid high for their services. If income were redistributed on an equalitarian basis Charlie Chaplin might go on collecting his £100,000 p.a. But it is doubtful whether famous surgeons would get huge fees for operations. It is certain that firms of solicitors could not make high profits by advising wealthy people on how to obtain quick and inconspicuous divorces.

(4) Finally, even if you ignore this you must remember that your computations of changes depend upon the assumption of fixed tastes and habits on the part of your consumers. It is really just an accident of history so to speak that certain things are demanded in certain quantities. Let there be a change in tastes an alteration of fashion and you are no longer comparing *social dividends of the same composition*. No doubt there is a sense in which you can say that the social dividend now is greater than the social dividend of the time of Queen Anne. But it is not sufficiently precise to provide a basis for extensive quantitative generalization.

For all these reasons, then, discussion of production from this point of view does not lend itself to exact analytical treatment. And there is yet a further reason why this general mode of approach does not always commend itself. It involves duplication of treatment and overlapping. For it is clear – is it not – that under capitalism at any rate there is an intimate relationship between the institutions of production & the institutions of distribution. We divide the product by means of money incomes. And the money incomes are the incentive to further production. It is a commonplace of elementary exposition that the processes of production and distribution are not really discreet [sic] – that the division made in the class room is only an expositional division.

It follows therefore that in dealing with the economic system from these two angles, while there are certain fields which are not common to the field of vision, there is a large field – the price system which is. If you adhere rigidly to the division you are bound to treat certain things twice over.

Because of all this – because of the difficulties of quantitative precision and because of the inelegance of a division which involves so great a degree of overlap – in recent years it has become the custom to approach the problem from rather a different direction. Instead of regarding the economic system as a machine for producing and distributing and inquiring concerning its

---

3 [A.L. Bowley, *The Division of the Product of Industry: An Analysis of National Income Before the War* (1919)]

potentialities and tendencies in these respects, it is considered simply as a system of quantities of goods of different descriptions – quantities of productive services – and analysis is directed to discovering under what conditions this system exhibits equilibrium – under what conditions there is no tendency for the quantities to alter or under what conditions they exhibit characteristics of orderly or periodic growth.

I say this is a recent habit – and it is true that it is only recently that this has come to be the avowed and central preoccupation of important treatises. See e.g. Pareto Cassel Knight etc.[4] But of course it is a treatment which has been implicit in many earlier systems. The idea of different tendencies to equilibrium. The idea of natural or normal prices etc., has dominated whole areas of economic theory since the days of Adam Smith and the Physiocrats. The whole theory of price has been developed essentially in terms of tendencies to equilibrium. The theory of distribution has been to a large extent on the same basis. The moderns simply make explicit the methodological assumptions of these earlier theories and generalize them.

This method has very important advantages over the other.

(1) First, it considers always quantities which – in conception at any rate – are precise. It contemplates the flow of quantities of commodities of like kind and quality – *their* distribution and production. How much bread is produced, how is it distributed. What is its exchange relationship etc. It never calls for contemplation of *aggregates* of different commodities. The social dividend of goods and services and the like. It may not be able to give a numerical value to the quantities it contemplates – this is a matter of availability of statistics. But there is nothing slippery and elusive about the conception.

(2) At the same time it has the very considerable advantage of asking its questions and giving its answers in a language much less question begging as regards causal relationships. The old approach led to a conception of economic phenomena in terms of single cause and effect. So and so is the cause of an increase in production. So and so is the effect of such and such a cause. And very often when the questions and answers were not simple to the point of banality this led to false views of the complexity of the economic system. The equilibrium approach tends to avoid all that. It views the various constituents of the economic system as mutually dependent phenomena and instead of asking what is the cause of that, it asks rather under what general conditions do these various things stand related to one another in such a manner in the theory of value. We no longer ask what is the *cause* of value. We ask rather what are the general conditions under which certain value relationships become prevalent. It is clear then that the approach by way of equilibrium analysis has much to recommend it. And in these lectures I propose very often to adopt it.

---

4 [V. Pareto, *Manuel d'economie politique* (1909); G. Cassell, *The Theory of Social Economy* (1923); F.H. Knight, *Risk, Uncertainty and Profit* (1921)]

But I think it would be wrong to imagine that it too is entirely without limitations, and that in every respect it is capable of superseding the older method. It is clear, for instance, that it provides no explanation of the distribution of personal incomes – as distinct from factor prices. We assume an initial distribution of property whatever form of equilibrium we are considering. Nor does it always provide a convenient framework for generalizations of a more practical nature – the effect of different institutions and laws – although it may help us some of the way in researching into these matters.

The fact is, I think, we need both methods. They are not rival, they are complementary. It is clear, I think, that the equilibrium approach enables us to get results of greater finesse and exactitude. But at the same time, I think, the other approach is necessary, if only to *interpret* the results of the equilibrium analysis and to show the significance in terms of relationships of the tendencies it discusses. A simple example will make plan what I have in mind. Take prices. In the equilibrium theory prices are one of the constituents of the general equilibrium. If prices were not what they are then the equilibrium would be different. So long as the equilibrium theory is strictly adhered to they are no more than this. But from the broader point of view of social organization it is clear that prices have a deeper significance. They are the impersonal indices which govern the direction of production. They provide the machinery whereby incomes are distributed. We miss the significance of the equilibrium analysis unless from time to time we relate it to these other questions.

Nevertheless, as I have said, it is the equilibrium approach that I propose to use most frequently in these lectures. This is purely for the very practical reason that you have been lectured to on other lines already. The Elements lectures are divided roughly on this basis. But it is partly for the reason that I do think that it is the better approach when dealing with the more abstract parts of our subject. For broad views and concrete applications the production-distribution analysis may be useful. But for refinement and new discovery the equilibrium analysis is more helpful, and I should be inclined to think that the traditional treatment – which has notoriously been rather at a standstill recently – is not likely to make further progress until it itself takes over more and more of the analysis of equilibrium. The discussion of production – utterly banal when treated as a classification and commentary on factors of production – becomes illuminating and exciting when carried on in terms of moving equilibrium.

Read

J.A. Schumpeter, *Das Wesen und Hauptinhalt der theoretischen Nationalokonomie* (1908)
Allyn A. Young, 'Some limitations of the value concept' in *Economic Problems Old and New* (1927)
A.C. Pigou, *The Economics of Welfare* (1929)
J.B. Clark, *The Distribution of Wealth* (1899)
[ADDED IN PENCIL:]
Gottfried Haberler, *Der Sinn des Indexzahlen* (1927)
J.M. Keynes, *A Treatise on Money* (1930)

2 The conception of equilibrium

Last time I was discussing alternative methods of Economic Analysis. Today I want to discuss more fully the conception of Economic Equilibrium.

What do we mean by Economic Equilibrium? I said last time that one of the criteria was stationariness of certain quantities. But this in a sense is a superficial description. If we are to use the conception fruitfully we must examine it rather more closely.

Suppose, our money incomes being fixed by the State, we were compelled to spend fixed proportions of those incomes on the different constituents of our real income: 20% on Food, 10% on Fuel, 30% on Shelter and so on. And suppose the prices of these commodities were kept constant by State decree. In such a case clearly the various quantities purchased would be constant. The requirement of constancy would be satisfied.

Or suppose that we were compelled by decree to take up certain occupations and by strict supervision our efforts were kept up to a constant standard. The quantity of services rendered in different branches of production would be constant. Again the requirement of constancy would be satisfied.

But in neither of these cases could we speak conveniently of equilibrium. The constancy would be *imposed*. There would be no real balancing of the various forces of change. It is only when the quantities contemplated are free to vary and do not do so (or if we are contemplating moving equilibrium, vary only according to certain "laws") that the conception of equilibrium is fulfilled. After all what use would it be to discuss the laws of such a state as I have depicted. History rather than scientific analysis would be the most useful explanation.

The conception of equilibrium then assumes a certain freedom in the economic system – not freedom in the philosophical sense necessarily but freedom in the sense that rigidity is not imposed from above or without. Labour does not flow from one occupation to another not because it is forcibly prevented but because the attractions elsewhere fail to counterbalance the attractions where it is. Commodities are not transferred – not because they are not allowed to be but because in the quantities in which they are possessed individuals do not transfer them on the terms on which they can be transferred.

But notice at once a certain limitation in our conception. We contemplate freedom but we do not contemplate freedom in all directions. In the theory of exchange I am free to vary my holdings of let us say coal and gold. I can diminish my stock of gold and increase my stock of coal by so doing. But I am not considered free to kill the coal merchant and appropriate his belongings. No doubt an equilibrium of this sort could be contemplated but it is not worth doing so.

It is important to bear this in mind when interpreting the results of our theorizing. We only contemplate equilibrium *within certain social restraints and limitations*. The statement that in such conditions the quantities considered will be in equilibrium does not take us very far in social theory. There is no penumbra of approbation about our laws. Equilibrium is not something good. It is just equilibrium.

It was one of the vices of the older economists that they sometimes neglected this caution. They sometimes assumed a greater degree of freedom to exist than was warranted by the circumstances and then having discovered *actual* tendencies to equilibrium, they would imply that these tendencies led to the best that could be hoped from a state of perfect freedom. This I think is what Mr Dobb has in mind when he urges that classical economics assumes classless individualism.[1] I am not clear that this is a fault that really can be imputed to the greater classics. Clearly it is a mistake which was committed by certain of their followers.

But there is a further restriction on our conception than this. We do not discuss *all* the possibilities of free change when we are discussing equilibrium – even when we have accepted as given the limitations of social environments. Clearly we do not do this for one group of possibilities is the possibility of innovations disturbing the equilibrium. If we were to discuss *everything* in the social milieu we should not be discussing equilibrium. For obviously things are not at rest they are ceaselessly changing. In considering tendencies to equilibrium we abstract from certain [of] the forces of change. To some of you this may appear to vitiate the value of analysis. How can any good be expected of an examination which leaves out what are often the most vital factors?

Of course this rests on a misapprehension not merely of the rationale of economic analysis but of the rationale of scientific analysis in general. Scientific analysis in general proceeds essentially by the method of isolation. It never attempts to examine the world in the lump. It ascertains that certain forces are at work and it asks how they would act in isolation. This is the case with the natural sciences. It must be the case with any scientific inquiry. The fact that the surface of a fluid exposed to the air is continually disturbed is no reason why we should not study the forces which tend to bring it to a state of rest.

But are there such tendencies in the economic system?

The answer is quite definitely yes. The analysis of equilibrium in markets, e.g., is not founded on *a priori* theory. It is founded on the fact of experience that tendencies towards equilibrium are discernible. We know as a matter of personal experience that when we are choosing between two alternative modes of procedure there is a point at which we do not choose to take more of one or less of the other.

---

1 [Robbins had reviewed Dobb's *Capitalist Enterprise and Social Progress* (1925) for *Economica:* ' The Dynamics of Capitalism' (March 1926) pp. 31–9.]

But enough of the theoretical justification of our procedure. That after all is a thing which must show itself as analysis proceeds.

The next thing that I want you to observe is that our analysis proceeds by stages. Up to now I have referred to the analysis of economic equilibrium as if it were one thing. In fact of course it is not one thing but many. We imagine different kinds of equilibrium at different stages in our enquiry and it is to the classification of these varieties that I want now to draw your attention.

Broadly speaking there are four main types of equilibrium contemplated in modern economic theory.

(1) In the first place you get what you may call equilibrium of exchange. In this case we rule out of consideration all possibilities of production and concentrate solely on discovering what happens if people are free to exchange the various stocks (or flows) of goods in their possession. A has 100 tons of coal, B 100 quarters of wheat. If they are free to exchange are they likely to do so? and if so under what conditions will their exchanging cease (or continue at a constant rate)?

This analysis can be subdivided into two parts.

(a) In the first we consider exchange between two individuals with stocks of two commodities.
(b) In the second we consider exchange between groups of individuals in different markets. Exchange throughout a complete economic system.

You can call these, if you like, simple and multiple exchange equilibria.

(2) Second, we consider what you may call equilibrium of production with fixed factor supplies Labour Capital etc. Here we begin to enlarge our view. Production is no longer ruled out of the picture. Hence there is a possibility of variations in the total supplies of different kinds of product. Instead of these stocks or flows being fixed by hypothesis we now inquire what determines the conditions under which they will not vary. But we retain rigidity as regards *factors*. The number of labourers of different grades is fixed. The amount of capital goods the amount of land, and so on and so forth

Here again, two stages of division are possible – though the division is not on the same lines as before.

(a) In the first place we may regard what may be called *simple production* – that is production where only one scarce factor is involved in any process: independent workmen using free raw materials.
(b) In the second stage we may regard what you may call *joint production*. Each product is produced by the joint use of at least two different factors of production. It is at this state that the more complicated problems of distribution emerge. How is the price of the product divided between the cooperating factors?

(3) Third, we again enlarge the possibilities. We now allow the quantity of *factors to fluctuate* – so long as the fluctuations are conditioned by the other elements in the situation. Labour may increase – if the increase is called forth by the rate of wages. Capital may continue to accumulate if it is called forth by the interest rate.

(4) Finally we change our view somewhat and assume that the supplies of factors are changing and ask in what way the equilibrium must move.

This is a field in which as yet little work has been done. But it should be clear that it is at this point that our studies really become most realistic. It is here undoubted that much of the most useful work will be done in the future.

Now all this may sound new and unfamiliar. It is worthwhile, I think, examining in what relation it stands to other modes of treating the subject.

[A] Take first its relation to the Marshallian analysis.

Marshall you remember divides his discussion of the problem of equilibrium into two sections corresponding to Books V and VI of the 8th edition of the Principles.[2] In the one he deals with the pricing of the products in the other with the pricing of factors of production. These divisions correspond to the old division between value and distribution. (Of course Marshall recognizes that distribution in the sense of pricing the factors of production is a problem of value in the broad sense. But for purposes of exposition he decides to separate them.)

Within these divisions he distinguishes various problems according to the length of period under consideration. In the theory of price e.g. he distinguishes four problems:

(a) The problem of market price. Given the supply in a market, how is price determined?

(b) The problem of short period normal price. The problem of what determines the price which be normal for a commodity within a period short enough to prevent new factors being brought into the industry.

(c) Third, the problem of long period normal price. That is the problem of what determines the price during a period long enough for factors of production to transfer into or out of the industry in response to changes in demand.

(d) Fourth, the problem of secular changes in price. The problem of what are the influences of changes in the supply of factors.

You remember he illustrates this distinction in terms of the fishing industry. What fixes the price of fish from day to day. That is a problem of market price. What fixed it within a short period say a year? That is a problem of short period normal price. What fixes it during a period when new boats can be built? That is a

2 [A. Marshall, *Principles of Economics* 8th edition (1920)]

problem of long period normal price. What will be the effects on the price of fish of changes in population etc. That is a problem of secular change.

Similarly with distribution there are short and long time problems. But here Marshall is preoccupied almost exclusively with the long period normal.

How does all this stand in relation to our classification?

There is one difference which it is important to recognize. Marshall's normal price theory has relation to particular products. He analyses one price at a time. This is clearly indicated by his disquisition on the shifting content of normal. What is a short normal period for one industry is a long one for others. The short time normal price depends on the production period.

Equilibrium analysis on the contrary deals with all prices at once. It releases the factors and watches what happens all along the line. No doubt it is possible to overemphasise this difference. But as we shall see later on, there are not unimportant differences between analysing one thing at a time – one industry at a time – and analysing one set of conditions all along the line.

But putting that on one side for a moment, there is a fairly obvious connection between the Marshallian scheme and ours. The theory of market price covers roughly the same field as our theory of exchange equilibrium.

The theory of short and long period normal price fit into second category. Equilibrium of production factors given the distinction between the short and the long is not made in our classification. *We deal with the differences when we deal with the mobility of factor supplies.* Similarly, Marshall's short period normal distribution comes under this heading. Marshall does not deal much with this. Clark's treatment falls exclusively under this heading – but more of Clark in a minute. Finally, Marshall's theories of secular price change and long period distribution come under our heading of Equilibrium of production factor supplies flexible. (Secular price changes might also come under the fourth heading "factors changing".)

If you like can tabulate these relationships in the following way:-

Equilibrium	Value	Distribution
Exchange	Market Price	
Production	Normal Price	Short Dist
Factors given	(short & long)	
Production	Secular Price	Long Dist
Factors flexible	Change	
Production	(Secular Price?)	
Factors changing		

[B] Now turn to J.B. Clark

Clark's celebrated theory is not really concerned at all with the theory of market price; his avowed object is to discover what he calls static laws of distribution. His employment of the term "static" has become popular, and it is important to understand what he means by it.

Clark surveys the economic system and discovers in it five main sources of change:

1)   Population changes
2)   Capital changes
3)   Methods change
4)   Industrial structure changes
5)   Wants change.

If we remove these from our assumptions, he says we shall contemplate the static state and discover static laws, and his Distribution of Wealth is devoted to this enterprise.[3]

Now it is clear that this hypothesis corresponds to our Equilibrium of Production factors given. So that it follows that J.B. Clark's Laws of distribution are to be regarded as being concerned with Marshall's Short period Normal Distribution Problem – the problem of what determines the prices of the factors of production when their supply is given. Now if Clark cares to call this the static state and generalizations based upon it static laws no one can gainsay him. There is no profitable dispute about terms as such in economic theory. But it is very important that you should bear in mind the limitations of this hypothesis – that the supplies of the factors are fixed – and it is very important that you should distinguish Clark's static state from another hypothesis with a similar name the stationary state of Marshall and the classics.

The stationary state of Marshall and the classics has this resemblance to Clark's static state that in it the various prices and quantities of factors are constant. But it has this important difference in that whereas in Clark's state the quantities of the factors are fixed by hypothesis in the stationary state of Marshall and the classics the quantities of the factors are free to vary but have come to rest because the tendencies to change are in equilibrium. In Clark's static state the supply of capital is given. It cannot vary. In the stationary state the supply of capital is constant but this is because the rate of return on new investment is less than the supply price of new capital. The stationary state therefore corresponds to our third hypothesis – Equilibrium of production factors flexible. If this is not recognized all sorts of confusions follow. As we proceed in our analysis these will come to light. At [the] moment notice that in two fundamentally important disputes of the past the distinction is fundamental.

Take first the theory of wages. If you are thinking of the static state – Equilibrium factors fixed – it is not untrue in certain circumstances to say that wages are determined by marginal productivity. Only the demand side is variable. If you are contemplating a flexible labour supply clearly this generalization is inadequate. Or again take the theory of price. If the factors are given then it is clear that real costs in the sense of sacrifices of leisure or pain incurred are not relevant. The

---

3 [J.B. Clark, *The Distribution of Wealth: A Theory of Wages, Interest, and Profits* (1899)]

Austrian solution of the theory of value is sufficient. If, however, the factors are free to vary, then in one way or another real costs have to be taken account of.

Read

J.B. Clark, The Distribution of Wealth (1899)
Alfred Marshall, *Principles of Economics* (1920) Book V Chapter V
J.A. Schumpeter, Das Wesen und Hauptinhalt der theoretischen Nationalokonomie (1908)
Die Theorie der wirtschaftslichten Entwicklung (1911) Chapters I and II
Frank H. Knight, *Risk, Uncertainty and Profit* (1921) Book II
Gustav Cassell, *Theory of Social Economy* (1923) Book I
[ADDED LATER:]
L.C. Robbins 'On a certain ambiguity in the conception of Stationary Equilibrium' *Economic Journal* (June 1930)

General outline of equilibrium analysis

3 Equilibrium of simple exchange

In my last lecture, I attempted to outline to you the main stages of the analysis of Economic Equilibrium. Today I want to commence to discuss in greater detail the first of these stages – the analysis of Exchange Equilibrium. I want to concentrate first on the simplest possible case Equilibrium of Simple Exchange. When I have done that I shall proceed to the discussion of Exchange Equilibrium in general.

Let us start by stating carefully the nature of the problem. We are to examine the conditions under which two individuals exchange commodities. A has a stock of corn. B has a stock of coal. And these commodities are the only commodities taken account of. We have to ask:

(i) Under what conditions will they exchange at all?
(ii) Under what conditions will their exchanges cease?
(iii) At what rate or rates will their exchanges take place?

Now at the outset of our enquiries it is definitely worth noting its limitations. Part of our inquiry at any rate relates to value. The whole of it is reminiscent of what is discussed in value theory. But the whole discussion is subject to the condition that the stocks of corn and coal are *definitely given*. It follows therefore that we shall get no help from theories of value which explain value in terms of the quantities of the production process. Whatever its validity over a wide field the labour theory of value has no place here. We do not necessarily banish the idea of costs in exchange – there will be more to say about that later – but production costs – labour abstinence outlays or what not – simply do not enter into the picture. The stocks of corn and coal are *given by hypothesis*.

That being understood we can proceed to the main business of analysis.

A. The first question, you remember, which we have to answer, is under what conditions will exchange take place at all?

It is clear, is it not, that each of the parties concerned must have some possible use for the commodity possessed by the other? A has corn, B has coal. In order that there may exist even the possibility of exchange A must have some use for coal, B must have some use for corn. If this condition does not exist then clearly no exchange is conceivable.

But obviously this does not carry us very far. Our knowledge of the dispositions of the two individuals must be more precise than this before we can generalize about the possibility of exchanges. We must know how A conceives of the possible uses of coal and how B conceives of the possible uses of corn in relation to coal.

We must therefore conceive that there exists for each of them a conception of the value of each commodity in terms of the other. So many units of corn worth so many units of coal. A scale of relative values you can call it if you like.

Now there are certain things which it is important that you should notice about this conception of relative scales.

(a)   In the first place, notice that the scale not only exhibits relative values, *it is itself relative to the quantity of the commodities possessed.* If A has 1000 quarters of corn and no coal he may think that 1 quarter of corn is worth 1 ton of coal. But supposing he has 80 quarters of corn and 20 cwt of coal he may now feel that 1 quarter of corn is worth 2 tons of coal. And if he had 50 quarters of corn and 50 tons of coal he might feel that 1 quarter of corn was worth ten tons of coal. That is to say the scale is not fixed. It alters with every alteration in the quantity of commodities possessed.

(b)   Second, notice in this connection that *the scale expresses unitary or marginal valuations.* It is conceivable that A may from time to time reflect on the worth to him of all the corn he possesses in terms of coal. He may ask how much coal he would be prepared to take for all his corn. But these shadowy computations would not be the computations he would have in mind if he were proceeding to exchange. He would then ask only given the stock I have how much coal do I want for a unit of corn. Or how many units of corn will I give for a unit of coal. It is the *marginal* not the *total* significance of the things exchanged that figure on the scale that is relevant.

(c)   Third, notice this relative scale simply *expresses the significance of one thing in terms of another.* 1 quarter of corn is worth 3 tons coal. I say nothing about its capacity to *measure* satisfactions. It is conceivable that it may be interpreted as doing this. But I am not making any such claim for it. Personally I find it very hard to think of measuring satisfactions. The notion seems to me to be open to very grave philosophical objections. But it is clear that whether I can say this satisfaction is three times greater than that and be deemed to talk sense or whether such a statement be completely meaningless, I can and do frequently say that thing – or a unit of that thing – is the equivalent to me of three units of this other thing. The scale expresses the significance of one thing in terms of another. It does not pretend to do anything more ambitious than this. It does not suggest that the units measure psychological or subjective magnitudes.

(d)   Fourth, notice that *the idea of this scale of equivalences does not in the least imply a rational basis of action.* It is not suggested that A is right when he thinks that 3 units of coal are as much use to him as one unit of corn. It simply means that he is prepared to exchange on that basis.

Thus, my relative scale of preferences may indicate that I would give 10 loaves of bread for one bottle of whisky and it may be that the loaves of bread would keep me alive while the whisky would just push me over into the paroxysms of delirium tremens. On any rational scheme of values therefore the loaves are worth more to me than the whisky. But we are examining equilibrium of exchange not a rational scheme of values. We enquire simply what A does.

Nor, strictly speaking, need we assume that A *actually reflects* about the matter at all. I have spoken as if at some time prior to the exchange A estimated to himself the relative worth of marginal units of corn and coal. But it was not *necessary* for him to do so. A may simply rush into the market in an unreflecting manner and buy without close on the wisdom of his purchases. That does not concern us. All that we need assume is that there is a relative scale to which his actions conform. That is to say, if we are pressed at all by the psychologists we can fall back upon mere behaviourism. We make no assumptions about mental processes at all.

It is important to bear this in mind when you are reading outside your subject. Economics is the happy hunting ground of the amateur and a man need only to have achieved distinction in his own subject to feel competent to make generalizations about ours. Thus, at the present day you will find prevalent a belief that economic analysis depends for its validity upon the making certain rather dubious psychological assumptions. And as psychological doctrines change very rapidly – they have changed almost every year since the war – it is very easy for a journalist out of a job, or a psychologist who is at a loose end for the time being in his own line to write what appears to be an extremely important book or article in which he makes it appear that the whole structure of economic science built up by the labours of a century stands in need of drastic reconstruction because of the important observations of chimpanzees made by Herr So and So or the highly significant monograph of Dr Stick on the influence of the grandmother on the habits of early adolescence.

Now no doubt in the past economists have deserved this sort of thing in that they have been too ready to pass beyond the proper confines of their subject and generalize at large about social and philosophical questions. But as a criticism of the inner structure of their analysis it is completely beside the point. We can build up the whole framework of economic analysis without any support from psychology. And though I am far from suggesting that in applying economics we should eschew aid from any quarter from which it may be forthcoming I think it is important to remember that the fundamental core of theory is a circle of inferences which at no point need imply any psychological assumptions whatever. No doubt it would be pedantry always to speak in behaviouristic terms. But it is important to realize that here is an impregnable line of defence from all the assaults of Philistines.

(e) Finally, notice that our assumption of relative scales for A and for B involves *no suggestion that these scales can be compared in any absolute sense*. I may say that A values one unit of corn as much as three units of coal and that B values one unit of corn as much as six units of coal. But that does not imply that B's want for corn is greater *absolutely* than A's. All that is implied is that *relatively* to coal B values corn more highly than A. A may "want" coal and corn more than B in the sense that he has greater need for them. But this is not what we are measuring. We are not assuming A to compare the use *to him* of corn as compared with the use *to B* of corn. We are assuming him to compare the importance *to him* of quantities of corn and coal. And we assume B to carry out a similar operation.

This again is important when you are considering implications. It is obviously possible to conceive individuals choosing between commodities for themselves. But it is not possible to conceive similar measurements *as between individuals*. You can't compare what goes on in my head with what goes on in your head. There is a vast (perhaps insurmountable) gulf between them. There are certain fields of applied economics where you assume that you can. E.g. In the theory of taxation you assume that a £ from a rich man is less than a £ from a poor man. That is an assumption which it may be highly desirable to make in democratic countries. But – Prof. Cannan, Dr Dalton[1] and many others notwithstanding – it is an assumption which is *not in the least* implied by the generalizations of the theory of value and equilibrium and it is an assumption of a totally different nature. In the one case you never go beyond what is objectively verifiable. In the other you make assumptions which never can be verified. It may be convenient to make it. But it is not a matter that can be demonstrated. The recording angel may be able to compare *different* experiences. It is not given to the sons of men to be able to do so.

So much for the implications of the relative scales. Now let us proceed to use them in relation to our inquiring what are the conditions of exchange of coal and corn between A and B. Let us draw up one or two imaginary sets of scales and see what will happen under the conditions supposed.

(i)   Suppose first, that A (who has corn) thinks that 1/3 of a ton of coal would be the equivalent for him of one quarter of corn. And B (who has coal) thinks that 1 quarter of corn would be the equivalent for him of 3 tons of coal.

We may tabulate this thus

	Corn		Coal		Corn		Coal
A thinks	1	=	1/3	*or*	3	=	1
B thinks	1	=	3		1/3	=	1

That is to say, coal is lower in relation to corn on B's scale than on A's. Or corn is higher on B's scale than on A's in relation to coal.

1 [See, for instance, E. Cannan, 'Economics and socialism' *The Economic Outlook* (1912) pp. 59–62; H. Dalton, 'The measurement of the inequality of incomes' *Economic Journal* 30 (September 1920) pp. 348–61.]

We may express this diagrammatically.
Suppose two scales measuring units of corn:

	A	*B*
3	A coal	
2		
1		B coal

The same thing can be expressed in a coal scale:

	A	*B*
3		B corn
2		
1	A corn	

But these can be combined.
Along X measure corn, along Y measure coal

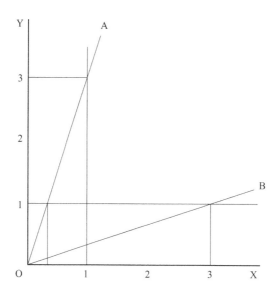

Clearly the conditions for an exchange are present. A is willing to part with 1 of corn for anything ever so little more than 1/3 of coal. B is willing to part with 1 of coal for anything more than 1/3 of corn.

Suppose they exchange on equal terms: A gets 1 of coal which he values at 3 of corn for 1 of corn; B gets 1 of corn which he values at 3 of coal for 1 of coal.

(ii) Now suppose that A (who has corn) thinks that 3 tons of coal would be the equivalent for him of one quarter of corn. And B (who has coal) thinks that 1 quarter of corn would be the equivalent for him of 1/3 of a ton of coal.

We may tabulate this thus:

	Corn		Coal	Corn		Coal
A thinks	1	=	3	1/3	=	1
B thinks	1	=	1/3	3	=	1

That is to say coal is higher in *relation* to corn on B's scale than on A's.

Clearly the conditions of exchange are not present. A is only willing to part with 1 of corn for 3+ of coal. B is only willing to part with 1 of coal for 3+ of corn. It is not that A and B have not the resources to procure a unit of each other's commodity. We may assume that A could give 3+ of corn for one of coal and B could give 3+ of coal for 1 of corn. But in neither case would the cost be equivalent to the gain.

Let us survey the results of our experiments and generalize. In the first case the possessor valued the thing he had relatively less than the potential acquirer. The corn man valued 1 coal as 1/3 corn and the coal man valued it as 3 corn. In the second case the possessor valued the thing he had relatively more than the potential acquirer. The corn man valued 1 corn as 3 coal while the coal man valued it as 1/3 corn. The coal man valued 1 coal as 3 corn while the corn man valued it as 1/3 corn. We can therefore say that exchange is possible when the things to be exchanged are valued less by their possessors than [by] their potential acquirers.

Now it is very important to be clear about this. The point is that the possessor values the thing less than the acquirer. This must not be confused with valuing the thing he possesses less than units of the thing he might acquire. In our example of possible exchange this was indeed the case.

A   (corn) valued a unit of corn less than a unit of coal 1–1/3.
B   (coal) valued a unit of coal less than a unit of corn 1–1/3.

But this need not have been so.
   E.g. Suppose the valuations are as follows:

	Corn	Coal	Corn	Coal
A (corn)	1	3	1/3	1
B (coal)	1	6	1/6	1

Exchange is clearly possible. If A gives 1 of corn and gets 4 of coal he is getting for 1 what he values at 1 1/3. If B gives up 4 of coal for 1 of corn he is getting for 4 what he values at 6.

The important thing, therefore, is not whether A values the thing he has more or less than a unit of the thing he might acquire but whether he values it less than B in terms of the thing in terms of which they are both valuing.

This comes out very well in the diagram:

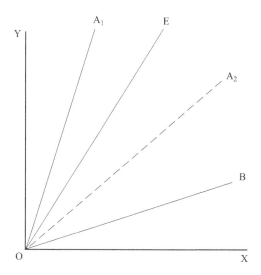

OE equals equivalent unit valuation.

It would be absurd to argue that in order that exchange should take place A's line should be always north of OE and B's south. All that is necessary is that A's line should be closer to the corn axis than B's.

Note for further reference symmetry of this with theory of comparative cost.

4 Equilibrium of simple exchange (continued)

Exchange, therefore, is possible when the commodity to be exchanged is valued relatively less by their possessors than by their potential acquirers and each party to the exchange has a supply sufficient to satisfy the requirements of the other. But now we have to decide the second question – how far exchange will go – at what point exchange will cease.

We must notice first the obvious fact that every exchange made *has the effect of diminishing the stock of the thing given and increasing the stock of the thing received*. A gives corn for coal. He increases his stock of coal he diminishes his stock of corn. What effect this have on the relative scale? Does he come to value corn less in terms of coal or more?

A priori we cannot say. But experience seems to suggest that the more he has of coal and the less of corn the more he will value corn in terms of coal and the less coal in terms of corn. Observation seems to suggest that the less we have of one thing the more we tend to value little bits of it in terms of another. And therefore we assume that this is so.

Here you see we are making an assumption closely similar to the famous law of diminishing marginal utility. But notice the difference.

(i) The Law of diminishing marginal utility pretended to be an exact psychological generalization. The more you had of a commodity the less satisfaction additional increments of that thing yielded. Ours is a formal law following from the assumption of diversity of ends.[1]

(ii) And again the law of diminishing marginal utility generalized in terms of capacity to yield satisfaction (or meet desire) it involved either the measurement of satisfactions or their comparison.

Our assumption begs none of these questions. We simply assume that the scale of equivalences moves in a certain manner and generalize on this basis.

---

1 [This last sentence replaced the following which was crossed through in ink: 'Our modest assumption has no pretensions to the status of an apriori law. We observe merely that this relationship between goods is the one which most frequently obtains and therefore we *assume* that it is so in discussing the conditions of equilibrium. We do not say that it *must* be so. We can think of cases where it is not so. Experience suggests simply that it is the most convenient assumption to make.']

To what conclusions does it lead us? A and B the possessors of corn and coal each value what the other possesses relatively more than what they possess themselves. They are therefore proceeding to exchange. As they exchange the stocks they originally possessed become depleted and the stock of the things they are acquiring become enhanced.

We have assumed that as this happens the value of the declining stock to each measured in terms of the augmenting stock will rise. Conversely the value of the augmenting stock measured in terms of the declining stock will fall. Thus A may start (as in our case (1)) of last time valuing 1 of corn as 1/3 of coal. As he exchanges the significance of corn will rise. After exchanging 10 quarters he may value 1 of corn as 1/2 of coal. And so on.

Sooner or later the difference between A's valuation of corn in terms of coal and B's must cease. *And at that point exchange will cease also.*

Suppose e.g. that after exchanging 50 quarters A values corn in terms of coal as 1:2 and suppose that B values the two commodities in the same ratio. There is no further incentive to exchange. A values a unit of corn as equivalent to two units of coal and so does B. There are no terms of exchange which would be advantageous.

Generalizing therefore we may say that *exchange will cease when the commodities exchanged stand in the same relation to one another on each of the exchangers' relative scales.* If we use the simple diagrammatic apparatus I explained last time, we may illustrate the situation thus:

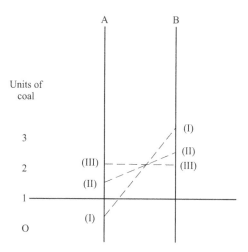

We start with A's valuation of corn in terms of coal low down on the scale at 1/3 and B's high up at 3. As they exchange the significance of corn grows for A and declines for B. Eventually exchanges cease when the two points are opposite one another.

Notice in passing how beautifully this example brings out the point I was making last time, that it is not whether a commodity is valued more or less than the other but whether it is valued relatively more by the acquirer than by the purchaser [sic] which determines whether exchange shall continue.

A starts by valuing corn as less than coal – 1/3. Gradually, the values become equivalent, and then corn definitely passes coal. But still the exchanging continues. For although corn is now valued more than coal it is not valued as much more by A as by B. Exchange only ceases when this relative difference has been wiped out.

Now there are certain misapprehensions to guard against in connection with this part of our theory which it is worth mentioning specifically.

(a) Notice first that we make no assumption about the rates at which the significance of the articles in question change for A and B as the stocks possessed by each vary. There is no suggestion of constant rates.

Thus in the example I have been discussing corn goes from 1/3 to 2 for A, while at the same time it only goes from 3 to 2 for B.

(b) Second, there is no suggestion that exchange only ceases when for each exchanger the *commodities exchanged* have equivalent significance.

Exchange does not cease when 1 corn = 1 coal for A. It ceases when corn is to coal as 1:2 and it ceases then because when the commodities have the same relation of the relative scales, there is no longer any incentive to exchange.

This point is important. In certain text books which pretend to explain these things in terms of utility theory, you come on the statement that in a state of equilibrium the marginal significances of *different* commodities are equal. This of course is wrong and a travesty of utility theory. If we are to use the terminology of this theory we can say that equilibrium obtains when the marginal utility of the same commodities measured in terms of the other commodities are equal for the two exchangers. Thus in our example if we were measuring the utility of corn in terms of coal we could say that equilibrium was attained when for A and B the marginal utility of corn was 2.

Or we can say that equilibrium is attained when the marginal utility of corn bears to the marginal utility of coal the same relation as the terms on which coal can be exchanged for coal.

Thus if the marginal utility of corn is to the marginal utility of coal as 2:1 and the terms on which corn can be exchanged for coal are as 1:2 then we can say equilibrium obtains. But we do not say that equilibrium obtains when for A the marginal utility of corn is to the marginal utility of coal is 1:1 because then – under the conditions we have supposed – exchange continues. B is still willing to part with coal at a rate of say 2½ to 1. So that in sacrificing 1 of corn which he values at 1 coal A gets 2½ coal – which has obviously more utility. So that even if we prefer to talk in terms of utility theory it is important to realize that the criterion of equilibrium is not equal utility for coal and corn but similar relationships at the margin for each commodity.

What has happened, of course, when the writers of elementary textbooks say that at a state of equilibrium marginal utilities are equal, is that they are unconsciously assuming that the units of commodities are not the units which are priced 1 lb. of flour and a pot of jam but the quantities which can be bought for constant outlay – a shillings worth of flour or jam. It is true that in an equilibrium of expenditure a shilling at each margin should have the same significance. *But this does not* imply that it purchases 1 physical unit of each commodity.

(For those of you who know mathematics the thing is simple. The statement we are discussing confuses marginal utility with marginal degree of utility – confuses $du/dx.\delta x$ with du/dx.[2] But the confusion should be plain without this technical distinction.)[3]

(c) Third, notice that of course it is possible for a whole stock to run out before equilibrium is attained. B may value corn so highly that when he has given all the coal he has the relative value of coal for him is still less than the relative value of coal for A. If he had more exchange would still go on. But he has not so it ceases. But this is not complete equilibrium.

Finally, two points of more general character.

(i) In the first place you may remember that at the commencement of the last lecture I said that while we ruled out all explanations of equilibrium in terms of production costs we did not necessarily rule out explanations in terms of *any* kind of cost. It should now be possible to see what was behind that cryptic reservation.

Clearly our whole explanation in terms of relative valuations implies an explanation in terms of costs. We exchange corn for coal so long as the costs (what we have to give up) are worth less than what on the terms secured we gain. A exchanges 1 of corn for 3 of coal so long as he values 3 of coal more highly than its cost (1 of corn). And in fact the whole theory of relative significance expounded in this way is in almost every formal respect analogous to the old theory of comparative costs in international trade. The scientific refinement introduced by the utility analysis is not the idea of utility so much as the idea of equivalence at the margin. The fact that the comparative cost theory measured in terms of labour, whereas we measure in terms of commodities sacrificed, is unimportant. The classics considered

2 See A.A. Young, 'Jevons's theory of political economy' *American Economic Review* (1912); P.H. Wicksteed, *The Alphabet of Economic Science* (1888) p. 46; I. Fisher, *Mathematical Investigations in the Theory of Value and Prices* (1892) p. 37.
3 This is also the distinction between Schumpeter's Wert and Wertintensitat.

production whereas we are considering exchange. The principle of explanation, however, is analogous. But there will be more to say on this later.

(ii) Second – a more technical point – in my example of corn and coal I have been assuming divisibility of the things exchanged. A is willing to give 1 of corn for 1/3 of coal, B 1 of coal for 1/3 of corn. Such divisibility is possible in the case of most simple commodities. But in the case of manufactured products it may be that stocks cannot be emptied continuously. The units are not divisible. In this case perfect equilibrium is not possible. A may have reached a stage when he values the two commodities as 1:1 and B may have reached a stage when he values them as 1:3, yet if exchange of 1 unit on either side takes place the positions on the relative scales may be reversed. A may value them as 1:3 and B as 1:1. The equilibrium is not perfect. It is wobbly at the margin.

Some people attach much practical importance to this sort of consideration. And no doubt indivisibility does prevent perfect equilibrium of expenditure. We might be unwilling to spend an extra shilling on a whole unit of a commodity but we might be perfectly willing to spend 6^d on an extra half if it were sold in halves.

In fact I think you can exaggerate this. Where things are not divisible in quantity, there are qualitative gradings which enable rough equilibrium to be attained. You may not be able to get 30/- worth of grade A boots at 40/- a pair. But you can probably buy grade B for 30/-. And so on.

(iii) Now it is time to turn our attention to the third problem. Granted that equilibrium is achieved – in the sense that no goods pass between A and B – at what rate is it achieved? At what rate do exchanges take place?

Notice there are really two questions involved here – the question of rate of exchange while exchange is proceeding and the question of the rate which secures equilibrium. Let us deal with them separately.

(a) First of all, let us examine the rate of exchange at the beginning.

To do this we may revert to our first example.
A regards 1 corn as equivalent to 1/3 coal.
B regards 1 corn as equivalent to 3 coal.

It is clear, I think, that *many* rates of exchange are possible.
A is willing to give 1 of corn for 1/3 of coal while B is willing to give 3 of coal for 1 of corn. At any rate, therefore, between 1/3 to 3 for 1 of coal both parties will gain more than they give up.
We may represent this diagrammatically thus:

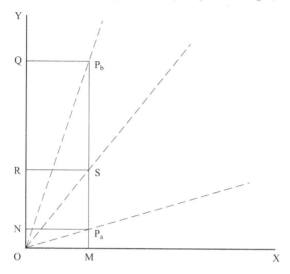

On two axes OX and OY mark off quantities of the commodities to be exchanged: on OX units of corn, on OY units of coal

Let OM measure 1 unit of corn. Then ON (= 1/3 coal) represents the lowest offer of coal that A will accept for 1 of coal.

Draw NP_a parallel to OX and P_aM to OY.

ON/OM = price per unit of corn $1/3 \div 1 = 3$

Therefore P_aM/OM = price per unit of corn.

But $P_aM/OM = \tan P_aOM$

Therefore A's limiting price = ON/OM or P_aM/OM or $\tan P_aOM$.

Naturally A will accept anything more than this.

Now let OQ represent the greatest offer of coal B is prepared to make for a unit of corn.

That is OQ/OM (= 3/1) is B's limiting price for corn

Or $P_bM/OM = \tan P_bOM$

Naturally, B will accept anything less than this, say OR/OM (or $\tan$ SOM) while as we have seen A will take anything more than P_aM/OM

so that between P_aM/OM & P_bM/OM or between $\tan P_bOM$ and P_aOM there is an infinite number of rates which would satisfy both parties.

The initial rate of exchange is therefore indeterminate. It depends on the relative degrees of bargaining ability possessed by A and B respectively.

If A is clever and B stupid at this sort of thing he may induce B to give him almost the maximum rate to which he is willing to go. That is the rate may be near tan P$_b$OM. If B is the astute bargainer he may give nearly the minimum A is prepared to take = tan P$_a$OM.

(b) But if the *initial rate* is indeterminate the *final rate* must be indeterminate too. For remember the scales of relative equivalences are *marginal* valuations & they change with changes in the quantities of each commodity possessed.

If A has 100 quarters of corn at the outset and 0 coal he may value them as 1: 1/3. Suppose now that he parts with 9 units of corn at a rate of 1/3. He will now have 91 units of corn and 3 of coal. But suppose he had secured a rate of 1:2. He would have 91 units of corn and 18 units of coal. It is most improbable that his relative valuation of corn and coal would be the same in each case. It follows, therefore, that his next minimum rate will depend upon his success in the last process of bargaining.

The same considerations apply to B. So that there is no reason to suppose that the final equilibrium rate is any more determinate than the initial one. We know that equilibrium will be reached. But we do not know *where* it will be reached.

There is one rate which, as Marshall has pointed out, is of peculiar theoretical interest, namely the rate which if it were hit on at the outset would make A and B willing to do business to the same extent. If much corn had to be given for one unit of coal it is improbable that A would want to go very far with the exchange. While if much coal had to be given for one unit of corn it is improbable that B would wish to go very far. There would be an intermediate rate at which they would be willing to do business to the same extent. Suppose it is 1 of corn for 1 of coal. A is willing to give 20 units of corn for 20 units of coal and B is willing to give 20 units of coal for 20 units of corn.

Or to use the language of the relative scale suppose that if A had 80 corn and 20 coal he valued corn at 1:1 and if B had a similar valuation after parting with 20 coal. Equilibrium would have been attained at a constant rate. But as we have seen there is no reason to suppose that such an equilibrium rate will be struck.

That is all I want to say for the moment about simple exchange. Let me summarize my conclusions.

(1) Exchange is possible between two individuals when the possessed commodity is valued relatively less by the possessor than it is by the possible acquirer and each possesses a sufficient supply to satisfy the wants of the other.
(2) Equilibrium is reached when the valuations are identical – when each commodity occupies the same place on both relative scales.
(3) The initial and final rate of exchange is however indeterminate. There is a theoretical equilibrium rate which if hit on at the outset would secure an equal disposition to exchange. But there is no guarantee that it will be attained.

Read

Alfred Marshall, *Principles of Economics* (1920) Appendix F Barter
J.B. Clark, *The Distribution of Wealth* (1899)

Philip.H. Wicksteed, *The Common Sense of Political Economy* (1910) Book I Chapters 1–4
   Book II chapters 1–3

The Alphabet of Economic Science (1888)

F.Y. Edgeworth, *Mathematical Psychics* (1881)

'On the determinateness of economic equilibrium', *Papers Relating to Political Economy*
   (1925) Vol. II pp. 313–19

Maffeo Pantaleoni, *Pure Economics* (1898) Part II chap I (Beware of loose terminology)

Frank H. Knight, *Risk, Uncertainty and Profit* (1921) Part II Chapter 1

Arthur L. Bowley, *The Mathematical Groundwork of Economics* (1924) Introduction and
   Chapter I Simple Exchange of Two Commodities

Allyn A. Young, 'Jevons's theory of political economy' *American Economic Review* (1912)
   pp. 576–89

5   Equilibrium of multiple exchange

In my last two lectures I have been dealing with the remote abstraction of simple barter. Today I want to turn to the more familiar problems of general exchange equilibrium.

Remember first the conditions of our problem. We are still dealing with given stocks (or given flows) of commodities. There is still no question of production. But whereas before we were dealing with two individuals and two commodities we are now to deal with m individuals and n commodities. And we are to ask under what conditions equilibrium arises?

At the outset of our enquiry, let us make one big simplifying assumption. Let us assume that one of the commodities in question is used as a general medium of exchange. That is to say let us suppose that ours is a community practicing the use of money. This is an assumption which has the merit of bringing our investigation closer to reality and at the same time of simplifying theory. We have seen already some of the theoretical difficulties of barter. We know from elementary monetary theory some of the practical difficulties of doing without money. The situation will be much easier to handle if we do not incur these difficulties.

Now let us survey the general situation. The various members of the community find themselves in possession of stocks[1] of different sizes of different commodities. Sometimes they may want to use these commodities themselves. But this will not always be the case. In many cases they would prefer to obtain other commodities. They will therefore sell the quantities they do not want for money and with the money they obtain buy the commodities they do want. That is to say the different members of the community will figure in two capacities. In some markets they will be sellers and on others they will be buyers. Our task is to discover the characteristics of their behaviour generally.

Let us concentrate first on the behaviour of buyers. And to simplify matters still further let us start by concentrating on the behaviour of a single buyer. We will deal with one consumer with a fixed income at liberty to spend this income on what he will.

---

1 Stocks or flows.

Now there is one point which it is important to notice at this juncture. Save in rare cases it is not possible for one buyer to affect the price of the goods he purchases by varying the extent of his purchases or by exercising skill in bargaining. Of course such things do happen in unorganized markets and the purchase of unique things. But these are of secondary importance and in a broad survey we may justifiably leave them out of consideration. It follows then that the terms on which our single consumer can get goods are *fixed facts of the market.* Market prices may fluctuate but the fluctuations are not of his making – Or so at least it will seem to him. That being understood we can proceed to analysis.

At this point the conception of a relative scale of valuations which I elaborated at such length last week again becomes appropriate. Just as when we were considering simple exchange we found the idea of scales of relative significance a help in discussing the situation so too now we are thinking of a more extensive system of exchange, a similar conception is useful. That is to say, we imagine that for our consumer there exists scales of relative significances which exhibits the significance to him at different margins of the various commodities he may purchase. Thus when he has x gold he may value 1 unit of bread as $1/20$ £ sterling 1 unit of coal as £10 sterling and so on –

There are one or two points about this conception which it is as well to note explicitly.

(1) The scale is *expressed* in terms of money. The units of other commodities are priced in terms of so many money units.

Thus if we were using the diagrammatic analysis I described last time, indicating position on the scale by distance along a perpendicular, the unit of measurement would be money, pence shillings or what not.

Pence	A
4	
3	Haircut
	Cup of tea
2	
	Tram fare
1	Daily Mail
0	

(2) But second, notice that the *valuation of money itself is implied in the relative scale.* If I value 2 of corn as the equivalent of 1 of coal I value 1 coal as 2 of corn. We saw in our earlier discussion that one scale implied the other.

This point is important to notice expressly because it has an obvious bearing on the theory of monetary value.

It may be that a man will value other commodities so much that he will get rid of all his money in a given period. He is then in the position of the man who valued corn so much that he parted with all his coal. But most of us find it convenient to keep some money by us and in spending our resources a point arrives when we value the "marginal" unit of stock of money more than any commodity we could get in exchange for it.

•   This is the way the celebrated Marshallian theorem fits into general equilibrium theory.

(3) Third, notice that there is no need for us to limit our conception of the goods entering into the relative scale to goods which are immediately consumable. We may buy goods which are durable, houses, tools etc. We may also buy rights to receive sums of money.

This last point is especially worth noting, for it conceals a problem with which we shall have to deal more fully later. Suppose we contemplate buying a piece of land let out for let us say 999 years at £100 p.a. At first sight you might be inclined to say that the position on the relative scale of this option is bound to be £99,900 – the sum of the rents + the sum of the rents which we compute could be got hereafter.

But a little reflection will show that we should not do this. We should never dream of paying now an infinite number of years purchase for a piece of land (or a debenture stock) yielding an infinite number of rents.

It is obvious that we should give less and the problem that we shall have to solve later on is why? The problem that is to say of capitalization. But meanwhile notice that rent yielders come into the circle of exchange and figure on the relative scale.

(4) Finally, notice that the positions of the various commodities on the scale are dependent on *all* the quantities possessed or supposed to be possessed. The extent to which I value bread will depend upon the quantity of other kinds of food I possess as well upon the quantity of bread in my possession *and on the quantity of money*.

So much for the relative scales of the individual. Now, observe that he is confronted as it were by another relative scale, the prices in the markets. It is clear that the market establishes a similar grading of commodities. A is worth 1/–, B 2/–, C 3/– and so on. We may call this the communal relative scale. When therefore our consumer goes out to spend his money, he will certainly find that possessing all money and no other goods there are many goods which are valued by the market in terms of money relatively lower than they are by him. Or to put it another way he will find that his valuation of money in terms of goods is relatively lower than the valuation of the market. It is obvious therefore that there will be an inducement to him to buy. As he buys his stock of money is depleted and his stocks of other things becomes augmented, gradually the advantage of buying will diminish and it will finally be extinguished when the commodities on his relative scale have the same relative position as they have on the communal scales of the market. Or – to put it another way – when the terms on which he can get goods correspond to the valuations he puts on these goods as compared with money.

Here we come again on the celebrated generalization of utility theory that in a state of equilibrium the marginal utilities of the different commodities 'measured' in terms of money are proportional to their prices – or that the final degrees of utility are equal. The relative scale may be conceived to express utilities in money. Units of money may be conceived to secure the last increment (not unit) of commodity. The only difference between the theories up to now is that we employ a terminology which refers to no psychological magnitudes and assumes no rationality of action. But I have discussed this point already.

Now let us enlarge our speculations and consider the case of buying in general. There are now *m* consumers as well as *n* commodities. Let us for the time being continue to ignore the community regarded as sellers. Let us suppose just that the stocks of commodities are given – that they are just there to be sold. Again we may suppose that there exist relative scales for each of the buyers to be conceived as we have already discussed. But we are now faced by the fact that before purchasing – or at any rate negotiations commence – there exists no communal scale of prices. How, then, does price emerge in the market? Here our theory comes into line with Marshall's theory of market prices. To see this it is easiest to have recourse to the familiar analysis of demand and price in the market.

Just as we have been able to imagine a relative scale for each individual expressing his willingness to exchange given varies quantities of income and commodities, so we can imagine a series of scales expressing his willingness to exchange – to buy given different stocks and given different terms of trade. To devise exact expressions for the way these scales behave would require very complicated formulae. For as we have seen every valuation is dependent upon not the only quantity contemplated as possessed of the commodity in question, but upon the quantity of other commodities possessed also – and therefore of the terms on which they are obtainable.

That is why Cassel and the mathematical economists generally insist so frequently that demand is to be expressed not only as $d = f(p)$ where p is the price of the commodity in question, but rather as $d = f(p_1, p_2 \ldots p_n)$.

But while recognizing the truth of this and realizing that it must be brought into the final solution, we may provisionally simplify matters by assuming that all the p's except p_1 are constant.

We are therefore free to draw up first demand schedules for all the buyers in a market and then to add them together to get the familiar demand schedule.

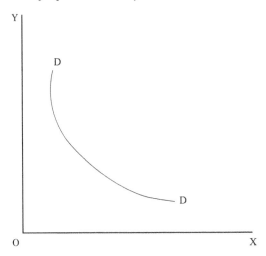

That being given, it is not difficult to see how the price is arrived at if the market is competitive. If equilibrium is to exist – if the market is to be cleared – the amount demanded must equal the amount supplied. The terms of trade – the price – therefore must be just such as to restrict demand to this quantity.

How far is this price determinate? If the market is competitive – that is if people know what is happening everywhere, so that a uniform price obtains and if the dealers hit on the equilibrium price at the outset, completely so. But if there is ignorance on the part of sellers or buyers and the wrong price is hit on and many transactions take place before it is discovered by the dealers, then we must imagine that the position and possibly the shape of the demand curve is affected and the ultimate price is not the equilibrium price at the outset. Probably in actual markets there is a good deal of minor indeterminateness of this sort knocking about. But clearly it is much less important than in the case of barter. At the moment, then, I propose to neglect it.

So much for price determination in one market. I hasten over details, as this part should be familiar. In exactly the same way we must conceive prices being determined in all other markets and since – as we have seen – it is not possible to regard the demand in one market as being independent of prices in other markets, if we are to obtain an exact view of the nature of the pricing process we must imagine them as being *simultaneously determined* by the general conditions of demand everywhere on the one hand and the size of the different stocks on the other. This is a process which can probably best be expressed by differential equations. It would be a waste of time to put these on the board, but those of you who can handle this sort of thing will find it useful to work through the explanation given in one of the standard works on mathematical economics – Cassel, or better Walras, Antonelli or Pareto.[2]

But now all this time we have been supposing supply to be a given. That is, we suppose the various members of the community to value any money more than the last unit of the stocks with which they come on the market as sellers.

This is a supposition which is unreal and unnecessary and we may now proceed to dispense with it.

Revert to our single market for a moment. Let us assume let us a say a fish market. The sellers are willing to sell all their fish if the price per fish is say 1/–. As the price falls, however, some of them decide that they prefer fish to money and withdraw part of their supplies from the market.

You have now a state of affairs in which demand and supply are both variable, both capable (as a first approximation) of being expressed by schedules or graphs. You know [the] accepted theory of the matter. At the point at which demand and supply are equal or at the intersection of the two curves price is fixed and equilibrium established.

But now does not this introduce a new complication? The demand curve as we saw ultimately depended on the relative valuations of different individuals of this commodity and money, given different quantities. Supply was given, a brute fact of hypothesis. Does not this upward sloping curve introduce a fundamentally new factor into the situation, something we have not yet contemplated? Not at all. *The supply curve here is just a disguised demand curve and depends, just as much as the demand curve, which is explicitly formulated, upon relative valuations.*

Let us look at this a little more closely.

Suppose an actual set of schedules.

Demand	Price	Supply
5,000	1/–	15,000
7,000	10d	12,000
10,000	8d	10,000
12,000	6d	8,000

The total supply is 15,000.

At this price the sellers are prepared to put all on the market. As the price falls they withdraw certain quantities. The price settles at 8d where supply and demand are equal.

---

2 [G. Cassel, *Fundamental Thoughts in Economics* (1925); L. Walras, *Elements d'economie politique* (1926); G.B. Antonelli, *Sulla teoria matematica dell'economia politica* (1886); V. Pareto, *Manuele d'economia politica* (1906), translated as *Manuel d'economie politique* (1909)]

Now observe that we could have represented this another way. Let us suppose that the sellers put the whole supply on the market without reserve. Then let us suppose that if the price falls below 1/– they reenter the market as buyers and buy out the quantities before reserved. This is not an unrealistic assumption. At auctions it is often done. Sometimes reserve prices are put on the goods. Sometimes the seller employs agents to big at low prices. Then if the higher price fails to materialize he has simply bought his own stuff and excluded the other buyers at lower prices.

We can then rewrite our table thus:

Price	Demand (buyers)	Demand (sellers)	Total demand
1/–	5,000	-	
10d	7,000	3,000	10,000
8d	10,000	5,000	15,000
6d	12,000	7,000	19,000

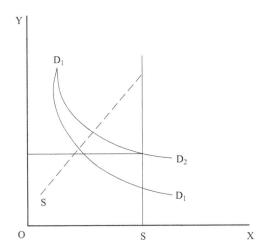

Clearly, if the total amount to be sold is 15,000 then the equilibrium price is 8d, which was what we learnt from the earlier table.

We can affect the same transformation of diagrams.

It is therefore clear that the phenomena of supply (production excluded) are of the same order as the phenomena of demand, both being dependent in the last analysis on the relative valuations of the buyers and sellers in the community.

It appears then that our separation of the community into buyers and sellers, although useful for purposes of argument, was theoretically unnecessary. The condition of equilibrium is merely that the various members of the community by buying in or selling out the different commodities concerned, bring their relative scales into harmony with the communal scale, that is to say with the relative scales of each other.

The difference between equilibrium here and equilibrium in barter is that here, where competition is active, price is determinate whereas under barter was determined only by relative cunning and bargaining power. But even this is only a difference of degree. Competition is never absolutely perfect in the sense postulated by pure theory. Under barter price is not indeterminate altogether. It is indeterminate only between limits.

6 Equilibrium of production

Factors fixed

So far in these lectures I have been dealing with the problem of Exchange Equilibrium – first barter then Multiple Exchange. I want now to enlarge the scope of our investigations and to proceed to the discussion of Equilibrium of Production – or that part of the theory of Equilibrium of Production which deals with Equilibrium of Production when the supplies of the factors of production are given. That is to say the relations I shall be contemplating in this and the following lecture are – roughly speaking – the relations contemplated in J.B. Clark's celebrated discussion of the Static State.

Let us just refresh our memories of the general conditions of the problem. So far we have been discussing equilibrium when the stocks of commodities exchanged are given by hypothesis. We are now to consider equilibrium when the stocks can be varied. Factors of production exist which can be turned to more than one use, so that if there is an impulse that way the stock or the flow of one commodity can be augmented, the flow of others being correspondingly diminished. That is a rough picture of the conditions we are to consider. Two things, however, need emphasizing a little further.

(1) First, we are considering production. Henceforward we shall think of our various quantities as flows through time. Hitherto I have used stock or flow as more or less interchangeable. But now (for reasons which will become clearer later on when we consider capitalization) I shall think always of flows – so much bread, so much fuel, so much meat per month or per year.

(2) The factors of production are given – their supply is as fixed as the supply of commodities was when we were considering equilibrium of exchange. Now there are two ways in which we can conceive this fixity.

   (a) Either we can conceive that neither men nor tools wear out and that their total number is given once for all during the period we contemplate.

   (b) Or we can think of a stationary population with constant age, sex and ability composition on the one hand. And a body of factory tools, materials etc., continually replenished by the application of a fixed proportion of existing capital and labour on the other.

Either way would give us what we want so far as fixity was concerned. But the second way although much closer to reality would impinge rather upon the problems I shall be discussing when I come to discuss Equilibrium of Production Factors Flexible. We should want to know why the population was stationary, and why capital was maintained in precisely a constant volume.

I therefore propose to adopt the more artificial hypothesis. Instead of assuming willingness to maintain population etc. stationary, I shall impose the fixity from without. I assume that the population is given and that the capital goods – factors of production – do not wear out. I shall assume too that neither capital nor labour can be put to making provision for the future by making *fresh* factors of production. That being understood we can proceed at once to analysis.

Now as I suggested when I was sketching the general stages of equilibrium theory it is desirable to attack this problem by stages. In this lecture therefore I want to make the further assumption that the various processes of production each involve only the use of one scarce factor of production. Thus we shall not consider the case of the producer using scarce labour to work up scarce raw material with scarce tools into a scarce final product – with all the problems of deciding how much of the value of the product is to be imputed to each of the factors. We shall consider only the case of workmen working up materials which are given in such quantities by nature that they are free goods. When we have learnt all we can from this it will be time enough to proceed to the more complicated case.

• Please do not be impatient at all these simplications. Some of you, I know, must feel that I am moving in regions utterly profitless to contemplate. And of course so they would be if they did not help later on. The point is that we are now dealing with problems so highly involved and intricate that if we do not simplify as much as we can we can still never get anywhere. Of course we may not get anywhere in any case – that is for you to judge – but I submit that if we do fail it is not because our mode of approach is unsatisfactory.

But now to work. Let us start by examining the behaviour of an isolated producer – Robinson Crusoe if you will. The factors of production are fixed. That is to say the length of time he works per day, per week and per year is given. And since we are only contemplating the use of one scarce factor today we must assume that everything else is free. There are as many oranges as he wishes – provided he will devote time to getting them. There are as many fish as he can desire, provided he will devote time to catching them, and so on.

That being understood it should be fairly clear I think that we are faced with a situation *not radically dissimilar* from that which we contemplated last time when we were considering an individual distributing his resources in the market. At first sight you might think that the two cases were poles asunder. *There*, we were dealing with exchange. *Here*, we are contemplating production. *There*, there was a multiplicity of persons. *Here*, we are dealing with a single individual. But a little consideration shows that these differences are largely illusory.

It is true that in the one case we are considering the exchange of money for goods and here we are contemplating production. But in both cases in order that something may be got something has to be given. There it was money. Here it is labour-time. But the difference is not great. Indeed, if we will we can conceive production as being a kind of exchange. The exchange of factors – the uses of factors – for the things they enable us to procure.

And there is a second similarity. In the market our purchaser was confronted with a series of options – prices – which it was not in his power to alter. The same situation confronts our producer. Oranges can be had at the rate of say two minutes an orange. Fish can be had at the rate of say four minutes a fish. We may therefore apply to the analysis of production the same apparatus of explanation that we learned to use when discussing exchange.

We may assume that a relative scale may be drawn up expressing the relative significance to Robinson of the different commodities he can procure. The time that it takes him to procure them per unit will be as it were the objective relative scale – not of the market – but of the environment.

And we can imagine distributing his time between the different occupations open to him in such a way as to bring his relative scale into harmony with the relative scale of the environment.

Thus let us suppose that there are two commodities procurable – oranges and fish. And that given a stock of time of say eight hours per day Robinson values oranges and fish as say 1 fish to eight oranges. Now if we assume as above that it takes four minutes to catch a fish and two to get an orange we may say that on the environmental relative scale 1 fish is the equivalent of two oranges. Clearly at the outset Robinson will be a fool if he goes for anything but fish. In four minutes he can get 1 fish or two oranges. But he values fish as the equivalent of eight oranges. If he goes for oranges rather than fish he is losing at the rate of which he values six oranges every four minutes so spent. Fishing therefore it will be for a time. But as the catch increases the significance of fish in terms of oranges (or time) sinks.

And probably (it is not certain for fish may be valued very high and oranges hardly at all) sooner or later 1 fish will be valued only as much as two oranges. It will be then time to consider orange picking. But the acquisition of oranges may sink then below fish after a short time and fishing will then be preferable.

And so the day will go on. No doubt the first day the adjustment would be very inaccurate and a good deal of time would be wasted switching from one thing to another. But as time went on we may assume that errors would be corrected and time would be distributed between the two occupations in such a way as to make alterations undesirable.

What would be conditions of such an equilibrium?

You may formulate it in two ways:

(1) Equilibrium would exist when time could not be withdrawn from onething and devoted to another without the cost being greater than the gain – that is when the significance of a minute in one channel was equal to the significance of a minute in another.

(2) Or equilibrium would exist when the commodities concerned occupied the same position on Robinson's scale as on the environmental scale – always assuming that the whole day was not exhausted before the initial disparity had not been remedied.

That is simple. But our treatment has concealed one or two assumptions which should be made explicit before we proceed.

(1) We assume that the tasks of fishing and orange picking are equally attractive to Robinson. If it were not so, if the fishing had to be done in a horrible swamp and the oranges could be picked in a sunny grove, then clearly there would be a complication. In considering the outlay of time on one thing or the other Robinson would as it were *debit* the fish with the unpleasantness and *credit* the oranges with the enjoyment. It would only be after doing this that he would distribute his time in the manner indicated in the first formulation of equilibrium. This is the complication envisaged in Adam Smith's doctrine of the tendency of net advantages rather than net earnings to a position of equality. It should be familiar to you all and I do not wish to dwell on it further here. I shall be referring to it later in another connection.

(2) We have assumed that *throughout the day* that Robinson can get either 1 fish or two oranges with an expenditure of four minutes. That is we assume that his efficiency does not change. But the complication is of minor importance. It is more difficult to generalize in terms of harmony of relative scales without undue complication of language for of course this circumstance implies that at different hours of the day the terms on which fish and oranges can be got vary – that the environmental scale changes. But it is just as easy to generalize in terms of equivalence of the yield of marginal units of time. In fact the same generalization holds. Time will be distributed in such a way as to make the yield of fish or oranges *per unit of time* of equal significance at the margin.

One final word on this particular example. How are we to understand costs? At first sight, it would seem that costs should be reckoned in time.

And no doubt this is one way of doing it. But if we consider further we see I think that *so long as time is not valued save for product*, that is so long as time worked is fixed and invariable we might as well go behind time to the alternative product. Thus if one fish takes the same time to catch as two oranges we sacrifice two oranges if we catch one fish, or one fish if we pick two oranges.[1] But this is by the way. There will be more to say about costs later on.

Now let us contemplate a more complicated situation. Let us admit a whole society to the island. Let us introduce money and the division of labour. But let us retain our initial assumption of fixed working days (they need not be the same for everybody) and free material factors. At the same time let us assume that there is no cooperation. Each workman produces and sells by himself.

The situation is now more complex. It is not now a question of one producer working for a product or series of products which he himself values. it is a question of a community of individuals each producing one good, selling it and with

---

1 We then judge the significance of the cost by reference to the relative scale.

the proceeds buying others. We have to ask under what conditions is there an equilibrium distribution of individuals between occupations and an equilibrium of prices.

Notice one feature of our hypothesis that is of great importance in this connection. We have left the employer out of the picture and the whole apparatus of contract. Each producer superintends as it were his own operations and brings his own product to market. It follows therefore that the sum of prices he gets for his product constitutes his money income. Remember he gets his materials etc. free. *The price problem and the income problem are one.* He is paid (by the market) the value of his product. There is no problem of imputation at this juncture. The demand for the product *is* the demand for the factor.

• You see here, I suggest, one of the advantages of our treatment. In the books which divide the problem of equilibrium into sections dealing with value and distribution respectively the connection between prices and income – money prices and money prices – is often lost sight of. By surveying the whole process at once we never lose sight of this connection. At the same time by viewing successively a series of models as it were approximating more and more closely to reality we understand at each stage the exact limitations of our generalizations.

But that [is] by the way – the question we have to answer is what are the conditions of equilibrium in the circumstances we are contemplating?

Assume that people have sorted themselves out into different occupations. Assume too competitive markets. They produce their goods and bring them up for sale. At this point our analysis of Exchange Equilibrium tells us what happens in the market. Once the goods are there they must be cleared. Prices are established which make demand and supply equal. The various producers are then in a position to survey their situation afresh. Probably the prices established will suggest the desirability of change for some of them. It may be that in one time A prices are such as to yield incomes higher that are being got by producers of similar skill and willingness to work. In another time B. If this is so there will be an incentive to change and we may assume that after a suitable interval of time has elapsed changes will take place. As the supply of work in A increases and the supply of work in B diminishes there will ensure a corresponding change in the price situation. The price of A will fall the price of B will rise. Equilibrium will be established when transfer is no longer rewarded by gain.

All this is familiar doctrine, and there is no need for me to waste your time in lengthy elaboration. It is sufficient to generalize and say that equilibrium in general will be *established when each producer is getting at least as much where he is as he could hope to get elsewhere.* But there are certain aspects of this generalization which it may be well to mention explicitly.

(1) In the first place, by getting as much we include of course the other advantages and disadvantages of production that I have alluded to already. The only

thing about these worthy of note is that they are essentially *subjective* influences. We cannot standardize the net advantages of an occupation in money terms. What is one man's meat is another man's poison. All that we can do is to regard them as being of the same nature as the individual valuation of the product – and to be taken account of in just the same way.

(2) Second, notice there is no suggestion that one producer will get as much as another. There is no suggestion that all incomes will tend to equality. On the contrary rather we should not expect this to be the case, (a) partly because of the different attractiveness of different industries, and (b) partly because we may assume that not all men have the same degree of skill at everything. We are not obliged to assume that there is only one factor of production – simple manual labour.

(3) Third, observe that I formulate the condition of equilibrium as being that each factor is getting *at least* as much where it is as it could get elsewhere. The "at least" is vitally important if our generalization is to be comprehensive. Some producers will have specialized skill which earns much more in one line of production than in any other. They will not only earn as much in that line as elsewhere. They will earn more. But the condition of their remaining is that they earn at least as much where they are as they could elsewhere.[2]

So much for simple production. One last word on the relation of what I have been saying to the older theories of value. Our discussion throughout has been in terms of demand (relative valuations) acting on disposable factors and securing an equilibrium position. What relation – if any – has all this to the theory propounded by some of the classics that when production was contemplated the ratios of exchange between different commodities was determined by their relative labour costs of production. What relation has all this to the Labour Theory of Value?

The Labour Theory of Value may be conceived to imply two things.

(1) Commodities have value because labour is embodied in them.
(2) Commodities exchange according to the relative quantities of labour going to their production.

The first proposition is obviously false. It was not held by any of the more respectable classics. Clearly things are not valuable because men work for them. Men work for them because they are valuable. But the second proposition is much more plausible and deserves further attention.

Suppose we take A. Smith's illustration it takes twice as long to kill a beaver as it takes to kill a deer. And suppose there is a market for both. It is not fairly plausible to argue that if beavers do not exchange for deer as 1:2 tendencies will be set in motion which bring it about that they do. Suppose e.g. they exchange as 1:1?

2 This has an important bearing on the theory of rent.

Obviously it will be better to get beavers by killing deer than by attempting to kill them directly. For it takes as long as to kill a beaver as it does to kill 2 deer. If therefore 1 deer exchanges for one beaver you can get 2 beavers in exchange, whereas by production in a similar time you can only get one.

Therefore people will change over. The supply of deer will increase, the supply of beavers will diminish and equilibrium will be restored with the exchange ratios equivalent to the production time ratios. Very plausible is it not? And granted its implicit assumptions true. For if the implicit assumptions are stated it will be seen to be only a special case of our general theory.

For in the first place it implies market values determined by supply and demand – the equating of individual scales to the communal scale. Secondly it implies our assumption of diminishing demand price – or diminishing relative utility – as the stock of deer increases and the stock of beavers diminishes the valuation of deer in terms of beavers diminishes. Granted these assumptions and also the assumption of production under conditions of constant cost the thing is true in the conditions supposed. We have seen something very similar when considering Robinson Crusoe arranging his efforts so as to bring his relative valuations into line with the objective conditions offered by his environment and his skill.

But quite apart from differences in the mode of statement – the assumptions not being made explicit – the thing is too narrow to explain any but the most exceptional cases. For further it assumes that:

(1) Occupations involve equal skill.
(2) They are equally attractive to all members of the community.

None of which things are necessarily given even in our limited universe as I have pointed out. And when you step outside – when you contemplate joint production – production using more than one factor of production the theory breaks down altogether – whereas the generalizations I have been making only need amplification and explaining to be equally applicable.

Read

Adam Smith, *An Inquiry into the Nature and Causes of the Wealth of Nations* ed. E. Cannan (1904) Chapter 8 David Ricardo, 'On the Principles of Political Economy and Taxation' in *The Works of David Ricardo* ed. J.R. McCulloch (1846) Chapter I On Value

Edwin Cannan, *A Review of Economic Theory* (1929)

Frank H. Knight, *Risk, Uncertainty and Profit* (1921)

Philip H. Wicksteed, *The Alphabet of Economic Science* (1888) pp. 116–124

H.J. Davenport, *The Economics of Enterprise* (1913)

J.A. Schumpeter, *Die Theorie der wirtschaftslichten Entwicklung* (1911) Chapter I

Friedrich Wieser, *Theorie des gesellschaftlichen Wirtschaft* (1923) Part II

F.H. Knight, 'A suggestion for simplifying the general theory of price' *Journal of Political Economy* (June 1928)

L.C. Robbins, 'The representative firm' *Economic Journal* (September 1928)

7 Equilibrium of production

Factors fixed (continued)

Now, so far we have been considering what I have called Simple Production – production that is to say involving the use of only one factor of production in each production process. Today I want to remove this assumption and to consider the more general case: Production involving the use of more than one scarce factor of production in each production process. Joint Production is the technical term I have given it.

Let us look more closely at the nature of the problem. Production is Joint. Two or more factors are involved in the different production processes. The different products are priced by a mechanism with which we are familiar. What we want to know is on what principles are the various process[es] of production organized. What determines the share of the proceeds of the sale of the finished product which goes to the cooperating factors? Now of course this is a very unrealistic method of putting things. In fact of course the question I have just put never actually arises. In practice the firms which receive the price of the finished articles will already have made bargains of one kind or another with many or with all of those engaged in its production. They will have agreed to pay certain sums as wages. They will have bought raw material. They will have rented their land or their factories – all this *before* the product is sold.

And of course it is very important to realize that this is so. No doubt the gap between the sale of the product and the contracts which fix the price of the factors is fundamentally important in the theory of industrial fluctuations. If our theory pretended at this stage to be dealing with the totality of facts in the distributive situation, we should have to take these things into consideration.

But it is equally important to realize a matter which my way of putting it brings out. The fact namely that whether there is a gap between the price contract and the income contracts or not, the price of the product provides the funds out of which the distributive shares are paid. In our former discussion – simple production – the price of the product *constituted* the income of the producer. The price problem and the income problem were one. In our present discussion things are indeed more complicated in this way, that the price of the product has to be *divided* between cooperating factors. There is a problem of the price of the product, and there is a problem of the price of the factors. But – short period disparities apart – it is clear that the price of the product *is* the outer limit of the price of the factors – that it constitutes the source of it of which they are paid and that – the volume of production remaining the same – one factor can gain if the others lose.[1]

And this is not a mere theoretical truism. It is a maxim which you do well to bear in mind in practical discussions of policy. It is often said for instance that upward changes in wages are a good thing because they increase general purchasing power and stimulate trade. Dr Ford has said so. Mr Wheatley says so continually.[2] But *assuming fixed factors* and fixed income the total "p.p." released by the sale of a product is constant, however it is distributed. Higher wages simply mean more spending power in the hands of workers less in the hands of rentiers. The same amount of "p.p." is released. Its distribution only is different. If we assume flexible factors then wages for the time being may encroach on capital. This means more demand for consumption goods – less provision for future. The cause of crisis and depression. Only if we assume different dispositions to hoard is the proposition conceivable.

But that is a digression. The question out of which it arose was the question what determines the prices of the factors of production when production is joint – and our other assumptions are given – and what is an equilibrium distribution of factors in these conditions. And I want to continue to put the question this way, not only for the reasons which I have already given but for others which should be more apparent later.[3]

Now of course we could conceive a world in which joint production involved complete rigidity in the forms of factor cooperation. So many men always had to use so many tools in order to turn so many units of product and if any one of the factors was left out the whole process of production would be disorganized. And no doubt even in the world we inhabit cases of this sort of rigidity do occur. When a horse and a cart are cooperating – so to speak – you cannot remove either the horse or the cart without upsetting the operation.

But in the main production is a more elastic thing than this. Different factors of production act as substitutes for one another at the margin. If you are thinking of the organization of a big concern you cannot think all the units of a certain kind of labour out of the picture. But you can think of *some* of them dropping out without greatly disorganizing the rest if substitutes are available in the shape, say, of a certain kind of machine or another kind of labour. That is to say over the broad field of production it is not inappropriate to assume variability of factor combination – substitution at the margin.

On the other hand, it is important to realize that this possibility only exists within *limits*. The combination of factors to produce a given product is not indefinitely

---

1 [Robbins added in the margin: 'This is a fact which has some bearing on problem of high monetary[?] theory. Omit this. Bring it in later on.']

2 [Henry Ford, the founder of the Ford Motor Company who advocated high wages for workers, and John Wheatley, a leftwing Labour MP who had been Minister of Health in the first Labour government of 1924]

3 It enables you (see Knight) to steer clear of the cost problem at this stage.

variable. Some combinations are less efficient than others. Variation is only possible at the expense of varying productivity.

It is this important fact which is sometimes described by what has come to be known as the law of diminishing returns.

Now there is no more protean "law" in the whole range of Economic Theory than the Law of Diminishing Returns. To understand properly its significance in every branch of theory in which it is used requires I think a not inconsiderable acquaintance with the history of theory. When I come back to deal in greater detail with the more technical parts of the ground we are now covering I shall examine it in some detail.

From our point of view it is sufficient to distinguish two variants of the law. The first runs as follows. If two factors of production x and y are used in combination and the quantity of one is varied the other remaining constant the return measures as an average of the variable factor first increases, reaches a maximum and then diminishes. That is the form in which you encounter the law in discussion of the population problem. It relates, as you see, to *average* productivity. But in this form it is not useful in our present discussion. I mention it only in order to distinguish it from the second, with which it is sometimes confused.

The second runs as follows: If two factors of production x and y are used in combination and the quantity of the one is varied, the other remaining constant, the additions to the product made by additional y's first increase, reach a maximum and then diminish. Here you see we are discussing *marginal* productivity – not the returns as a whole measured as an average of the varying factors but the difference to the returns as a whole made by additional increments of the varying factor.

What is the basis of this law? Quite clearly experience. If you could increase the quantity of products indefinitely by only proportionally increasing the quantity of one of the factors contributing to its production, the world would be a much easier place to live in than it actually is. All the corn needed could be grown in one field. All the cloth made in one factory all the supervision done by one supervisor and so on. The thing is obvious as soon as you think of it. We only put it into precise forms in order to assist more complicated thought later on.

Hence I think it is a little pathetic to watch the experiments which are sometimes made to "verify the law of diminishing returns". Of course it always is verified and gullible economists put a footnote in their books referring to the important experiments at X –. But such activities are quite superfluous. The experiment is made every time we try to get more out of a certain factor than it will yield and have to increase our holding.

No doubt, it is very interesting to [word missing] *the rate at which* productivity changes. Experiments of this sort are not at all superfluous. But to experiment to discover whether it diminishes at all – that is reminiscent of Swift's Laputa.[4]

---

4 [The flying island in *Gulliver's Travels* (1726) whose inhabitants had mastered magnetic levitation but made measurements with compass and quadrants rather than tape measures]

But now let us watch the "law" at work in the system we have constructed. Let us start as before with the behaviour of a single producer – a small farmer perhaps, hiring labour and land and using little machinery. We will neglect the apparatus of contract and the possibility of dynamic frictions – we are considering static conditions where these complications are unnecessary.

Three fixed facts confront our producer.

1)   First, the price of his product. That is given by the general conditions of demand and supply in the market in which he sells.
2)   The relative scale of prices of the factors of production he uses. He buys these in a competitive market so these too are fixed.
3)   The productivity of the factors he uses. The technical properties of the various kinds of land and labour at his disposal and their laws of variation. These too he cannot alter in the absence of new knowledge how to use them.

Now let us watch his behaviour as he organizes his business. Let us suppose that he only uses one grade of labour and one of land. Clearly he must have some labour and some land. That much is obvious. Labour cannot produce without land. Land will not produce without labour. We need not worry about the "first" stages of his activities therefore. Some land and some labour will be used. But gradually he will come to be more careful. The question is how much land and how much labour will he hire in the end?

Let us consider labour. As he goes on adding labour to his land, its marginal productivity will diminish. The additional quantity of product will be less. At the same time the prices both of labour and of product will be constant. Surely this gives us our clue. *So long as the value of the marginal product is greater than the price he has to pay for it he will go on hiring labour.* For clearly there will be a profit in so doing. He will stop when the profit is obliterated.

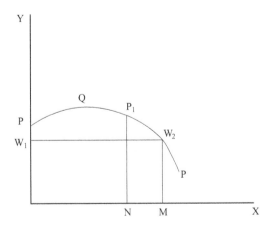

The thing can be represented diagrammatically thus. Along OX represent units of labour applied to a constant [amount] of land. Along OY represent rates of yield at the margin and rates of pay of labour. Then PP_1 represents the variation of marginal productivity. First it rises, reaches a maximum at Q and then declines. At the same time let W_1W_2 represent rates of pay for the labour employed. It is bought in a competitive market hence it is constant. So long as OP is greater than OW, there is a margin of profit to be gained by engaging additional labour. Employment will therefore be pushed up to the point OM where MW = MP.

One word about the measurement of productivity. I have equated productivity to wages in the illustration above. Is this not illegitimate when I have spoken throughout of productivity as something physical? Ought we not to distinguish physical and value productivity? Of course we must. And of course in all but rare cases as Marshall makes it clear it is to the value of the additional product rather than to the physical product itself that the entrepreneur will look. The process will not always be so simple that the product can be measured in sheep! But no harm is done so far by the failure explicitly to distinguish the two concepts. Because while we are considering one producer we assume fixed prices for his products. *Hence variations in physical productivity will be proportional to variations in value productivity.*

So much for labour. We can conceive the same computation applied to land. If the price per unit of labour is less than the value of the marginal net product then the farmer will extend his land holding. Thus, in an equilibrium position, we must imagine that the marginal productivity of the factors he employs will be proportionate to their prices – the situation, you see, is still analogous to equilibrium of multiple exchange. But why does he not go on expanding for ever – adding land and labour in amounts which keep their marginal net products proportional to their prices? This is a question which is bound to arise sometimes and it is as well to indicate the answer here and now although its full examination must be deferred.

The answer is to be found in the same generalization that has helped us up to now. *Returns to managerial ability diminish.* As his business increases the amount of supervision the entrepreneur is willing to give to each part is diminished. We are assuming fixed factors so we must assume fixed willingness to work on his part: if he extends beyond what we may call the optimal size for him the concern will become relatively inefficient.

But more of this hereafter.

Now let us very briefly generalize the theory. We need not be long for it is just a matter of extending what has already been said. Assume as before a random distribution of factors. Assume too that contracts are made only for one production period. No dislocation arises beyond one process. Now suppose the first production period over. The goods are made and brought to market. We know already what happens here. Equilibrium prices are established which equate supply and demand. Now the entrepreneurs or the leaders of production have an opportunity of surveying their position. At the same time the owners of the factors they use, labour and material instruments, can reconsider their contracts.

Let us suppose that in one time wheat growing prices are high and labour is relatively short, and that in another time coal digging prices are low and labour relatively abundant. The wheat growing entrepreneurs will realize that if they extend their employment of labour there will be a profit. The coal diggers will realize that theirs is the converse position. The demand of wheat growing for labour will increase, the demand for coal digging will diminish. At the same time, if there is mobility there will tend to be a movement of coal diggers from coal digging to agriculture.

What will be the result of this? It will be twofold.

(a) The *physical productivity* of wheat growing labour will diminish at the margin and the physical productivity of coal digging labour will increase at the margin.

(b) The supply of wheat being increased and the supply of coal being diminished the price of wheat will fall and the price of coal will rise. That is to say, the *value productivity* of wheat growing labour will fall and the value productivity of coal getting labour will rise.

And *this process will go on until in each occupation the physical productivity of labour of that grade as measured in value terms is proportionate to the price which has to be paid in the market for that kind of labour.*

Notice I do **not** say until physical productivities are equal. I refrain from saying this because, of course, the other advantages or disadvantages of the different occupations might not be the same. In an equilibrium, it might be necessary to pay a higher price for labour of a certain grade in coal digging than in agriculture. If this were the case physical productivity at the margin would not be equal.

Such is the celebrated marginal productivity theory of distribution. I have illustrated in terms of labour but of course the thing could be generalized so as to cover all cases. All that we have to do is to repeat our generalization of last time. *Equilibrium exists when each factor is earning at least as much where it is as it could hope to get elsewhere* – remembering that as much means total gains not merely money income – and adding that *when production is joint and the factors are variable the marginal productivity of factors will be proportionate to their price.*

Now of course this is not all there is to say about this very important matter. I shall be coming back to returns and costs in a later lecture. For the moment perhaps it will make clear what the theory involves if I discuss one or two of the more familiar objections to it. Most of these objections relate to the theory when applied to the explanation of wages. People don't like to think that labourers are rewarded according to their marginal efficiency. They don't mind what happens to the other factors.

(1) First, it is objected that this is not a complete theory of wages.

To which it may be answered that few people have ever supposed that it was. Marshall e.g. explicitly says it is not a theory of wages but throws light on one of the causes determining wages. And remember that in the context in which I have developed the theory, it should be abundantly clear that it does not pretend to exhaustiveness. This for two reasons:

(i) The hypotheses we are examining – Production factors fixed – rules out of consideration all repercussions of price on alternate supply of labour.

(ii) *Even within the hypothesis it is only one of the conditions of equilibrium.* It all depends upon the price of different commodities and upon the supply of the different factors where the appropriate margin is.

(2) It is sometimes urged that the theory assumes conditions of variability which are not true to life. That in fact the proportions in which the factors can be combined are fixed and not variable and that to remove a labourer or two from a given combination as we do in our hypothesis would so disorganize things as to make it impossible to assume that other things remain equal. This is really an objection to the suitability of the theory to explain facts rather than to the logic of the theory itself. And all that can do in a case like this is to go to the facts and examine them. Personally I am convinced that over the broad field of industry variability does exist. No doubt there are cases like those regarded as typical by Mr Hobson and others but they seem to me the exception rather than the rule. The theory works as a first approximation.[5]

(3) Closely allied with this sort of objection is another also fathered by Mr J.A. Hobson, which depends upon the choice of ridiculous arithmetical illustrations. It is forgotten that the theory refers to variations which are relatively small viewed in relation to their effects at the margin and arithmetical illustrations involving large variations are considered. It is shown that variations of this sort involve distributions of product which more than exhaust the total production and it is believed that this reduces the theory to an absurdity. If any of you are inclined to this sort of thing I suggest that you read Edgeworth Collected Papers Vol II p 381[6] – Here I content myself with saying that objections based on arithmetical inductions involving large and disconnected variations have no relevance on theories which consider variations which are small and continuous.

4) Finally, some people object to the theory because they think that to say that a factor is rewarded according to its marginal productivity means that it gets what it morally deserves. This is all J.B. Clark's fault. He thought it did. But no other economist that I know has ever thought so. It is obvious to me at any rate that the man who thinks that a system of distribution which gives Einstein less than the Editor of the *Sunday Express* is morally perfect is a moral imbecile. But I do not think he is an intellectual imbecile if he thinks that in competitive conditions incomes are "determined" (in part) by marginal productivity.

---

5 [J.A. Hobson, *The Economics of Distribution* (1900)]

6 ['Applications of the differential calculus to economics' *Papers relating to Political Economy* (1925) Vol. II pp. 367–86]

Read

Frank H. Knight, *Risk, Uncertainty and Profit* (1921) Part II Chapter II

Philip H. Wicksteed, *The Common Sense of Political Economy* (1910) Chapter IX

Alfred Marshall, *Principles of Economics* (1920) Book V Chapter VI and Book VI Chapters 1 and 2 Books VIII and IX

J.B. Clark, *The Distribution of Wealth* (1899)

Thomas N. Carver, *The Distribution of Wealth* (1904)

H. Schultz, 'Marginal productivity and the general pricing process' *Journal of Political Economy* (1929)

Fred M. Taylor, *Principles of Economics* (1924) Chapters 9–12

F.Y. Edgeworth, 'Laws of increasing and diminishing returns' *Papers Relating to Political Economy* (1925) Vol. I pp. 61–99

Application of the differential calculus to economics' *Papers Relating to Political Economy* (1925) Vol. II pp. 367–86

8   Production

Factors flexible

Last week we were dealing with Equilibrium of Production when the ultimate supplies of the factors of production are given – the static state of J.B. Clark and others. I want now to remove this assumption of rigidity of factor supplies and examine the wider conditions of equilibrium resulting. That is to say, I want to pass from the examination of J.B. Clark's static state to the famous stationary state of Marshall and the classics.

Outwardly, as you remember, the appearance of the two systems is similar. All the various quantities – prices of products, factor prices, quantities of commodities, quantities of the factors [-] are constant. Year in year out the same things happen. But in the one case the factor supplies are constant because they are given. In the other case they are constant because there is no incentive for them to alter. As I say, it is this latter case that I now wish to examine.

We are approaching reality in successive hypotheses – successive approximations. We have already done much of the work which it would be necessary to do if we were attacking this problem from the beginning. We have examined Exchange Equilibrium. We know how commodity prices and quantities are held in equilibrium. We have examined Equilibrium of Production with fixed factor supplies. We know how the demand for factors operates. What remains therefore in the present investigation is to examine the new complications introduced by the hypothesis of variable supply.

Two broad divisions of inquiry at once suggest themselves corresponding to the two broad classes of factors of production.

1)   In the first we will examine the flexibility of labour supply.
2)   In the second we will examine the flexibility of supply of material factors of production.

We shall then very broadly survey the part these may be conceived to play in the general conception of equilibrium.

Production: factors flexible: labour supply

I pass then to consider the effects on our conception of equilibrium of the hypothesis of a flexible labour supply. Now labour supply is a complex notion, which it is necessary to analyse carefully.

(1) In the first place we must observe that we are dealing with a supply of *services* – a rate of flow of services rendered in time. There can be no question of a stock of services. The idea is meaningless. We can only conceive of the stock of people who render the services – the labour force.

(2) But secondly notice this supply can change as a result of several different causes. It can change because of a change in the size of the labour force. Or it can change as a result of changes in the quality of the labour force. Moreover it can change as a result of changes in the disposition of the labour force to supply their services – either by way of variations of hours etc., or by way of harder or slacker work within the hour. Extensive and intensive changes.

Broadly speaking these fall under two headings:

(i) Changes in the labour force
(ii) Changes in the supply of services from a given labour force.

For the remainder of this lecture I want to investigate the former kind of change. Next time I shall analyse the latter.

I turn then to changes in labour supply due to changes in the labour force. Let us concentrate first on quantitative changes. We can deal with quality later. Let us assume, too, that we are only dealing with one kind of human factor. That the working population is a homogeneous labour supply. This too is a simplification which we can dispense with later.

The question we have to ask is: What are the conditions of equilibrium granted such an hypothesis? Or to be more specific – to concentrate more on the *new* element in our problem – can we formulate a generalization showing the relation of the labour supply conceived as variable in this matter to the rest of the elements in the equilibrium?

Let us suppose for a moment that we are contemplating a state in which the labour force consists of creatures who are not free agents. Let us think of what would happen in a slave state in which labourers were produced and treated exactly as we treat slaves.

Clearly two considerations would influence slave owners:

(i) Maximizing their own gains
(ii) The cost of producing labourers.

They would therefore push the production of labourers up to just that point at which the marginal productivity of labour was equal to the marginal cost of producing and maintaining labourers. We may illustrate the matter by the apparatus we used last week.

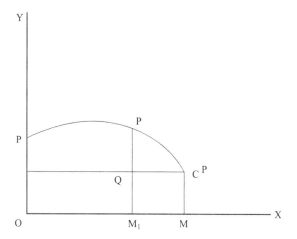

Along OX measure labourers working a constant amount per annum; along OY measure the productivity of labour and the cost of producing labour.

Then it is clear that if the slave owner is in possession of OM_1 labourers it will pay him to breed some more, since there is still additional profit to be made by so doing. He will stop when MC = MP. I have drawn the cost curve horizontal, as is appropriate when considering competitive conditions and a single slave owner.

It is possible of course that if all the slave owners bred more slaves the increased demand for food would necessitate resort to poorer soils or more intensive cultivation. In that case the *collective* cost curve would slope upwards and costs would be different at different margins. But the same generalization would hold. Supply would be pushed to such a point at which marginal cost of production and marginal productivity were equal.[1]

Now of course this is not the whole of the story. The breeding of slaves demands capital, and we have said nothing about that. Moreover, obviously the point at which marginal costs and marginal productivity are equal will depend on the quantity of material equipment available. Equilibrium might be reached with a small or a large population according to variations in these factors. But at this stage it would be tedious to explore such matters in detail. It is worthwhile, however, looking a little more closely at the notion of cost of production thus conceived.

1 Knight suggests that Classics assumption was constant cost. I think it is clear that Ricardo at least realized that costs increased. (*Risk, Uncertainty and Profit*, p. 153)

(1) Notice in the first place that it is a *physical* quantity. We may depict it as a value magnitude, but clearly behind the veil of money we conceive a sort of basket or series of baskets of food, fuel, shelter etc. necessary to keep the beast alive and efficient.[2] It is clear that the classics so conceived it when they thought in terms of the sub[sistence] theory. Movements in *money* wages were supposed *inter alia* to be due to movements in the price of food.

(2) But second, notice that this physical quantity will vary under different conditions.

    (a) It will vary first according to the physical requirements of the slaves. A race of giants would need more than a race of dwarfs etc.

    (b) It will vary second according to climate. A giant will not eat so much at the equator as at the north pole.

    (c) It will vary third according to the work for which the slaves are required. This is a minor detail at this point.

    (d) It will vary fourth with the death rate among slaves. If of a family of four children only two survive to an age when the slave can be useful then the cost of producing a slave must cover the cost of producing two which dies[sic]. Clearly the cost of production must cover the risk of death from disease etc. If the death rate falls the cost of producing slaves will fall also.[3]

And so I could go on refining the conception. But for the moment it will do. It is clear that in the circumstances we have been contemplating a clear connection exists between the supply of labour and the other quantities in the Economic equilibrium. But now the question we have to answer is this: Do similar relations arise when labourers are not owned and bred like cattle but are free agents in the labour market? Has the model of the slave state any significance for the interpretation of the state of affairs under capitalism?

The belief that it had was widespread at one period of our science. At one time indeed it was treated as almost axiomatic. "In all sorts of work," said Turgot, "it must come about and it does come about that the wages of the worker are limited to that which is necessary to procure their subsistence."[4] It was this belief that finds expression in Adam Smith's discussion of the stationary state. If wages were long above subsistence level then labourers increased their numbers and forced them down. He thought it was possible that continued accumulation of capital might delay this state of affairs for a long time, but eventually when the rate of interest had fallen so low as to make it no longer worthwhile to save, labour would catch up with capital and the stationary state would set in with

2 This leaves out interest, which I think is expedient at this point.

3 This will affect interest charge.

4 [Edwin Cannan quoted this, in French, from Turgot's *Reflexions sur la Formation et la Distribution des Richesses* (1770) in his discussion of subsistence theory of wages: *Theories of Production and Distribution in English Political Economy* (1917) p. 232]

wages at a level sufficient only to enable the labourer to keep alive and to bring up a family sufficient to keep the working population constant given the prevalent death rates. The same thing is behind the First Edition of Malthus' celebrated Essay on Population.

Of course there are differences. There is no longer deliberate breeding. *The instinct of Sex takes the place of the desire for profit.*

The death rate is probably higher. The slave owner would not breed *more* than was necessary to bring in the maximum profit. The wretched labourer unless restrained by institutions which are either miserable or vicious goes on breeding and if the supply is so great as to press the productive margin below the cost margin then death steps in. The positive check comes into play. But in the main the conceptions are not dissimilar.

Now of course there may be parts of the world and there may have been periods of history when an assumption of this sort was not a bad approximation to the truth. But of course it certainly does not apply to western conditions now. And it is probable that there are long periods of earlier history when it was not applicable.[5] At any rate it was not long before this theory was abandoned. Malthus conceived a check which was not miserable or vicious – the check of late marriage. Torrens observed that what is necessary is partly a matter of convention – that if the labourer has expensive habits the minimum which will induce him to reproduce his kind is higher.

Out of these developments sprang the idea of a natural – a normal – rate of wages, a rate which kept population steady – fixed not by *physiological* necessities but by *psychological* disposition. A new hope had dawned for "the friends of humanity" – a new conception had been added to the theory of equilibrium. The "static rate" was in a new sense a variable. James Mill thought that wages might by due limitation be raised to any heights deemed desirable.

Now of course this idea of an equilibrium supply price for labour which depends on the labourers' standard of living is much *subtler* than the crude subsistence theory. It is much more in harmony with our conception of equilibrium as depending on choice rather than physical necessity. And of course it includes all that was true in the other theory.

Clearly there is an idea behind it which is sound. Clearly men have powers of restraint over their multiplication not possessed by rabbits. Clearly the motives guiding men as free agents are not the same as the motives guiding slave owning entrepreneurs. Nevertheless there are grave drawbacks inherent in the theory which seem to me to render its usefulness open to question.

(1) It assumes a preoccupation with the financial aspect of child rearing, which seems to me to be totally out of touch with reality. I do not object to the abstract assumptions as such – how could I – but I do urge that assumptions

5 See e.g. A.M. Carr-Saunders, *The Population Problem: A Study in Human Evolution* (1922).

must be *suitable* either by way of contrast or similarity to illuminate some aspect of reality. The "non economic" factors influencing the size of the family seem to me to be so overwhelmingly powerful once you get away from those people whose multiplicative habits still conform roughly to the Malthusian assumption that I am sceptical, whether we really help by making this particular assumption.

(2) Also notice that even on the view of its most intelligent exponents we cannot regard the "natural rate" of wages – this equilibrium supply price – as something given independently of the way it is reached.

According to the best Ricardian view the natural rate and the market rate tended to come together. We should say that marginal productivity and marginal cost tended to become identical. But this did not mean that the market rate gravitated to a natural rate which was *fixed*. It was one of the hopes of the classics that owing to the continued accumulation of capital the market rate might be kept above the natural rate so long that the labourers learnt expensive habits and the natural rate was thereby raised to the level of the market rate.

Now of course there is nothing inherently absurd about the idea of an equilibrium price which varies with the time taken to approach it. On the contrary such ideas are among the most valuable of the recent additions to the theory of money. Still in this particular connection I submit that this indeterminateness of the natural rate is another factor working against the adoption of the notion in general equilibrium analysis.

(3) When one reflects too that in fact the labour force is not one homogeneous body but a heterogeneous collection of different grades each recruited from different classes with different average tendencies to multiplication this view is surely reinforced. The assumption either of a natural rate or a series of natural rates expressing a rigid connection between population and wages is unsuitable for dealing with the modern situation. It is not impossible to conceive; it is inappropriate to the facts.

Of course you must not misinterpret this scepticism. What I have been saying applies essentially to the idea of labour supply in a closed community. I am far from denying the influence of a rise in the rate of wages in one area upon movement into that area. That is however a question of adjustment within the general system rather than flexibility of the system as a whole.

In recent times a certain school of thinkers reacting against the classical idea of a positive connection between the rate of wages and the size of the labour force has attempted to suggest the existence of an inverse relation. As incomes rise the labour supply as influenced by the birth rate falls off, so it is urged. Now of course I would not wish for a moment to dispute the *statistical facts* which are the basis of this generalization. Of course it is perfectly true that speaking broadly in Western communities the higher up the income scale you go the lower the number of births to the average family. But it is a far cry from the ascertainment of this fact to the view that when people's incomes rise their habits as regards multiplication change. Clearly this *may* happen. But it does not follow from the mere statistics. From the mere statistics it would be just as justifiable to infer that those who limit their families rise higher in the income scale. And common sense suggests that this too may happen.

Clearly, I think, the possibility of a reduction of the willingness to bring children into the world through acquaintance with more civilized habits of living, though important in a programme of social reform, is not suitable to provide a basis for an abstract theory of equilibrium. It is not the quantity of real income which matters. It is the habits of the social group to which incomes of a certain level give class and clearly that it is a matter of history and social institutions.

And while I am on this point, may I say that it is just as well to be careful in applying this argument in the context of practical reform.

Some of the more enthusiastic advocates of family allowances e.g. have almost suggested that raise incomes by family allowances the less children will come into existence.

Now[6] I myself think that there is much to be said for family allowances in the abstract. (I make no comment on their desirability in the present political situation.) But I think that this is carrying the argument quite obviously too far.

It is one thing to urge that when people attain by means unconnected with the possession of children a higher standard of living their rate of multiplication tends to fall off. It is quite another thing to urge that this will happen *when the possession of the increased income is contingent upon the having of children.* I do not urge that this thing is logically impossible. Obviously it is not. It might be urged that all that was necessary was the impact of payment for children already there. But it is clear that the probabilities are much heavier against the one course of events than against the other.

[THIS PARAGRAPH IS CROSSED THROUGH:] As I say I myself have much sympathy with the view that money spent on the training and nurture of children is a highly remunerative investment. And on the whole I am not greatly worried by the fear an increased population – clearly the tide is in the other direction – any repercussions of such systems of family allowances as are possible in this country would be only a tiny ripple in the other direction. But it is a pity to bolster a good cause by an argument of such dubious theoretical validity.

So much for wages and labour supply. My general conclusion is the negative one that the connection is so attenuated, so overborn by other dynamic factors, that we simply make the analysis of economic equilibrium unnecessarily unreal by attempting to include it in our equations.

And if this is true of the connection between the quantity of the labour force and its price how much truer is it of the connection between price and quality. We

6 [At this point Robbins pencilled in the margin: 'This involves an analytical blunder' and crossed through the rest of the paragraph.]

may if we like enunciate the qualitative view that up to a point higher incomes are conducive to greater efficiency and better nurture and training of the young. But beyond that we are helpless. These are matters which in any analysis of tendencies to equilibrium it is better to take as given. They are not unsusceptible of scientific study. But they do not lend themselves to this kind of analysis. *For us they must be independent variables.*

But what about the other source of flexibility in labour supply, changes in extensity or intensity of work? That as I hope to show next time is a matter which can be treated in a more positive manner.

Read

Adam Smith, *An Inquiry into the Nature and Causes of the Wealth of Nations* ed. E. Cannan (1904)

David Ricardo, *On the Principles of Political Economy and Taxation*,(1817) Chapter V On Wages

T.R. Malthus, *An Essay on the Principle of Population* 1st edition (1798) reprinted 1926

Alfred Marshall, *Principles of Economics* (1920)

F.W. Taussig, *Principles of Economics* (1929)

L. Brentano, 'The doctrine of Malthus and the increase of population during the last decades' *Economic Journal* (1910)

Eleanor Rathbone, *The Disinherited Family: A Plea for the Endowment of the Family* (1924)

D.H. Macgregor, 'Family allowances' *Economic Journal* (March 1926)

Enrico Barone, *Principii di Economia Politica* (1929) Chapter II

9 Production

Factors flexible: labour supply (continued)

Last time I discussed the problem of the relation between labour supply as affected by changes in the quantity and quality of the population and labour incomes and decided that no such clear functional relationship existed as would justify us in introducing a hypothesis of this sort into our conception of stationary equilibrium. Variations in labour supply due to variations in the population, we decided must be treated as independent variables. Today I want to turn to the other sources of flexibility in the labour supply – the amount of work done by given labourers. For the sake of simplicity I assume at first that all variations of this sort are extensive – come about through changes in the time worked, the intensity of the work done changing only consequentially upon such changes.

At once the question arises is this not another case where the variation is better treated as independent. We have spent a whole lecture discussing population and labour incomes only to discover that no connection can be suitably considered in relation to equilibrium theory. Is not the quest of a relationship between hours and wages likely to be similarly ineffective? Is there any reason to suppose that in the world of today a connection of this sort is apparent? The question is natural. And I grant that a very strong case can be made in favour of scepticism. Clearly in the modern world the time a man works depends largely upon trade custom, legislative enactment, Trade union regulation and so on. At first sight it does almost seem as if the idea of a balance between work and leisure on the part of the individual were worthless to contemplate. But I submit there is this important difference between the case we are now considering and the case we considered last time.

In the case of population and wages we came to the conclusion that *even if we abstracted from frictional influences* the influence of the size of the labour income on the disposition to bring children into the world was vague and weak. It did not seem worthwhile, *assuming* it because there was no reason to suppose that even if it were isolated it would be clear or easy to define.

But in the case of hours and wages I submit this is not so. It is true that the tendency towards reciprocal influence is restrained and overlaid by all sorts of contractual and technical hindrances. But if these were removed there is every reason to suppose that we should find it acting strongly and as contractual and technical frictions are always, as it were, having to contend with it. So that if we discuss it further as it would show itself under our hypothetical conditions, *we shall not be discussing something whose existence can be questioned.* We shall merely be examining in isolation a tendency which is actual and powerful in the world of reality.[1] That being understood, we can proceed with clear consciences.

Let us start once again from the simplest possible hypothesis. Let us revert to our Crusoe Economics and imagine as we imagined a week ago the behaviour of Crusoe on his island arranging his productive activities. Let us suppose as before that time is the only thing to be economized. The oranges and the fish that he gathers can be had in unlimited numbers if he is willing to devote time to their production. But there must be this difference between the situation that we are contemplating now and that which we contemplated before. Then we assumed that the supply of labour, the amount of work Robinson would do in a day, was *fixed.* Here we assume it is *flexible.*

That being understood, the analysis is simple.

Let us suppose that the only thing he can produce is oranges at the rate of say four an hour. At the beginning of the day he may perhaps value 1 orange at the rate of 30 minutes of time spent in doing other things. As he can get an orange with the expenditure of 15 minutes the exchange is worthwhile: he proceeds to pick oranges. As the stock of oranges accumulates its significance in terms of the diminishing stock of time diminishes. An orange shrinks in significance from 30 to 25 to 20 and so on.

And when its significance has shrunk to 15 minutes then clearly the time has come to stop exchanging – producing. The marginal significance of oranges measured in terms of time is equivalent to the terms on which oranges can be procured. To go further would be irrational. It would be to procure for 15 minutes what is valued at less than 15 minutes – clearly a loss.

That is to say the length of day worked will depend upon the point at which the marginal significance of oranges – that is real income – is proportional to the cost, the terms on which they can be procured.

But now the question arises how are we to conceive cost. Some economists have suggested that we must look to the absolute pain of labour. When the marginal utility of product is proportionate to the disutility necessary to procure it, they say, then you have equilibrium. But against this it may be urged quite rightly that work may not involve disutility in the hedonistic sense. The whole working day may be above the zero of pleasure. And if this is so what becomes of the idea of cost? Do we throw it overboard altogether?

Clearly not. Clearly even if all work is pleasurable, the time taken by work cannot be devoted to leisure. *There may be no incurring of pain but there must still be a sacrifice.* You cannot have your cake and eat it. You can't spend three

---

1 Not unnaturally changing the supply of work one does has clearly more intimate psychological connection with income than changing the number of children one decides to have.

hours on orange picking without sacrificing the possibility of spending those hours on something else – without alternative *opportunities*. And it is that kind of sacrifice that I have taken into account in the example we have been considering. In order to get real income (oranges) Robinson has to sacrifice time – time which he might have devoted to something else. He stops work when the time which he has to sacrifice is worth as much as the thing which he gets by the sacrifice.

It is quite easy to generalize this example. Suppose once more our groups of independent producers producing with the aid of free goods and selling their own products. Assume as before that they have produced and brought their goods to market. They survey the results of their sales. No doubt there is a need for reshuffling but we will ignore that. We have dealt with that before. The point I want to concentrate on is this. Probably they will find that the remuneration they are getting per hour is not in harmony with the cost in time of production.

Say e.g. a group values money as 5/– an hour – we assume that each member has the same valuation – and suppose an hour's product at present prices yields 8/–. Clearly it is an opportunity for an extension of the work done. Accordingly this is done. The supply of the product increases, its price falls. At the same time the relative significance of money in terms of time falls also. Sooner or later the value of income at the margin in terms of time will correspond with the terms on which income can be made. Marginal significance will be the same as marginal cost. Equilibrium will be established. And so we could go on. It would be easy to extend the generalization so as to cover the case of joint production. But it would be tedious to fill in details, which you can quite well fill in for yourselves.

Let us instead examine the relation of supply of labour to its price a little more carefully. It is possible to express this in the form of a supply schedule. But it is more illuminating, I think, if we regard the connection as we have regarded it already, namely as an exchange of effort or time for income. We have seen already that the supply curve has always something suspicious about it. It suggests that there are forces at work different from the forces behind demand. If therefore we regard the process of production from the point of view of work as the exchange of effort for income we can proceed to think *demand schedules for income in terms of effort*, and we are thus led to the vitally important conception of elasticity of demand for income in terms of effort.

This conception is fundamental, and it is therefore worthwhile spending some time examining it in detail. It may best be represented by the apparatus of coordinate geometry. You can demonstrate in this way propositions which it would be tedious in the extreme to prove by arithmetical examples. The easiest apparatus – easiest because it is most familiar – is the unitary demand curve.

Along OX measure units of income; along OY the *price of income in terms of effort*. (Suppose oranges are real income and the price of oranges not money but effort. The thing is then seen to be completely symmetrical with the ordinary demand curve.) Let DD express the quantity of income that will be bought at various effort prices. Suppose the price to be Oe_1. Then OI_1 income will be bought for a total expenditure (of effort) of Oe_1PI_1 (price times amount).

Given a curve of this sort, it is easy to understand the conception of elasticity of effort demand. If the elasticity of demand is equal to unity then all the effort rectangles will be equal.

If e is greater than 1 then the rectangle formed at a lower price will be greater than one formed at a higher price.

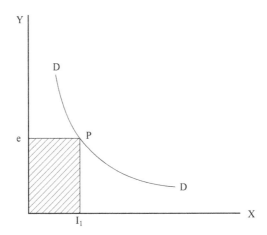

If e is less than 1 then the rectangle formed at a lower price will be less than one formed at a higher price. In simple English, if Robinson's effort demand for income has an elasticity equal to unity, then whatever the effort price of oranges, he will work the same length of time.

If it is greater than unity then he will work longer if he can get oranges at a low effort price, then he will if they are dearer.

If it is less than unity, he will work less if he can get oranges cheap than he will if they are dear.

The same thing can be expressed in *integral curves* if you prefer that sort of thing.

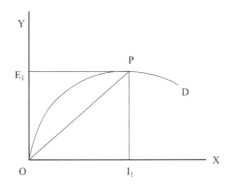

Along OX measure income, along OY effort (total effort). Then OD will express the varying relationship between income and effort. Thus for an income of I, E_1 effort will be expended. The price (demand price of income in terms of effort) is therefore $OE/OI_1 = OQ/OI = \tan QO_x$. While OD is still rising e is greater than 1, that is the effort outlay increases as the price falls. At Q which is the maximum e = 1 and if it continued horizontal would continue to do so since E would be constant when it falls e is less than 1.

All this enables to see at a glance the effects of a tax on income.

A tax of so much in the £ is clearly a reduction in the yield per unit of effort, or – to put it in the form appropriate to this discussion – *an increase in the effort price of units of income*. If before the tax you could get £ at a price of 1 hour and the tax removes 4/- clearly you will have to work more than an hour to obtain a £s worth of income. Hence, we can show the effects of a tax simply by supposing the effort price of income to be altered.

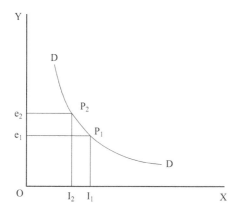

Let DD exhibit an individual's demand for units of income in terms of effort. Let Oe_1 be the price at which he can get income. Then equilibrium will be established with OI_1 income and $Oe_1P_1I_1$ effort expended.

Now suppose a tax to be imposed such that the price of income shifts from Oe_1 to Oe_2. Then equilibrium will be reestablished with income OI_2 & $Oe_2P_2I_2$ effort expended. If the elasticity of demand is greater than 1, then $Oe_2P_2I_2$ will be less than $Oe_1P_1I_1$. Less effort will be expended in consequence of the tax. If the elasticity of demand is less than 1, then $Oe_2P_2I_2$ will be greater than $Oe_1P_1I_1$. More effort will be expended in consequence of the tax.

The same thing can be shown on the integral apparatus.

We may show the price of income in terms of effort by a slope OP_1. Then to get OI_1 income OE_1 must be expended. Suppose the demand curve to cut the income slope at this point: equilibrium is established (OD is below OP_1).

A tax is then imposed. OP_1 the income slope has to be redrawn at a steeper angle – rotated to the left. The new equilibrium point is Q_2. Since OD shows

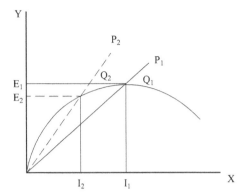

elasticity greater than 1 up to Q_1, E_2 less than E_1. If the income slope had cut the total demand curve further on when it had become inelastic, the converse effect would have been witnessed. Thus:

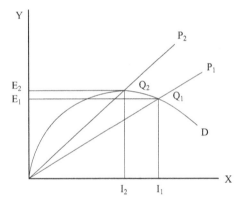

It is sometimes asserted – it has been so asserted by Professors Pigou and Knight[2] – that a man will always work more if his income is reduced by a tax. And this assertion is justified implicitly by appeal to the law of diminishing utility. Because the marginal utility of income falls as income increases it is urged therefore the elasticity of demand for income in terms of effort is less than unity. Now it is with very great diffidence that I venture to differ from the two greatest living authorities on theoretical analysis, but I am forced to do so.

2 [F.H. Knight, *Risk, Uncertainty and Profit* (1921); A.C. Pigou, *The Economics of Welfare* 1st edition (1920); Knight and Pigou both wrote to Robbins when he published his article 'On the elasticity of demand for income in terms of effort' *Economica* 10 (June 1930) pp. 123–9: see Editorial Note below.]

The conclusion does not seem to me in the least to follow from the premise. The law of diminishing marginal utility may indeed imply that the utility curve or the demand curve has a negative inclination. But it does not at all imply that it exhibits an elasticity less than unity. That is not a matter of the diminution of rates of utility. It is [a] matter of the rate of diminution about which the law says nothing.

Take the unitary curve of demand we have already discussed.

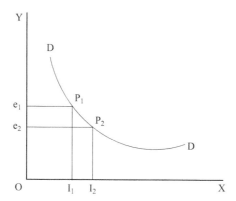

If we like, we may take this effort demand curve as expressing the relative significance of units of income measured in terms of effort. It should be clear, I think the "law" (what I call the assumption) implies that DD slopes downwards. But it does *not* imply that $Oe_1P_1I_1$ is necessarily greater than $Oe_2P_2I_2$.

Mr Knight attempts to prove his position by the following reasoning:

> Suppose that at a higher rate per hour . . . a man previously at the perfect equilibrium adjustment works as before and earns a proportionately larger income. When now he goes to spend the extra money he will want to increase his expenditures for many commodities consumed and to take on some new ones. To divide his resources in such a way as to preserve equal importance of equal expenditure in all fields he must evidently lay out part of his new funds for increased leisure i.e. buy back some of his working time or spend some of the money by not earning it.[3]

Very plausible and rather beautiful is it not? At first sight it appears overwhelmingly convincing. Where then is the catch? Why does Mr Knight's argument lead us to a result at variance with the result of our own investigation?

---

3 *Risk, Uncertainty and Profit*, p. 117.

The reason I think is this. Mr Knight has forgotten that *the change in the rate of incomes implies a change in the effort price of all commodities constituting real income.* The money price is the same, the effort price is diminished. If you think of real income in terms of say oranges and regard the process of producing oranges as an exchange of effort for oranges (as we have done earlier) then the problem is simple. If the effort price of real income (oranges) diminishes as in Mr Knight's example, surely it is entirely a matter of elasticity whether more or less effort is given for them. Just as if the money prices of oranges change, it is a matter of elasticity whether more or less money is expended on them.

Or we may put the same objection another way. Mr Knight forgets that when the real income obtainable for an hour's work increases, *the income price of leisure (the cost of leisure per unit in terms of income sacrificed) increases.* Now when the price of leisure (or any other commodity) rises, it is not at all clear that more of it will be bought – even out of an increased income. And surely this has been borne out by common experience. It is perfectly true that sometimes the offer of a higher wage results in less work being done – or the imposition of a tax involves more work being done. But it is highly paradoxical to urge that no offer of higher wage rates can reduce a *permanently* increased supply of work.[4]

Surely the conclusion of experience bears out the conclusion I have tried to bring home to you by highly abstract reasoning, that sometimes a higher wage will elicit more work, sometimes less; sometimes a tax will elicit less work, sometimes more. That is to say, it is all a matter of elasticity of demand for income in terms of effort.[5]

Read

L.C. Robbins, 'The economic effects of variations of hours of labour' *Economic Journal* (March 1929)

H.J. Davenport, *The Economics of Enterprise* (1913)

Edwin Cannan, *Wealth* 3rd edition (1928) Chapter I

Philip H. Wicksteed, *The Common Sense of Political Economy* (1910) Chapter IX

Frank H. Knight, *Risk, Uncertainty and Profit* (1921) p. 117

Hugh Dalton, *Public Finance* 5th edition (1929)

Editorial Note: *The Principles II notebook also contains a four page note of the diagrams. When Pigou, on reading Robbins's article 'On the elasticity of the demand for income in terms of effort' in June 1930, wrote to Robbins to say he thought Robbins had misunderstood his argument, he also commented*

---

4 In the language of the supply curve, the supply curve turns back at *once*.
5 In Expanded Course deal with kinds of labour factors. This comes in "Elements". There is no need to deal with it in detail.

that he thought diagrams were unnecessary to prove Robbins's point. Robbins explained in his reply that the note he had submitted to Economica *had originally been part of a course of lectures and 'consisted merely of the diagrams & the critique of Knight whose work I used as a supplement to Marshall for teaching purposes. I decided to publish it . . . because so many students failed to grasp the diagrammatic exposition that I got tired of having to lend out my notes.' (Susan Howson, Lionel Robbins [2011] page 172)*

10 Equilibrium of production

Factors flexible: material factors

Last week we commenced to examine the conditions of equilibrium when factor supplies are flexible – the hypothesis which we have agreed to call the stationary state and having discussed the general nature of the problem we went on to examine in some detail the flexibility of the labour supply –

Now it would be possible for me to linger still longer on this side of the question. To discuss the various kinds of labour – the doctrine of non-competing groups and so on. These things however are very simple and are quite well treated in the general textbooks. It is better I think since we have limited time at our disposal to turn straight away to the other side of our problem – the flexibility of supply of material factors of production. Accordingly my lectures this week will be devoted to this matter.

Now the first question which arises in this connection is the question how are we to classify the material factors of production. Are we simply to remain content with one general class, lumping the services of land with the services of factories, stores of petrol. Or is a subtler classification desirable? And if so on what is it to be based. That is the question I want to examine in this lecture.

In the traditional treatment of this part of our subject you find that the factors of production are divided into three Land Capital and Labour. The question we have to ask is: is this a suitable classification for the purposes of our inquiry? We have dealt already with the supply of services. We have seen that there is not one but many kinds of human service. We may therefore leave out of the question the heading labour and concentrate on the classification of material factors. But notice en passant how odd the old classification sounds: Land Capital and Labour. A stock of land a stock of capital a flow of labour services. Clearly it should have been either the services of land the services of capital and the services or simply Land Capital and Labourers. This point is not as trivial as it sounds.

But more of that hereafter. Recognizing that the significant thing in production is the use of the productive agents – that what we are ultimately concerned with is the flow of services of land labour and capital - let us proceed to examine the division of material agents more closely.

At once we are struck by a curious ambiguity of conception.

Land is not difficult to conceive. There are difficulties in the technical conception to which I am returning later. But in the rough we know what is meant by land agents. But capital, on the other hand, is a much more slippery conception. We ask ourselves what do we mean by capital? And instinctively I think nine out of 10 of us tend to think in terms of sums of money and money valuations. This man has a capital of £X, that man of £Y and so on.

And certainly, if we turn to the world of affairs, that is the usage that we find. The capital market deals in sums of money. Capital accounts deal with money valuations. Capitalists are men with a command of large sums of money.

Clearly the conception of land and the conception of capital as we find it in everyday affairs are not at all homogeneous. We think of land in physical units – so many acres – we think of capital in terms of value – so many £ sterling. Moreover, the two classes thus conceived are not mutually exclusive. The *business* use of the term capital, at any rate, *includes* land values. No joint stock company yet found has ever issued a balance sheet in which the value of the land owned has been excluded from the catalogue of its capital assets – when it was proposed to liquidate the war debt by a Capital Levy, no Labour politician explained that landowners would not be liable.

It is fairly clear therefore that when the older economists divided material agents into land and capital they meant by capital something rather different from what is meant by that word in the rough and tumble of everyday speech. That they were thinking not of the value of property rights but *of the material things in which property rights were held* – or some of those things. And of course it is notorious that they did. The reasons for the change were various:

(a) Partly they were due to the exigencies of the interest controversy. As you know, Aristotle and – following him – the casuists of the Middle Ages had attacked interest urging that it was unnatural. Money – for the use of which interest was paid – did not breed money. It was barren metal. Hence it was wrong to take interest. And when the church was at the height of its influence on secular affairs, interest accordingly was prohibited. Now of course in a capitalist society the lending and borrowing of money have very important functions. It was inevitable therefore that as industry and trade developed there should be a revolt against the mediaeval prohibition. And it was inevitable that the apologists of interest should come to emphasise not the money – the capital sum of the debt – but the concrete things that money would buy.

(b) That was the first reason for the break with traditional usage. The second was also connected with the interest controversy. About the beginning of the 18th century a certain school of thinkers, notably the philosopher John Locke, urged the theory that the rate of interest depended upon the amount of money – in the sense of units of currency – in circulation. This clearly was a wrong view – at any rate of the long run problem – for although variations in the quantity of money affect the value both of principal and income while the change is taking place in the end they are both equally affected.

Hence there was an obvious incentive to economists of the time again to emphasise the things behind money. To change the significance of the term capital from simply money valuation to the things actually valued.

There were other reasons for the change with which I need not worry you. The important thing is that in 1776, with the publication of *The Wealth of Nations*, the change was actually made. Adam Smith used the word "Capital" to designate that part of a man's Stock which yields revenue. And from that day to this, confusion has resulted.

Capital then, in the sense in which it is used by the classical economists, means not values but things. Not property rights but the things in which property rights are held. To that extent the classification is redeemed. Land and Capital are at least a similar kind of conception. We are not classifying factors into acres and £ sterling. But why the division between land and capital in the sense of goods? We have seen that business practice values Land as other capital assets. Why, if the transition from values to things must be made, why not have one class capital goods to form the material counterpart of capital values? This is the question we have to examine further.

Let us first be clear what is meant by the distinction. By land is meant not what we think of when we think of the estate market. The classical definition implies something very much narrower. Land is taken to be that part of land in the market sense which is not due to human effort: the unimproved powers of the soil *plus* – note the addition very carefully – improvements which do not have to be maintained. In addition to this, other scarce natural agents are sometimes included. By land the economist sometimes meant water. "By Land," says Marshall, "is meant the material and the forces which Nature gives freely for man's aid, in land and water, in air and light and heat".[1]

By capital on the other hand is meant material agents which are "not-land" in this technical sense I have just explained. There were other aspects of the definition with which we need not at the moment concern ourselves – whether consumption goods were to be included, whether houses used as dwelling places were social capital, and so on and so forth. The history of all this is important in any close view of the problem of capital and interest, but in this context we need not worry greatly about it.

So much for the distinction. Now what of its usefulness? What is the rationale of the division between land and capital? Two main reasons seem to have justified its use in the past. (1) In the first place it may be urged that land and capital give rise to two different sorts of income: Rent and Interest. (2) Secondly it is urged that land is fixed in supply while capital is variable. Let us look at these arguments separately. We shall not be wasting time for we shall be passing in review certain aspects of some of the knottiest and most hotly contested points of theoretical economics.

(1) Take first the argument that land and capital give rise to two different kinds of income: Rent and Interest. There can be no doubt, I think, that here you have the historic reason for the rise of the separation. The contract to rent a piece of land and the contract to borrow money arose in two different parts

---

1 [*Principles* 8th edition (1920) p. 138]

of the economic system, in land owning and in commerce, and when the term capital came to be used for material goods rather than sums of money, it carried with it the association of the interest contract.

Now of course there is a profound difference between the rent and the interest contract. In the one – the rent contract – you undertake to pay so much per annum for the use of a piece of land and return it physically intact. In the other you undertake to pay so much for the use of a sum of money and return the money intact. But it is a difference of commercial and legal convenience. The rent contract concerns a relatively permanent instrument which can be seen and identified easily and whose condition can be physically measured. The interest contract arose in the sphere of commerce – where you borrow money essentially to part with it. It would be most inconvenient to say I will borrow enough to buy so much corn, and I will return you the value of that physical quantity at the end of the year. It is much easier to think in money terms. But these are matters of origin and convenience. Rent and interest in this sense are not *analytically* restricted to different types of goods. *They are two different modes of expressing one and the same thing.* Rent is the yield per physical unit. So much per annum per acre. Interest is the yield per unit of value. So much per cent. They are as it were two different aspects of one and the same thing. You can see this perfectly well if you reflect that a rent can always be expressed as interest. You can say I get £20 per acre for that field or 5% on the money I put into it. And the yield on a non-land material agent like a piano or a motor boat which according to the definition ought to yield interest only can be expressed as a rent – a higher price.

It is clear then that the distinction between Rent and Interest in the ordinary meaning of these terms does not correspond to the distinction between land and capital goods other than land. It corresponds to our distinction between instruments physically considered and the present value of those instruments.

(2) But now turn to the second reason for the distinction. Land is fixed in supply, capital is not. Now as we shall be seeing there is an important distinction between material agents whose supply schedules are rigid and those whose supply schedules are rigid [sic]. *The only question is whether it is convenient –* whether it is conducive to clear thinking – *to redefine land so as to make it the label of this class of agents.* And here I think the classics were definitely at fault. Most of the land which comes into the market is as much "made up" as the tools which are used in its cultivation. A market garden is just as much a produced means of production as a cotton loom. And *the supply of land in this sense is capable of increase or diminution.*

Why then did the classics think fixity of supply was the peculiar characteristic of land?

(i) Partly of course because they were living at a time when during a short period resort was had to greatly inferior soils. The limitations of the land surface were very obvious in England during the Napoleonic Wars.

(But of course, this was a cause, not a justification. If in a short period there is great pressure for other capital instruments they likewise show diminishing returns.)

(ii) Partly because their land concept was ambiguous. Marshall, you remember, defines land as the totality of nature. One could cite other classical definitions in the same sense.

Now of course, the supply of land in this sense is fixed – at least there is every justification for supposing this to be the case.

But – and this is the point I am trying to bring out – *land in the sense of the totality of nature does not come on the market*, and it is not a scarce agent of production in the ordinary sense of the word. What does come on the market are different pieces of nature. Land in this sense – either unimproved as in the case of virgin forest, or worked up by human labour into fields, brick-walls, factories, saucepans, gold rings, bags of corn and so on. There are "original powers of the soil" in a field used for growing turnips. There are original powers of the soil in the saucepan used for boiling them, and no doubt it is useful to distinguish between unimproved nature and the transformation man achieves. But it seems inconvenient to use the same title – land – to designate both unimproved nature and one of the things nature is "improved into".

What we need to do, I suggest, is to classify factors of production on the material side according to their variability of supply.

We shall have a class whose supply is fixed once and for all. Marshall's hard bright meteoric stones and urban sites characterized by definite geographical features. All the sites within a mile's radius from St Paul's e.g.

We shall have a class whose supply is fixed upwards but can be used up. Mineral deposits come here.

We shall have a class whose supply is fixed downwards but can be increased upwards. Here come the permanent improvements of the classics.

We shall have a class whose supply is fixed both ways.

All these classes save the first can be subdivided according to the rate at which the supply can be depleted or increased.

In this way, I think we retain the important feature of the classical classification without incurring the disadvantage of using a term to denote one of our classes which is usually thought of in connection with a class of agents which falls into the others. Where the classics went wrong was not in supposing that there was an important difference between agents whose supply is rigid and agents whose supply is flexible, *but in assuming that land which comes into the market so nearly possesses the characteristics of rigid supply that it only needed a little redefining to make it a suitable label for this class.* In fact, of course, the difference between Ricardian land and ordinary agricultural land in an old country is enormous. It has been suggested that only 5% of the land values in the English countryside are Ricardian. The remaining 95% are the values of produced means of production which, if left unprovided for, would speedily deteriorate.

But if we do this what is to become of the term capital? Is it to become the generic title of all these classes, or are we to allow it to relapse – so to speak – into its ordinary business sense? Clearly we do not want to be pedantic about the mere use of terms. If the thing helps if used in an unorthodox way we ought not to make any fuss about it. And I would not pretend that there do not arise arguments when it would be absurd to refrain from using capital in the sense of real material agents. None the less I am inclined to believe that we do well whenever possible to revert to business and accounting usage. As we shall be seeing next time, capital value is a concept which is quite important enough for us to wish to keep it as free as possible from ambiguity.

Moreover, it is not unimportant for us to realize that capital value in the various senses in which it is used in business and accountancy is by no means restricted to material things. It is not correct to suggest that capital goods and capital value are parallel concepts. You can see this quite clearly if you examine the concept a little further.

Capital in business relates either to a sum of money which has been invested, a proportionate claim on a dividend: I hold x of ordinary shares in so and so. Or to the present value of certain rights – that is to the sum of money which would be released by the sale of those rights. Now it is clear that in either case we may be thinking of the purchase or sale of material things – I invest in a new rubber company and they buy plant; the company is sold and the purchase money covers its machinery. But it should be equally clear that it may not – a new company may spend money on the acquisition of patent rights; an old company may be sold and the main thing it has to sell is goodwill. Again it is clear that capital may be invested in persons – we invest capital in our children's education. Or think finally of the phrase export of capital. Does it cover the movement of material factors of production? It may – we may send steel rails to the Argentine. But it may not – we may render shipping services to Argentine wheat exporters and refrain from bringing home the payment. It should be clear, I think, that there is quite enough to do analysing the meaning of all these things without giving the term 'capital' any heavier burden. As far as possible, therefore, I am in favour of the accounting concept.

But what has all this to do with equilibrium theory? Why have I devoted a whole lecture to remote questions of exegesis and nomenclature? That is a question I hope to answer in the next lecture.

Read

Alfred Marshall, *Principles of Economics* (1920) Chapter IV Income. Capital FrankH. Knight, *Risk, Uncertainty and Profit* (1921) Part II Chapter II

Frank A. Fetter, 'The relations between rent and interest' *American Economic Association Papers and Proceedings* Vol. 5 (February 1904)

'Recent discussion of the capital concept' *Quarterly Journal of Economics* (November 1900)

Alvin S. Johnson, *Rent in Modern Economic Theory* (1903)

Irving Fisher, 'What is capital?' *Economic Journal* (December 1896)

The Nature of Capital and Income (1906) (or *Elementary Principles of Economics* (1911))

H.J. Davenport, *The Economics of Enterprise* (1913) *Value and Distribution* (1908)

J.A. Schumpeter, *Die Theorie der wirtschaftslichten Entwicklung* (1911) Chapter III

Eugen von Böhm-Bawerk, *Kapital und Kapitalzins Erste Abteilung: Geschichte und Kritik der Kapitalzins-Theorien* 4th edition (1921)

11 Equilibrium of production

Factors flexible: material
factors (continued)

Last time I commenced to discuss the supply of material factors of production
under stationary conditions, and as a preliminary investigation I examined the
traditional division of factors of this sort into land and capital. Broadly speaking
the conclusions I tried to suggest were twofold:

(a) That "land" is an unsuitable label for the class whose supply is rigid and that
it is better to classify on the analytic basis of flexibility of supply than on the
"substantial" basis of whether the factor is or is not a produced means of production. All material factors are composed of "land" in the sense of natural
stuff; the important question is how rapidly can their number be increased or
diminished.
(b) Second, that it is better to restrict the significance of the term capital to its
business meaning, sums of money invested or the present value of the rights
conferred by ownership.

Now today I want to proceed to the discussion of the conditions of equilibrium.

The broad conditions of our problem are familiar to you. What is the relation
between the supply of the various classes of material agents and the other elements in the general equilibrium? At once our classification becomes useful.

So far as the class of agents whose supply is fixed once and for all there is no
functional connection between supply and price. The price *per annum* is determined by the general conditions of demand for such agents. Our discussion of the
productivity analysis was designed to throw light on this.

The capital value – the price that you have to pay here and now for the possession outright of such an agent – we will discuss later.

So far as the class whose supply is fixed upwards but which can be exhausted
downwards is concerned, we must leave it out of our consideration of stationary
equilibrium. Clearly the equilibrium cannot be stationary if one of the quantities
is continually changing. This, I think, is a grave reminder of the limitations of
equilibrium analysis of this sort. The thing can be worked into a theory of moving
equilibrium no doubt. But it has no place in the stationary state. This makes the
stationary state a very unreal place to live in – so to speak. No one can pretend it

is a very accurate picture of reality. No one can say that I have even suggested that it is. But I do suggest that it is the most convenient way of examining the working of forces which must be active in any economic system. So I propose to go on with the analysis.

So far as the other two classes are concerned however we have still to solve our problem. How far will this supply be pushed? What will be the relation between their annual yield and their quantity?

Now let us start as before with the simplest possible case. Let us revert to our Crusoe Economics. We may suppose that Crusoe is now surveying the possibilities of his situation for some time to come. Hitherto we have always discussed his behaviour in regard to the immediate product. At his disposal are his own powers of work and the various natural features of his environment. Now he may decide that it is best to live from day to day, picking his oranges and catching his fish, using the factors of production at his disposal for providing only for the present. If he does this then we know all that we need to know about the conditions of equilibrium. He uses his time and the scarce factors in such a way as to secure equimarginal significance in every use. But he may decide on a more ambitious plan. That is to say he might decide to use some of his labour and some of his material factors *indirectly* in more lengthy – more roundabout – methods of production. Instead of spending all the time picking and eating, he may decide to spend part of the time planting and tending.

This has two implications:

(1) It means that his present income and leisure must be diminished – you cannot give time to planting without taking it from picking or eating. it means that he has got to go without present income in order to carry out these indirect operations.
(2) But secondly it means that in the end – if he has chosen the right technical methods – he will have a larger income.

For it is a well-known empirical fact that the more productive ways of using the factors of production take time, and indeed that if you have a given collection of original factors the only way of getting more out of them – inventions apart – is to resort to more and more lengthy production processes – to defer further and further into the future the moment when their final product matures. This is the simple and obvious fact behind Böhm-Bawerk's celebrated theorem of the greater technical efficiency of roundabout methods of production.

B.B. has often been misunderstood because of his use of the term 'roundaboutness'. People thought in terms of methods of production which were unnecessarily complicated like a Heath Robinson creation and whereas of course what he meant was merely that in order to resort to modes of production of a *technically justifiable complexity* the uses of the factors of production had to be deferred and that the longer you deferred them – the longer you were prepared to *wait* – the greater range of technical choice was open to you.

But to return to Crusoe. He has the choice of using his time and tools either for making provision for his day to day needs or making provision for greater product in the future. In so far as he chooses the latter, devotes time and the uses of available factors to indirect production the volume of material factors will be augmented. For example he decides to make a spade.

Herein we see the real nature of the distinction between saving and spending – in ultimate non-monetary terms (I am not thinking of Mr Keynes terminology)[1]. Saving is using the factors of production to make provision for the future. Spending is using them to make provision for the present.

This point is important. It is sometimes suggested that saving consists in accumulating stocks of consumable commodities and then living on these stocks while productive instruments are brought into existence. Thus Roscher e.g. illustrates the process of capitalist accumulation by an imaginary case in which a fisherman resolves to build a boat and in order to do this accumulates a stock of 100 fish and – to use Cannan's vivid description – then proceeds to build the boat while living on this stinking putrefying diet.[2] Of course this is all wrong. What happens of course is that the fisherman resolves to fish a little less every day and devote the time so saved to canoe building. *The fish he saves – goes without – thus never actually come into existence.*

But to return to the choice which Crusoe has to make. We may assume that the instruments which he makes are useful in helping him to secure the various things he wants. We may assume too that the more he has the less their marginal productivity. This follows from the Law of Diminishing Returns which we have studied in an earlier lecture. He will, that is to say, have a series of options open to him. If he only saves a little the marginal productivity of the new instruments will be relatively great. If he saves it will diminish. At the same time in using the factors of production in making such provision he is forgoing to that extent the possibility of present income. The more he saves the more present income he has to forgo.

Now just as we have conceived the process of production in the present as a process of exchanging time for goods or the goods not produced for the goods actually made, so we can conceive this business of making provision for the future *as an exchange of present income for future*. And we can imagine relative scales showing Robinson's relative valuation of present and future incomes granted the possession of different flows of these amenities. Thus we may suppose that it is conceivable that if he thought his needs would be greater later on than now he would be willing to give two units of present income in order to get one unit of future income. The thing is conceivable – people do not always value the present more than the future. But the case depends upon the assumption of increasing needs.

---

1 [In *A Treatise on Money* (1930)]
2 [See E. Cannan, *A Review of Economic Theory* (1929) pp. 129–32, where he is discussing Wilhelm Roscher's *Zur Geschichte der englischen Volkswirtschaftlehre* (1851)]

If we rule this out and assume equal needs at the future date when the income would materialize then we are justified in assuming I think that from the outset ratios of exchange would be in favour of the present. This seems to follow from our assumption of diminishing relative significance.

Assume for a moment that incomes at both periods are equal. Then if our assumption holds it follows that the relative marginal significance of $1 - \Delta x$ is greater than the marginal significance of $1 + \Delta x$. Hence in order that exchange may take place the terms must be more favourable than 1:1 for the present. And as we consider a greater and greater sacrifice of present income so we must assume that the ratio turns more and more in favour of the present.

We can think of this changing ratio in two ways:

(a) Either as a falling demand price for future income in terms of present.
(b) Or as a rising supply price of present sacrifice.

Either way expresses the same fundamental thing. I shall be returning to this later.

Now let us resume the Robinsoniad. On the one hand Robinson is confronted with the fact of diminishing productivity of present sacrifice. If he sacrifices x units of income now he gets $x + 5$ units of income in the future; if he sacrifices $2x$ units he gets $2x + 8$ units and so on. On the other hand we have his relative scales of significance of present and future income. It is surely not difficult to see what he will do: he will exchange present for future income until the rate of return and his rate of preference are equivalent. Suppose e.g. he values 1 unit of present income as 1.05 units of future income. And suppose he can get for such a sacrifice 1.10 units. Clearly the exchange is inadvisable. But as the supply of present income is depleted its marginal significance rises. At the same time the productivity of sacrifice falls. When they come together there is equilibrium.

So much for Crusoe Economics. Before we go on to deal with more complicated conditions one further elucidation is useful. I have spoken as if Robinson could only devote saving to the creation of new tools. This was useful for purposes of illustration but it would be misleading if you regarded it as exhaustive. He can of course accumulate stocks. If his needs are greater in the future than in the present this may be worthwhile. 1 coconut next winter may be worth 2 coconuts now. If by storing he gets 1 for one storing is worthwhile and will be carried out until the ratio of significance is 1:1. Or he can spend time on improving himself. He can invest time which would have been devoted to procuring income in the present to educating himself to procure higher income in the future. Such possibilities would compete with the production of tools. And expenditure of present income on future income would be divided between in such a way as to secure equimarginal advantages.

But now let us turn to the more complicated world of competitive industry. Let us start by examining the affairs of one tiny unit in the system. Let us suppose a working peasant farmer who markets his goods but who otherwise does most of the work himself. He is possessed of a certain quantity of material agents of production and he himself supplies the work which cooperates with their services to yield his annual income.

Now he may devote all these resources to the maintenance of his present equipment and the securing of his present annual income. (Some of the tools will wear out. If he is not to encroach on capital – that is run the risk of less income in the future – he must devote some time and materials to their maintenance but for the moment we neglect this.) But he may devote time and resources to improving his material equipment – say to ditching his fields.

If we contemplate the effect on his product say corn of such improvements we may imagine that small investment of this sort will enhance greatly the size of his crop. Larger will have a small marginal yield and so on. The effects can be exhibited as a declining productivity curve expressed in value terms, price being constant. How far will be carry this process?

Two considerations are important.

(1) First, the immediate cost in terms of present income. Each ditch dug will mean so much time and other resources utilized which might have been devoted to getting income in the present.
(2) Second, the fact that in all probability he will not value a bushel of wheat next year as much as a bushel of wheat now. His relative scale will exhibit a tendency for the present to be valued more highly than the future, other things being the same.

Hence, he will only push his savings up to that point at which the rate of return on sacrifice is equivalent to his valuation of sacrifice in terms of future product.

We may exhibit this in diagrammatic language thus.

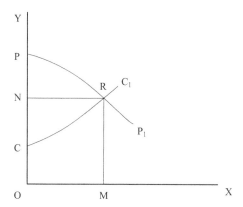

Along OX measure units of income sacrificed. Along OY measure the value productivity of sacrifice at the margin and the significance at the margin of present sacrifice in terms of product in the future. Then PP expresses declining value productivity of ditch making, CC the significance of present income in terms of future income. Equilibrium is clearly established at R where with OM units of present income sacrificed the productivity of sacrifice is DN or RM and the value of sacrifice is similar.

That treats the matter in terms of our Crusoe economics. We can however exhibit it in a more realistic fashion.

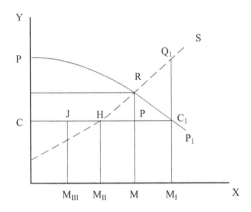

Along OX now measure units of ditching. Along OY measure the value productivity of such units – the earnings of the marginal length of ditch.

At the same time measure the money cost in terms of income sacrificed of units of ditching on the same axis. Then PP exhibits value productivity and CC the money cost of ditching.

At first sight you might imagine that ditching would be pushed to the point M_1 where the money cost of ditching is equal to the value it will bring in – to OM_1. But this is not likely to be so. For, as we have seen, it is most improbable that the peasant will value the marginal income he sacrifices now to get OM_1 – i.e. OC – as equivalent to the return M_1C *which will come only later on.* On the contrary he will probably value it as M_1Q_1. He will regard it as equivalent to more than the present cost.

To get the point of equilibrium then we must draw a new curve SS_1 exhibiting the conditions of supply of the cost of ditching. It is conceivable that at the outset he might so value future income that the ratio of exchange would be in its favour. This is expressed by drawing the curve below CC. When e.g. OM_{111} units of ditching are dug, the marginal cost $M_{111}U$ might be valued as less than an equivalent addition to income in the future – by JI. But once M_{11} ditching is done income in the future is valued less than income in the present and the curve goes on rising. Equilibrium is therefore attained at OM – the present cost being PM at the margin and the surplus of the rate of return over cost RP.

The same conditions can be shown with the rate of time preference (as it has been called) exhibited as acting on the demand side rather than on the supply side. It is worth while doing this both because it brings out the substantial identity of the cost and time preference theories (of which more next time) and because it brings our discussion one stage nearer to reality.

Let us suppose now that our peasant, instead of doing the ditching himself and estimating how much it costs him in present income, goes into the market and buys labour to do the work for him – investing capital (which he saves out of income) in the process. We can exhibit the value productivity of ditching and its money cost in the same way as before.

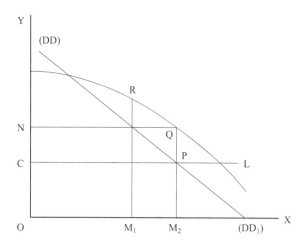

Now if there were no interval between investment and its product, the productivity curve would provide us with a demand curve for that particular individual. But as we have seen it is improbable that a man will invest capital (sacrifice present income) only to receive back the *same* amount at a later date. He will not value the future value product as highly as its present equivalent. There will be a discount on the future.

Hence we must redraw the demand curve DD_1DD_1 cutting the productivity curve fairly high up and thus exhibiting a discount on the future. Thus a yield M_1R in the future is not valued as M_1R but as MQ and so on. Equilibrium therefore is attained at OM where the discounted productivity curve cuts the present cost curve. The future marginal yield MI is greater than MP the present marginal cost. But there is no inducement to continue buying since the extra-marginal *discounted* yields are below the present extra-marginal costs. Notice that NIPC = Interest and COPM = total amount invested. The rate of interest is therefore NIPC/OOPM x 100.

Now let us shift once more our point of view and survey matters from the point of view of social equilibrium. The factors of production at the moment are given and the income they are capable of producing in the present.[3] To augment the income of the future the income of the present must be sacrificed. The factors of production must be used to make provision for the future.

In the modern world this adjustment is secured through the expenditure of money. People spend in such a way that some of the factors of production cease to produce present income. Instead they produce income in the future, that is they use their income for capital investment.

Now the productivity analysis enables us to understand the options which are open to them. And the analysis of this lecture shows us how individual entrepreneurs will expend their incomes. If all entrepreneurs provided their own capital resources we could extend this as we did, the individual productivity analysis to describe the social determination of the rate of interest. As the volume of investment grows the value productivity must be conceived to fall faster than the physical productivity. Equilibrium follows when value productivity and the supply price of sacrifice are coincident.

But in fact it is more realistic to proceed by way of the analysis of the loan market.

The important thing to notice here is that the demand is demand for free capital money to invest. And the *borrowers* of capital constitute the demand side. What they offer is income in the future for income sacrificed in the present (capital). They will be willing to offer then anything less than the marginal value productivity of what they borrow. Supply comes from savers. They are sacrificing present income for future. We may expect therefore that they will ask at least as much as their present valuation of future income. We may anticipate too that their supply curve will slope upward. Equilibrium will be attained when the rate of return on present sacrifice and the rate of discount on the future are equal.

All of which may be expressed again by a diagram of intersecting curves.

OY rates of return; OX quantity of loan capital. DD represents the demand price for capital (income sacrificed), SS the supply price of capital. Equilibrium is attained at P, OR being the rate paid and OM the amount (rate of flow forthcoming).

This way of putting the matter is sometimes thought to beg the question, since it takes for granted the cost of the things that the borrowers will buy with their loans – which cost it is said already implies a rate of interest.

But this rests on a misapprehension. The cost of the goods bought is the price of the factors of production employed or the price of the present income relinquished. *The reason why the price of the new agents is not equal to the sum of*

---

3 Minor inaccuracy here. Flexibility of labour supply left out of account in order not to complicate exposition.

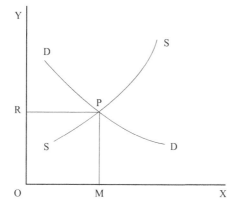

their future products is because the demand is not great enough to push them up to it – which again is due to the scarcity of capital seeking investment. It is true that in a sense everything depends on everything else. But this is the fundamental lesson of the theory of equilibrium. To exhibit mutual dependence is not in the least to argue in a circle.

But more of this hereafter.

12 Interest rates, capitalization and the equilibrium of production through time

I now wish to draw your attention to yet another set of price relationships in the economic equilibrium – the relationships namely of the present prices of goods maturing into consumption goods at different points of time in the future. This brings me back to the general influence of the equilibrium rate of interest. But first we must make a further investigation of the nature of production and the way it is organized in time.

Let us for the moment ignore the complications I introduced last week in regard to what may be called the seasonal irregularities of production. Think the seasons out of the picture for the time being. Revert to our former suppositions. Later on I shall show you how we can reintroduce the additional complications. That being understood we can proceed.

Now the first thing to realize is that *every production process take time*. It is only the most primitive production processes such as scooping water out of a brook to drink with one's hands which can be said to synchronize with the processes of consumption to which they minister. All other kinds of production involve using existing factors of production in advance. From the beginning of the productive process to the moment of consumption the technical nature of production involves delay. *The productive process takes time.*

That is to say at any point of time – or if you will cross section – there will be in existence not merely a series of consumption goods – the goods of the first order – the end products of the productive process, but also a series of production goods at different stages in the process of production. Some will be on the point of becoming consumption goods. Some will be a year behind, some two years.

Take e.g. a properly organized forest. Suppose it to be in stationary equilibrium. We can think in terms of rows of trees.
There will be a set of rows ready for cutting 1931.
A set of rows which will be ready a year hence

two years hence, and so on until you come to a set of rows just planted.
[If life of tree is 20 years – 20 sets of rows of equal numbers (making allowance for probable decay etc.)

In stationary equilibrium as many trees planted as cut. Total number of trees = number cut per year and length of production period.]

Tree example helpful in certain ways. But very important to remember that a one-year old tree is a different commodity from a tree two years old.

Important too to remember that goods of higher temporal orders often change altogether as they come down through time. E.g. steel plates may be two years off consumption as part of Cunard liner., but they undergo transformations before then. Next in the time series may be steel plates in another place. Then part of the hull (bare), then part of the painted hull etc.

Böhm-Bawerk's concentric circles.[1]

(See Edgeworth)[2]

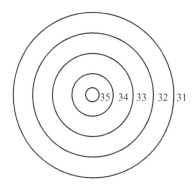

Goods maturing at once *present* goods. Goods maturing later on *future* goods – goods of "higher" temporal orders.

Now another distinction – some goods only yield use once – others endure some time – some last forever. Position of perishable goods in temporal series unambiguous. Coal used for melting pig iron. But in case of durable goods, we must look upon them as consisting of *series* of future goods – services this year and so on. And *these* uses must *themselves* be given appropriate temporal grouping.

E.g. a dwelling house yields services of first order now and in 1932 '33 '34.

So does a suit.

But an iron foundry existing in 1931 yield[s] services in 1932 which will "ripen" say in 1933 and again services in 1932 which will ripen in 1934 and so on.

Thus our instantaneous photography of the state of the world at the moment – if interpreted properly – will reveal a very complicated series of "time" relationships *in the economic sense* between the physical goods existing apparently contemporaneously.

---

1 [*Positive Theory of Capital* (1890) Book II Chapter V The Theory of the Formation of Capital].

2 ['The theory of distribution' *Papers Relating to Political Economy* (1925) Vol. I pp. 43–5].

Now it should be quite clear from what I have said in earlier lectures that these time relationships will be reflected in the price system.

Two points must be remembered:

(1) "Future goods" derive their value from the "present goods" they will eventually become. The sapling is valued because it will become a tree etc.
(2) But second, that value is "contracted" because it accrues only in the future. Or to put it in more general terms, it will be – or may be – different if it accrues in the future, the contraction being the agio – discount – positive (or negative) on future income – in other words the rate of interest – the cost of holding through time.

Thus, at any time a set of ratios of exchange will establish themselves between the goods of different temporal orders which other things being equal will in stationary conditions be a reflection of the rate of interest.

Take e.g. our example of trees. Suppose the price of a row of trees ready for felling now is £100. Suppose that the rate of interest is 5% and no labour required after planting. The trees which will mature in 1932 will be worth £100 too in 1932 – since we assume static conditions. But in 1931 the 1932 trees will be a year off maturity. They will be worth less. If the rate of interest is 5% they will be worth £95. The ratio of exchange will be 95:100 and the price margin will be 5 – the rate of interest. Similarly, with the trees of higher temporal orders. The further back the greater the contraction of price. The rule being that the price must be such that the prevalent rate of interest compound interest on the investment will amount to the value of the tree at maturity.

Now take the case of durable goods which render services through time. Take e.g. a machine. Its services will be valued at so much per annum.

But they are spread out through time. Its present worth therefore will *not* be £100 x the number of years the house will last, for this would treat all *future* services as equivalent in value to the *present*. Rather the future services will be *discounted* according to the rate of time preference (interest) prevailing.

Let us take a numerical example to fix our notions more precisely.

(I take the figures from B.B. p. 343 – – P.T.C.)[3]

Suppose the machine lasts six years. Suppose services value £100. Its present value *not* £100 x 6. But (taking rate of interest of 5%) £100 + 95.23 + 90.70 + 86.38 + 82.27 + 78.35 = £532.93.[4]

Now let us push this a little further to see how the use of the machine yields a *net* income.

At the end of the year the £100 worth of service has been rendered.

The machine has lost that much value. But at the same time the value of the other services has grown. They are nearer maturity. The service which was worth 95.23 is now worth £100; that which was worth 90.70 95.23 –

---

3 [E. von Böhm-Bawerk, *The Positive Theory of Capital* (1891)].
4 Utility obtainable in advance.

But the sixth year's service is no longer there – the machine has only five years to live. Hence the net loss is the loss of the sixth year's service – the *most remote* service. (That is 78.35.) The machine is now worth $100 + 95.23 + 90.70 + 86.38 + 82.27 = 454.58$. The loss in value is 78.35 which must be made up out of the £100 realized, leaving 21.65 which is 5% of 432.93, the sum which the good became worth when the £100 was deducted.

Some may find this hard – business of remote uses. Think of the trees illustration – the forest as a machine turning out finished trees.

Each year yields row of mature trees. If value to be kept constant each year row of saplings should be planted. (Value of saplings discounted value of trees they will become) Difference between a row of trees and *the* machine – the row of trees completely used up in transformation into next year's trees. The machine gives off uses for several years which themselves valued on discount principle. The forest as a whole equal to the machine. Each tree is like the materials the machine uses.

That shows us the case of the capitalization of goods of a limited durability. Suppose the good is infinitely durable – Ricardian land.

Then the last service is an infinite distance away; its value is therefore infinitely small. Hence there is no loss of value during the year.

Each year's service detaches itself and there need be no deduction for loss of value of the good as a whole. The rent is *net*. There is no depreciation.

Notice next that this time element principle enters into the remuneration of the original factors of production. According to the marginal productivity principle each factor receives what its contribution is worth at the margin. But this is not to say that it receives the value of the *final* product. The entrepreneur quae capitalist buys labour at one point of time and sells its product at another point of time. The difference is interest.

Take e.g. the case of the forest. Says it takes £1 a year to plant saplings. Suppose the owner sells the saplings at the end of the year.

Then we may suppose that the saplings will sell for £1–1–0 5% interest.

But the labourers who planted the saplings will not get £1–1–0. At the time they did the work the saplings were only worth £1.

It is this phenomenon which gave rise to the exploitation theory of Marx and others. They urged that the labourer did not realize the full value of his product. This true if by full value they meant value quae consumption good.

But not true if by value meant *present* value. For a sapling now is not a sapling a year hence. If the labourers had capital they could wait for full value. If they haven't capital they can't. There may be a basis of a sociological theory of exploitation. But it cannot be the basis for an analytical theory. It is clear that if they had capital – command over present factors – they would have to weigh the productivity of using factors for income now or income later on. I.e. they would have to separate interest from wages as book reckoning.

But this brings us to a fresh viewpoint – a viewpoint which exhibits with most beautiful clarity the universality of one of our main guiding notions throughout. I have just said that labour (and the same thing applies to land) is rewarded according to the *discounted* value of the final product it helps to make. At the same time it is obvious that in a continuous economy labour and land are used in production of goods of *different* temporal orders.

• At different points on the concentric circles. Labour is used for planting the saplings, it is used for sawing the full-grown trees.

How comes it then that labour is *equally* rewarded at different stages?[5]
 At first sight this is a paradox. Two considerations help us:

(1) The law of single price. In a comp[etitive] market single price prevails. If labour more highly rewarded in one line than another, shifting –
(2) But how does entrepreneurs profit equally of goods of different temporal orders have different prices and labour has single price.

The thing to remember is that the longer processes are "more productive" – but (given static conditions) more productive at a diminishing rate. This *is* the law of diminishing returns as it shows itself in the use of capital.

At each stage at the margin the product of labour has the *same* present value. The product of a day's labour felling trees has the *same* value in the present as the product of a day's labour planting trees. Assuming mobility etc. The difference in value of the work done in the latter case only accrues over time. Labour is therefore distributed between work on goods of different temporal orders in such a way that at the present rate of interest the present value of what is done at the margin is the same. Considerations of this sort give us the clue to what happens when the amount of saving changes.

If there is more saving available (more willingness to dispense with present income) then clearly labour remaining the same longer processes can be embarked upon. If you are willing to wait 20 years you can have a fir. If you are willing to wait 40 years you can have an oak. A greater product will accrue at the end of the longer period.

How will this show itself in exchange relationships between goods of different temporal orders? There will be a diminution in demand for goods for immediate consumption. An increase in demand for goods at earlier stages. The price margins will diminish in the later stages and increase in the higher stages because they provide greater product. This will provide a definite incentive to transfer factors to higher stages – to make methods of production more "roundabout". Equilibrium will set in when price margins between goods of different orders are again equal. But they will now be narrower.

The same thing can be put another way. Saving increases. The rate of interest falls. Longer processes are more productive. But have been exploited already up to the margin at which value of returns the same as rate of interest. With fall in rate of interest can be extended. This more familiar way of putting it. Notorious

5 Of course assuming homogeneous labour.

that when interest falls more profitable to install capital equipment, plant longer growing trees, build channel tunnels etc. The converse if saving diminishes, if people consume capital.

Thus, whole structure of production through time affected by changes in saving available – rate of interest.

This surely throws important light on industrial fluctuation.

In world of practice savings made available in money. Some margin at least for banks to vary amount make available. Forced savings and inflation. Now suppose money rate of interest below natural rate – rate at which voluntary savings would be cleared – owing to extension of credit. Incentive to embark on longer processes. Building machines etc. Boom in construction industries. Inflation proceeds. Forced levies become ineffective. People are not really willing to save more. Gold drains.

Hence, prices of consumption goods rise relative to prices of goods of higher orders. The longer processes become unprofitable. People no longer willing to buy the machines etc. Cassel's way of putting it – not enough capital coming forward to carry real capital being produced. Crisis [and] depression. This [is] the Austrian theory of fluctuation. Mises. Hayek.[6] Does it not help explain what has been happening in America[7]

---

6 [L. von Mises, *Theorie des Geldes und der Umlaufsmittel* (1924); F.A. Hayek, *Geldtheorie und Konjunkturtheorie* (1929)].

7 [As Robbins commented in his preface to Hayek's *Prices and Production* (1931) pp. XI–XII].

13 The supply of material factors (continued)

Now the next thing we have to do is to relate what has been said already to more familiar theories relating to the same subject.

The supply of Material Factors is a problem which in the traditional treatment has been usually dealt with under the two headings Rent and Interest (See e.g. the treatment in Marshall) according as the supply in question was supposed to be fixed or flexible. So far as the theory of rent is concerned what I have said already about the place of factors whose supply is fixed is roughly similar to the traditional theory. It differs superficially in two respects:

(1) I have not used the title "land" to cover the class of factors concerned. I have given reasons for this in the lecture in which I discussed the classification of the factors of production.
(2) I have explained the price of such agents in terms of the general productivity analysis whereas in the traditional treatment it is usually discussed in terms of what may be called the rent analysis.

This might be thought to be a more fundamental difference. But in fact as I hope to show in a later lecture it is really no difference at all. The rent analysis is simply the productivity analysis from rather a different angle. Each concentrates solely upon the demand side. Each employs the hypothesis of dosing one factor with another. Each proceeds upon the supposition that substitution is possible. What difference remains is largely a matter of exposition.

But this is a matter to which I can more conveniently revert when dealing more intimately with the cost of production.

So much for the treatment of agents in fixed supply. The treatment of agents in flexible supply demands more extensive discussion.

In the orthodox textbooks, as I have indicated, this comes under the general heading "Interest". This I think is unfortunate since it tends to suggest that only the return to factors whose supply is flexible is capable of being conceived as interest, whereas as we have seen the return to any factor of production can be conceived as so much percent of the capital value.

Still for better or worse this is how the question has been treated and it is our business to discuss the relation of the theory expounded last time to the traditional treatment of the interest problem.

The traditional treatment of the interest problem has generally consisted of attempted answers to the question Why is interest paid? Attention has been given too to the question What determines the actual rate of interest? But in the main it is true to say that the chief interest has been displayed in devising answers to the former question.

In recent years certain mathematical economists – Pareto is the chief in this respect – have been in the habit of dismissing this enquiry as if it were ridiculous to undertake it. The rate of interest, *they say*, is a price like all other prices and it is absurd to ask for the particular causes which make it what it is without at the same time asking what causes make all other prices what they are. Such reflections have their uses no doubt but in this case they seem to me to miss the point. No doubt from the strict standpoint of mathematical equilibrium theory it is absurd to speak as the rate of interest were determined independently of the other elements in the pricing system.

But it is not this question which the historical discussion of interest is chiefly concerned with. The historical discussion is not concerned so much with what fixes the rate as with what causes interest to be paid. The historical discussion takes its complexion from the old days of medieval casuistry when the taking of interest was still a deadly sin, and the best people held the view that Aristotle had shown interest taking to be unnatural by suggesting that money was barren. It was not then the question What fixed the rate? It was the question Why should any rate be charged at ? – which was urgent. And from that day to this that has been the main question which has roused controversy.

Now whether all this controversy has been worthwhile or not, it is not set-tled by the equations of an equilibrium theory, and in point of fact I think you have here a very good example of the limitations of the mathematical approach. The equilibrium theory may well tell you how the rate of interest is fixed. But it does not tell you why interest is paid. It does not tell you what interest is the price of.

Now some of you may feel that this is a very trifling question. Interest is paid you may answer for the use of capital and that is the end of the matter. Capital goods are scarce therefore it is natural that they should have a price. Why worry further about the problem. Properly interpreted of course the answer is a correct one. It is the answer I should expect you to give if you understood my last lecture correctly. It is perhaps the only answer which would be necessary in a world in [which] old controversies did not cast their shadow over present theories. But let me try to put the matter to you not as it appears to you now fortified by the subtleties of modern treatment but as it put itself to say such a comparatively modern writer as the Austrian Böhm-Bawerk and see if even you will not be a little puzzled.

It is easy enough to see why rent is paid said the Austrians. Land is scarce and has utility in securing goods for consumption. It is given by nature and therefore it has no cost. Its value is determined by the value of its products. But when we come to interest the problem is not so simple – they said. Interest is the price paid for a produced means of production, not a piece of land given by nature but a plough, a spade, a factory machine.

Now, of course, it is obvious that such things have utility – that there is a demand for them – we do not deny that. Nor do we deny that they will have a price – a higher price that their owners will be able to charge for their uses.

But at the same time it must be remembered that such things can be produced – at a cost. And what we do not think obvious is why the sum of the annual prices which are paid for their use should be greater than their cost of production, why there should be a net product – a *reinertrag* remaining after the cost of production has been liquidated. A gross product yes – we understand that (*rohertrag*). What remains to be explained is the net product. Why the sum of the prices paid for the use of a produced means of production should be greater than the cost originally incurred to produce it. Why is not the value of the product imputed back (attributed to) the cost [of] goods. Why does the production of such goods proceed up to the point at which their value is equal to their product?

Now no doubt the answer is not difficult in the light of our recent analysis. We see that the securing of produced means of production means an outlay in the present for a return which is in the future. *Hence the supply is not pushed up to that point at which the sum of the anticipated products measured in value terms is equal to the present cost.* It is pushed only to that point at which the *discounted* sum of those products is equal to present cost. But it has taken much time to achieve this solution and the earlier search was by no means a quest of the obvious. It will still throw some light on the present theory if we examine some of the other solutions.

(This is not antiquarian research of the kind that is so unpopular. The theories I shall discuss are all comparatively recent. The names of Smith and Ricardo are not going to put in an appearance.)

Five main theories have been put forward to explain the phenomenon of interest besides the one I have expounded. They are:

(1) The Exploitation theory
(2) The Productivity theory
(3) The Abstinence theory
(4) The Time Preference and Agio theory
(5) The Dynamic theory.

Two of these I think are definitely false. The others I think have all considerable truth in them. They all illuminate one aspect of the problem but they are incomplete. The theory I have put forward combined these different suggestions and is sometimes known as the eclectic theory. One of the reasons why some of you found what I had to say last time so hard was perhaps because I used a terminology drawn deliberately from different theories at different points of the exposition. That was because I wanted to bring out the underlying identity of the propositions involved. But now let us look at these theories a little more closely.

(1) I take first the exploitation theory

This theory is attributed to Marx and Rodbertus and other writers of the German School. Interest or surplus value, it holds, is a payment reaped by the owners of capital in virtue of their power to exploit the labourers. Labour is the producer of all wealth. But since the capitalist system labour like other commodities is remunerated according to its cost of production and since labourers produce in a day more than is sufficient to feed them the owners of capital are able to appropriate the surplus value so produced to their own sinister enjoyment. This theory I regard as false. In fact, I would be prepared to say that it is almost unique among the theories of the past in the past in that it has no feature in it which is worthy of retention. It is mere dogma and illogicality. And as Keynes says, the wonder is that anything so dull and so wrongheaded could have dominated men's minds for so long.

Take the concept of labour remuneration. We have seen that it is not useful to assume that there is any connection between the supply of labourers and their cost of production. But from Marx's point of view this was not so obvious. In his day it was legitimate for an intelligent man to hold that this view was a useful first approximation to the facts. As you know, this view was taken by the classical economists. But did Marx appeal to such a hypothesis? Not a bit of it. He totally rejected the Malthusian Theory of Population – of course if it had been true it would have meant the end of communist ambitions: that is why the Bolsheviks are anxious to disseminate knowledge of contraception – but to reject it was to reject the only logical foundation of a subsistence theory of wages. It is not really possible to explain wages in terms of a universal buyer's monopoly. Yet this is what Marx attempted to do. Moreover his theory implied that surplus value was only reaped by the capital invested in the employment of labour. Capital invested in the buying of machinery returned its own cost but nothing more. That is to [say] the theory implied that the rate of interest would be different in different industries according to the amount of "circulating capital" employed as compared to the amount of "fixed capital" – which in view of the known tendency of capital to seek a common level is absurd.

It was on this rock that the theory foundered. Marx realized that here was a contradiction that that needed explaining. But in Vol I of *Capital* – the only volume published in his lifetime – he contented himself with saying that this was a nice riddle for proletarian economists to try their wits on. In Vol III which was patched up out of his manuscripts after his death by Kautsky, he makes a feeble attempt to solve the problem which only involves an abandonment of his labour theory of value. See B.B.[1]

Nowadays nobody believes in this theory. It may be true that the fact that one class possesses property and another does not can in a sense be described as

---

1 [E. von Böhm-Bawerk, *Capital and Interest* (1890) Chapter XII The Exploitation Theory].

exploitation. (It may not.) But *who owns* property is one thing; *why a price is paid for its use* is another. The absurdity of the hypothesis of exploitation as an explanation of why interest is paid is seen if one reflects that the problem would still arise in a society of classless individualism – the sort of thing some people would have you believe America to be – or even in a socialist community. See Cassell or Henderson.[2]

(2) I turn then to the productivity theory

This theory holds that interest is paid because capital is productive, and that the rate of interest depends upon the productivity of capital at the margin. Now we have seen already that the productivity of sacrifice plays an important part in the general determination of equilibrium.

But it clearly going too far to say that productivity is *the cause* of interest. It is only one of the conditions. Böhm-Bawerk may quite legitimately say that such an answer does not tell us why the value of the product "capital" is not at once imputed back to the things out of which it is made. Why is there a net product. Why is the sum of the higher prices greater than the cost?.

Moreover, the form in which it used to be put the productivity theory was inclined to be circular. Interest was said to depend on the supply of capital and its productivity at the margin and the supply of capital was conceived – not as the sums of money which people were willing to supply at the time in question but rather the total supply of capital goods in existence measured in value terms. Conceived in this way the theory is circular. For it is fairly clear that the value of capital goods – existing instruments of production – is dependent upon the rate of interest and alters with every alteration in its level. (This is the problem of capitalization to which we shall be returning later.) To argue from capital value to the value productivity of capital is to assume what has to be proved. Still it is not necessary to expound the theory thus. And if capital is defined as I have defined it, as power to direct the factors of production, then the supply of capital and its marginal productivity are the important factors in determining the rate of interest.

(3) I come now to the celebrated abstinence theory

This was put forward by Senior in the [eighteen]thirties.[3] Senior suggested that interest was paid because the productive process involved postponement of consumption and since this was painful it had to be paid for just as painful labour had to be paid for. An extension of the Ricardian theory of Real costs.

Now this, for its time, was a very ingenious and subtle theory, and it was a great advance on any theory that had then been put forward. And in essence it is very like the theory I have propounded.

---

2 [G. Cassell, *A Theory of Social Economy* (1923) Chapter VI; H. Henderson, *Supply and Demand* (1922) Chapter VIII].
3 [N. Senior, *An Outline of the Science of Political Economy* (1836) p. 58].

a) In the first place it emphasises that interest is paid because people are not willing always to go without present consumption for an equivalent future gain.

b) It defines interest as the price not of capital in the old sense (capital goods) but of what Senior called "abstinence", which is substantially equivalent to my definition of capital as money directed to the provision for the future.

(Marx and others have made fun of the term abstinence. No doubt it is absurd to think of the abstinence of a Rothschild – as if abstinence implied a positive sacrifice. For this reason, modern writers Macvane Marshall and others have used the phrase "waiting".[4] But this is itself not altogether satisfactory. And Mr Robertson's Lacking is worse.)[5]

The theory is, however, open to two objections.

(a) It does not bring out the part played by productivity.

(b) It conceives abstinence as something absolute – a real cost. The modern theory does not enquire into this. It simply emphasises the fact that saving involves not spending – that devoting present income to providing for the future means going without income in the present and it measures the increasing resistance to this in terms of the diminishing significance of future income.

The relation between the old abstinence theory here and the theory I have expounded is exactly the relation between the old theory of utility and the modern theory of relative significance – a considerable difference in the end but a difference mainly in emphasis and philosophic background.

(4) Finally I come to the Time preference or Agio theory

The theory namely that interest is paid because men discount the future and are therefore unwilling to exchange present and future income on equal terms.

This theory which in essence was anticipated by Galiani and John Rae has been expounded in modern times by Böhm-Bawerk Irving Fisher F.A. Fetter and others. In the form in which it is propounded by Irving Fisher in his *Rate of Interest* Part III, I have no exception to take to it. In substance it is not in disharmony with the modern form of the abstinence theory. I showed last time how the discount on the future could be exhibited as a rising supply price of abstinence or sacrifice or a falling demand price for present sacrifice in terms of future income. The one mode of demonstration is that adopted by Landry and the abstinence school, adopted by Fisher and his followers. Both exhibit the same fundamental fact: that present and future income are exchanged against one another on other than equal terms. Thus far I have no quarrel with the Agio theory. My only complaint would be that, like the abstinence theory, it does not give sufficient prominence to the productivity of

---

4 [Marshall, *Principles of Economics* (1920) p. 193n, citing S.M. Macvane, 'Analysis of cost of production' *Quarterly Journal of Economics* 2 (July 1887) pp. 481–7].

5 [D.H. Robertson, *Banking Policy and the Price Level* (1926)].

sacrifice. Irving Fisher does indeed work in the idea of productivity in his second approximation but he is so terrified of the word that unless you are on the lookout, for it may entirely escape your notice. Fetter succeeds in writing a whole treatise on Principles without anywhere leading you to suppose that productivity has anything to do with interest.

In a sense of course this is justified. It is true that even if there were no technical productivity of sacrifice one can conceive a capitalization rate arising. But an interest theory which neglects the most characteristic reason for capitalist accumulation must be held guilty of emphasizing the wrong abstractions.

There are however more serious defects in the theory as expounded by Böhm-Bawerk.

(a)   Böhm-Bawerk gives you to suppose that the preference for present goods over future goods is something universal and inevitable, that men have always a tendency to consume everything at once and leave the future unprovided for.

This, of course, is absurd. Of course you can conceive savage conditions where forethought is entirely absent.

But this is not the sort of case on which to base general assumptions. Speaking broadly it is wrong to say that there is a tendency for men to consume all they have in the present.

You can see this if you think of an extreme example.

Suppose a man shipwrecked on a raft 50 days from land with 50 days provision on the raft. Is there the slightest reason to suppose that divorced as he would be from any possibility of augmenting his total income he would show any disposition to eat all the provisions at once? Clearly he would ration himself severely. There would be no preference for present goods. The rate of time preference would be zero.

Now of course this is an extreme and absurd example, but it points to the way in which to approach the problem. Instead of thinking of the matter as a choice between "all or nothing now" and "nothing or all later on", we have to think rather in terms of disturbances of an income stream equally distributed through time.

This is Landry's solution, and Fisher's, and it is very important to distinguish it from Böhm-Bawerk's.

(b)   Secondly Böhm-Bawerk and others sometimes give one to imagine that the rate at which the future is discounted is constant – that whatever the amount saved the ratio of willing exchange with the future is the same. This is a grave misapprehension. There is not *one* rate. There is a series of rates according to the amounts conceived to be possessed in the present and the future – the marginal cost of saving is not constant.

We saw this when we were drawing the supply curve of sacrifice. We found it had an upward inclination – whereas if this way of putting the matter were correct the curve would be parallel to the x axis, thus:

OY cost per unit; OX units of capital.

The same point can be illustrated by a construction of Carver's.

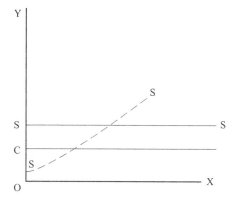

Measure years along OX, values along OY.
Let A_1O_1 = present value of present units of income.

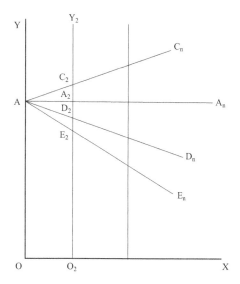

Let the present value of future units of income be measured along the successive perpendiculars to OX.

Thus the present value of O_1A_1 a year hence is measured along O_2Y_2.

The rate of exchange therefore between present and future will be measured by the ratio between O_1A_1 and the line expressing its value a year hence.

Or the rate of discount will be measured by the slope of the line connecting O_1A_1 with O_2E_2 or whatever the top of the line in question may be.

Now if it were right in speaking of *the* rate at which the future is discounted we should have to believe that however many A_tO_1s were saved the discount slope would always be the same.

In fact, we must suppose that it will swing continually downwards.

It may start as AC, showing a premium on the future, but it will gradually swing round in a clockwise direction, showing that as more OAs are sacrificed the marginal valuation of future OAs diminishes.

Read

Eugen von Bohm-Bawerk, *Capital and Interest* (1890)

The Positive Theory of Capital (1891)

Nassau Senior, *Outline of the Science of Political Economy* (1836)

Gustav Cassell, *The Nature and Necessity of Interest* (1903)

Irving Fisher, *The Rate of Interest* (1907)

Frank A. Fetter, *Economic Principles* (1915)

Adolfe Landry, *L'Interet du Capital* (1904)

Edwin Cannan, *A Review of Economic Theory* (1929)

Eugen von Bohm-Bawerk, *Karl Marx and the Close of his System* trans. Alice M. Macdonald (1898)

14 Supply of material factors (continued)

I come finally to Schumpeter and the Dynamic Theory of Interest.

Put baldly this amounts to a denial that in stationary conditions produced means of production can earn a net product – a *reinertrag*.

Schumpeter takes his stand on Böhm-Bawerk's analysis of the productivity theory of interest and declares roundly that no sufficient answer has been provided to it. There are only two factors of production, he says, Labour and "Land" (Boden) or Natural agents. In stationary conditions therefore he holds that the value of whatever is produced by the aid of these instruments must be "imputed back" to them. There is no room for interest and a third factor of production.

But how then does interest arise? Nobody denies that interest is paid. Schumpeter clearly has to provide an answer to this question. His answer consists of an extension of the Clarkian (or the Mathematical) Theory of Profits. According to Clark, Profits – the margin between costs and receipts only arise in a state of dynamic change. In stationary (or static) conditions there is no profit because costs and prices are identical. Profits are the extraordinary gains which accrue when the equilibrium is disturbed and the compensatory forces have not had time to reassert themselves. Suppose e.g. that things have been in equilibrium. There occurs a change in taste that leads to an increase in the demand for, say, coal. For the time being the price of coal rises and the producers of coal make exceptional gains. These tend to attract new labour and capital and equilibrium is once more restored with costs and prices equal. The transitory gains of the period of disturbance are described by Clark as "Profits".

Schumpeter's theory of interest follows along these lines. Ruptures in static equilibrium in his view are due to the action of entrepreneurs who force society to accept new processes and products. But in order to do this, they need the aid of capital – capital being defined in the sense I have given it earlier in the lecture. They are therefore willing to share with capitalists some of the dynamic surplus which accrues to them and this constitutes interest. But, and here we come back to that part of the theory, as soon as the dynamic change is carried through the surplus disappears. There is no room for interest in the stationary equilibrium.

Now there are certain features of this theory to which I have no objection. I have no doubt that in practice many of the incomes which go by the name of profits – the incomes of ordinary shareholders e.g. – are of this transitory nature. I am in substantial agreement too with Schumpeter's usage of the term capital. I have explained earlier why I think that the breach with business and accounting tradition made by Adam Smith was misleading. On this matter, I think Schumpeter's views are very enlightening.

But with the main thesis – that interest is not a static phenomenon – I cannot agree. On this matter I want to state my views more explicitly.

Let me start by removing a possible misunderstanding.

Of course if interest is defined as the yield of new saving – in the sense of net additions to the capital resources of the community it may be agreed that in a stationary equilibrium – where by definition there was no *new* saving – that kind of interest would not be present. But if by interest is meant the return to capital of any sort – then I think Schumpeter's view must be repudiated. And this for several reasons:

[(1)] In the first place, it seems to me quite illegitimate to assume dogmatically that the value of the products of a produced means of production must be imputed back to the agent from which they come.

Granted that if the product were produced simultaneously with the produced means of production this would be so. But when the products are strung out over time it seems to me quite gratuitous to *assume* that the sum of their values must be imputed back to the thing which produces them. The burden of proof surely is with those who hold that it must be. In fact we know that normally people are not willing to give an indefinitely large number of years purchase for a rent yielder. Why should such a curious state of affairs be regarded as normal under stationary conditions?

(2) Secondly the suggestion that ultimately all values must be imputed back to land and labour, *Arbeit und Boden*, seems to me quite illegitimate.

This is where the core of truth in the abstinence theory is useful.

It may be absurd to say that abstinence is a factor of production. The fact of postponement of consumption – waiting – is not *physically* productive.

But it remains true that unless people are willing to abstain – postpone consumption – accumulation will not take place. And since we have seen reason to suppose that beyond a point such abstention involves a sacrifice, a sacrifice of present income more highly valued than the equivalent amount of income in the future, there is no reason to suppose that this saving will be done unless it is remunerated.

(3) But this brings me to what I must regard as the final and absolutely crushing argument against Schumpeter. So far from it being impossible to conceive

a stationary state in which there is interest, I am prepared to argue that it is almost impossible to conceive a stationary state without it. For, other things being given, it is the equilibrium interest rate which keeps the stationary state stationary. If it were not what it is, either there would be net accumulation, in which case society would be "advancing", or there would be net decumulation, in which case the thing would be running down.

But how is this you may ask, how can people consume capital? And the answer is by precisely the reverse operation to that by which they accumulate – by turning factors of production which are devoted to the service of the future back to the service of the present. The possibility exists because of the physical depreciation of instruments. Every year a certain proportion of the existing factors of production have to be devoted to maintaining intact the existing equipment of society. Crusoe would have to devote time to keeping up his ditches. The machine society has to devote time to keeping up its instruments. Is it really conceivable that this sacrifice of possible income in the present is going to be made unless it is productive in the future? Are you always to have your cake without eating it if having it does not enhance your income indirectly? Clearly not. If there were no interest in the stationary state the stationary stage would cease to be stationary.

This refutation of Schumpeter links up very closely with Cassel's celebrated proposition that the lower limit of the interest rate depends very closely on the expectation of human life. This doctrine is expounded in detail in Cassel's own writings. It would be tedious for me to bore you with the details. Broadly speaking the doctrine is this. It is worth while saving for any income in the future – or keeping your present capital intact – if the rate of income you can get by so doing is greater than the income you could get by gradually encroaching on your capital until your death. It may be worth giving £10,000 now for £1,000 per annum (10%) because you expect to live more than ten years – and if you lived on your capital instead of keeping it intact you would be through with it in a little more than ten years. But if the rate falls to 1% the income you can get from investing £10,000 is only £100. Clearly even if you hope to live another 50 years you could more than double this income by steadily encroaching on your capital.

Or to put it another way, buying an income in the future for the sacrifice of present income may be expressed as giving so many years purchase.

If the rate is 5% then when you give £100 for an income of £5 p.a. you are giving 20 years incomes – (20 x 5) – 20 years purchase.

Clearly the length of time you expect to live – or the length of life you expect for your successors – will influence your judgment.

If the rate is 5 you give 20 years purchase. If it falls to 1 you give 100 years purchase. Hence Cassel argues that if the rate fell to much below 2 1/2% a great many people – particularly those who have only a few years to live – would cease to save and begin to consume capital. To buy annuities would be of course the most expeditious way of doing this.

This would curtail the supply of capital annually coming forward and the interest rate would rise. Hence he argues the probability that the rate of interest will ever become zero is absolutely negligible. Of course if the monkey gland treatment were to turn us all into Methuselahs it would be a different matter. Reflections such as these, I suggest, very powerfully reinforce the case against Schumpeter.

Now finally I come back to certain refinements which I want to introduce into my original statement of the Eclectic Theory. Let us revert to the diagram by which I explained the formation of interest in the capital market.

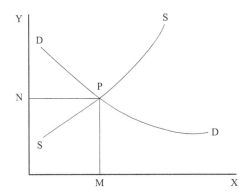

What exactly does this represent?

Equilibrium with OM capital and ON rate of interest.

Now recollect that as a rule diagrams of this sort represent *rates* of supply and rates of demand per annum. Now, as we shall see in a minute there is a sense in which it can be argued that this is the right interpretation of the diagram in a *state of final equilibrium*. But suppose we are thinking of the market position at any moment. Then the interpretation is more difficult.

D.D. represents the diminishing value productivity of capital – what would be the productivity of different instalments at the margin? S.S. on the other hand represents rates of supply per annum. Now is not this an incongruent position? Does it represent an equilibrium necessarily?

For suppose OM is saved one year – have we any reason to suppose that it will be all destroyed that year so that next year the rate of demand can be represented by the same demand curve? Obviously not. The situation you see is analogous to the problem of equilibrium of demand and supply of anything durable, gold or houses, as a picture of a final equilibrium. When no net additions are being made to the stock the diagram will do – interpreted as depicting *rates* of demand and supply. But it will not do for the intermediate stages.

What are we to do? Let us take a simple case, gold, and let us see if we cannot construct an apparatus which will exhibit the determination of equilibrium.

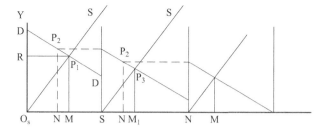

In the sort of apparatus of pigeon holes shown above, treat each box as a set of coordinates of the usual sort. Let DD exhibit demand for a year and SS the conditions of supply for the same period. Thus, in that year OM will be produced and sold at MP. Now if gold were permanently durable or houses, OM demand would be satisfied and the next year's production would have to satisfy demands now extra marginal But we may assume some waste. Suppose at the end of the year only ON remains. Then in drawing the demand curve for the next year (or unit period) we must assume that demand starts from that level.

This may be represented by projecting NP_2 on the new Y axis and then drawing the demand curve parallel with the old.[1]

Draw the supply curve as before. The new equilibrium will be OM_1 at a price MP_3. Follow out the same procedure for the subsequent year.

Then we may assume that the ultimate point of equilibrium will be reached when OM, the amount produced in the unit period, is equal to ON, the wastage from the previous period – the demand price and supply price being coincident.

At this point the yearly rate of supply is equal to the yearly rate of demand. The old interpretation of the diagram is valid.

Now supposing we cut out these diagrams and set them up in three dimensions. As before we measure quantity produced per unit period along OX and price along OY. We may set out successive time periods along OZ.

Suppose that we continuously reduce the period of observation. Eventually, we get instead of disconnected curves continuous surfaces so:

and the equilibrating price a path on the demand surface.

Our old friend the two-dimensional exhibition of equilibrium is thus seen to be a cross section taken at that point on OZ at which rates of supply and demand come into equilibrium.

All this is in terms of gold. If the same sort of construction is to hold for material equipment in general we shall have to complicate it to this extent that we can

---

1 We assume that population etc is stationary.

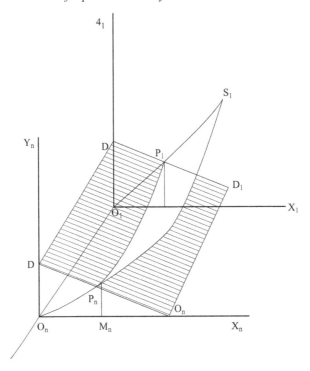

no longer assume the supply curve to be constant. More income. More (or less) saving. Each successive curve will have to have a slightly different position. Apart from this, however, the thing will do. No doubt it too is only an approximation of a rather crude order. But I suggest it does make the matter clearer than the usual two dimensional apparatus.

Finally, one word about capitalization. We have seen how the present value of *new* capital goods is equal to the value of the present income that has to be sacrificed to secure them. Capital goods – material instruments already in existence – have the present value determined by their future yield and the prevalent rate of return on new sacrifice. Thus Ricardian land which has no cost of production will have a present value determined by its annual yield and the number of years purchase which it is customary to give for future incomes in the capital market. At any time you can *cash* your land into that amount of capital which will secure an equivalent income at the current rate of interest. That is the common sense explanation. If you like you can push further and show how the rate of interest itself depends partly upon the volume of income provided by perpetual income yielders. But that is a refinement which is very well expounded in Fisher and Fetter, and there is no need for me to go into it.

Read

J.A. Schumpeter, *Die Theorie der wirtschaftslichten Entwicklung* (1911) Chapters I and II.

Gustav Cassell, *The Nature and Necessity of Interest* (1903).

Frederick Lavington, *The English Capital Market* (1921)

F.H. Knight, 'Neglected factors in the problem of normal interest' *Quarterly Journal of Economics* (February 1916).

T.N. Carver, 'The place of abstinence in the theory of interest' *Quarterly Journal of Economics* (October 1893).

Irving Fisher, *The Rate of Interest* (1907)

15 General review of equilibrium theory

I have now reached the end of my elementary treatment of Equilibrium Theory, and I want to devote this lecture to reviewing in broad outline the doctrine I have expounded upon and its place in the general system of economic science.

Let me start by briefly recalling to you the steps we have taken.

(1) After a couple of lectures explaining briefly what I intended to do, I commenced by an analysis of exchange equilibrium. This fell into two parts:

   (a) In the first I examined the conditions of simple exchange or barter. This enabled me to draw your attention to the fact of choice as the fundamental determining factor in the matters of exchange and to the concept of determinateness in exchange equilibrium.

   (b) I then passed to an examination of multiple exchange. The problem of market price. Here the leading threads of discussion were: (i) the fundamental identity of the forces underlying the demand and supply curves. I showed you how we could transform the latter into the former – sorting out as it were the psychological factor of relative valuation from the physical facts of the stocks available; and (ii) the interdependence of all markets.

(2) The second stage of my enquiry was the conception of equilibrium of production when the supplies of factors were given. Here again there were two subdivisions:

   (a) In the first I discussed what I called simple production. This enabled me to exhibit the idea of production as an exchange of productive services for product. It also gave me an opportunity to investigate the remote circumstances when the labour theory of value can be regarded as valid.

   (b) Then I went on to joint production. What I had to say here was chiefly concerned with the idea of marginal productivity.

(3) Having done this, the way was clear for the final stage: the analysis of equilibrium when supplies of factors are free to vary. This was treated in greater detail. The problem of labour supply was discussed under the two heads population and supply of work per labourer. The problem of material factor

supply resolved itself into a restatement of the theories of rent and interest shorn of a terminology which makes them misleading and emphasizing their relation to the general idea of equilibrium. This has constituted my last four lectures. I do not want to recapitulate in detail.

Such is the theory I have been trying to explain to you. Before we go on to the series of special studies with which I design to finish this course, I want to do three things:

(I)   First, I want to underline certain leading notions which run through this equilibrium analysis.

(II)   Second, I want to indicate its relation to certain other systems of analysis.

(III)   Third, I want to set out clearly its precise limitations and to explain how in spite of these it seems to me to assist our comprehension of reality.

(I)   First of all, then, for the leading ideas:

(1)   First and foremost comes the idea of *mutual dependence* – the mutual dependence of all the elements in the system of equilibrium. This is an idea which is of course implicit in the very notion of equilibrium but you have to think through the various pieces of analysis we have undertaken to realize fully its implications.

We see it first in the treatment of exchange equilibrium. The stocks of commodities are given and the psychological makeup of the exchanging parties. So too the initial distribution of stocks. But the amounts actually demanded and the prices obtaining in the various markets are reciprocally dependent on each other. Alter one element in the situation and all the others must alter. (Horizontal and vertical.) We see this dependence extending as we introduce new complications into the hypothesis. In the static state supply of commodities becomes a variable. At once it plays a double part. On the one hand it constitutes the demand for other commodities, on the other it varies according to the terms on which they can be obtained. The proportions too in which the factors are combined is a variable. It too depends on prices and prices depend on it. Finally in the stationary state the supply of factors also becomes a variable. Prices of commodities depend on the supply. Supply depends on the factors of production, the supply of factors of production depends on the price, and so on.

Once this conception of reciprocal influence is thoroughly grasped, one's whole conception of causality in the economic system is revolutionized. It is no longer sensible to ask e.g. what is the *cause* of value? – whether it is to be looked for on the demand side or the supply side. It is obvious that there is no one *cause*. There is simply a series of conditions given by the state of the world at a given moment. The rest is a process of mutual adjustment. Of course we are still at liberty to speak in terms of single causes when we are discussing the behaviour of the elements we have agreed to consider as *independent* variables: changes in population, tastes, invention etc. No doubt here too in the ultimate analysis is the idea of causation in the old unilateral sense is philosophically untenable. But we are not making enquiries into these metaphysical ultimates. For our purposes it is more convenient to regard them as variables subject to more arbitrary controls.

This idea of mutual dependence is particularly important to bear in mind when you are thinking of what is sometimes called marginal analysis.

Modern Economics is sometimes described as marginalism – by e.g. J.A. Hobson – and language is not infrequently used which suggests that the various margins contemplated are regarded by modern analysis are regarded as having special causal significance. Prices are determined by the marginal cost, interest *depends on* marginal productivity of free capital etc. Such language is very misleading.

True, we do tend to look more to the significance of *small* variations. We recognise that over the wide field of economic analysis it is here that the attention of entrepreneurs, purchasers, etc is focussed. But we do not regard the margin as causal. Marshall is continually insisting that prices are fixed *at* the margin not *by* the margin. And even this degree of emphasis is a little misleading. The inframarginal units are conceived to be just as important as the marginal units. If the inframarginal fertility of land were not what it is the margin would not be where it is. If you bear in mind this idea of mutual dependence there is no fear that you will fall into such misconceptions.

(2) The second leading idea has been *the conception of all processes in the system of equilibrium as forms of exchange.* Production is an exchange of the uses of factors for product: the provision of effort an exchange of leisure for the production of work, the provision of capital the exchange of present income for future income.

   (a) On the one hand, it enables us to realize the psychological side of the equilibrium as very fundamentally an equilibrium of choice – a weighing of this rather than that. The idea of the relative scales expressing the significance of different alternatives which assisted us to solve the simple problems of barter is seen to [be] as applicable to the solution of the most complicated problems of flexible production.

   (b) On the other hand, it enables us to formulate a clear and consistent conception of costs as the alternatives we have to forego in order to attain what we choose. The cost of corn was coal, the cost of oranges [was] the fish which the time which procured the oranges would have secured. The cost of income from work is the leisure we forego in securing it, the cost of income from new accumulations of property the income we forego in making the accumulation. We value the product in terms of the cost and the cost in terms of the product and the act of choice is seen to be the ultimate indivisible fact on which we base this side of our analysis.

(3) This brings me to the third feature of this analysis, the *sorting out at each stage of the psychological from the technical* influences.

When we discussed exchange equilibrium, we saw the way to amalgamate the demand and supply curves so as to leave as it were as a crude deposit the stock in the market. When we discussed the static state the productivity analysis was carefully split up into the two notions of physical and value productivity. And so too in the interest problem – the technical element was sifted out from the element of time discount or valuation of sacrifice.

Our equilibrium at every stage has been seen to be what Pareto calls an "equilibrium of tastes and obstacles".

(4) Finally, by proceeding at every stage from the hypothesis of Crusoe Economics and only going on to the analysis of equilibrium in society, I have tried to show in what way the fact of social cooperation complicates the economizing of individuals. This leads to three observations which I think are of importance:

(a) First, it shows that there is no need at any point in our analysis to make comparisons of psychological magnitudes as between individuals.

(b) Second, we see that when we are looking at this from the point of view of the whole the choices of individuals fall into the class of subjectively motivated conditions, the technical facts into a class of pure objective conditions, yet when we think of the point of view of individuals we must realize that *for him* other people's choices are as fixed as the technical obstacles.

(c) Third, we realize that whereas man in isolation works for *his* product, man in society works for the value of his product – lots of little bits of other people's products.

While there is competition this introduces no disharmony, when competition vanishes and demand is inelastic this may involve grave conflicts of social interests.

So much for the leading ideas of the analysis.

Now what of its relation to other systems? Let us proceed gently from the more to the less similar systems. Naturally I undertake no systematic comparison – I do not want to bore you – I indicate merely salient points of similarity and dissimilarity.

(1) Let us start with Cassell. On the whole there is very little difference between what I have said and the positive views expressed by Cassell. The general view of the pricing process which he presents is of course quite consistent with the view I have given which derives more specifically from Knight, Wicksteed and Davenport. The terminology is different. Cassell is always talking about scarcity as if it were something unfamiliar. But Cassell's scarcity is of course only supply in relation to demand. The fundamental equations which he uses are in line with those of all equilibrium theorists.

My chief complaint against Cassell is that he so frequently throws the baby out with the bath. I do not object to his extrusion of psychological considerations and hedonistic utility theory. I have tried to do this myself. But he extrudes too much. He deprives himself of the opportunity for detailed examination of the facts of choice on the one hand and the combination of productive factors on the other hand. Scarcity becomes too much of an incantation. He does not explain sufficiently the way scarcity shows itself. He breaks (or pretends to be break) too violently with traditional analysis.

(2) Now take Marshall. My complaint here is the opposite.

The view of equilibrium I have tried to give you could be constructed piece by piece almost entirely from Marshall. Those of you who read chapters 1 and 2 of Book VI – The Preliminary View of Distribution – will have no difficulty in recognizing the picture. Cassell's accusation that Marshall did not recognize the interdependence of things is rubbish. No one has done more than Marshall to make us alive to them. My criticism of Marshall is that he clings to closely to traditional moulds [sic] of treatment and terminology, that he pretended that there was no difference between him and the classics, that he tried to vindicate even their most paradoxical views while himself advancing theories which were really dissimilar. Moreover, in at least one case – the theory of real costs – I think he allowed his penchant for the old definitely to distort his judgment. But there will be more to say about Marshall when we come to special studies.

(3) As regards Clark and the productivity theory, I have indicated already its relation to the system I have developed. Clark's productivity theory is essentially
a theory of equilibrium in what he calls a static state – a state in which the
supplies of factors are given. So far he fits into the system. But on the questions of utility and interest I think he is definitely misleading.
(4) The same stricture of limitation must be passed on the utility school of
Vienna. It is essentially a theory of the static state.

Within those limits, of course, in its time the work was pathbreaking. Its influence on Wicksteed was considerable. But its views of utility and of attribution are often crude and misleading. The Austrian theory of utility is replaced in our system by the theory of choice and the relative scale: *relative* rather than *absolute* utility. The theory of attribution – Zurechnung – gives way to the productivity analy-sis. The important feature which remains is the concept of opportunity cost first formulated by American D.I. Green Q.J.E. 1894[1], but in essence it is essentially Austrian.

(5) Fifth and finally, what of the Classics conceptions?

Now germs of an equilibrium theory are clearly discernible in the Classics. Adam Smith's celebrated Chapter on Wages and Profits, with its insistence on the tendency of net advantages to equality, contains the outlines of a theory of

---

1 ['Pain-cost and opportunity-cost' *Quarterly Journal of Economics* Vol. 8 (1894) pp. 218–29].

this sort.[2] Ricardo's working out of the Labour Theory of Value (as Davenport has suggested and as has recently been proved by the publication of the notes on Malthus)[3] is clearly conceived in opportunity cost terms. The value of commodities was proportional to their real labour costs because if it were not so there was shifting.

Again, the idea of a stationary state is clearly classical. In so far as it is used by Marshall it is obviously classical in origin. Nevertheless we are a long way from the Classics. The treatment of the demand side is postclassical. The idea of simultaneity in prices in postclassical. The productivity analysis in its modern form is not classical. Our analysis of the supply functions is vastly different from theirs – save in so far as it derives from Senior. The study of the Classics is important, but it is important as much for the way it illuminates modern theory *by contrast* as for the positive guidance it offers.

Finally I want to state definitely the limitations of the analysis.

These fall into two classes:

(1) Limitations within the field of stationary equilibrium defined as I have defined it;
(2) Limitations due to the nature of this hypothesis itself.

Let me explain what I mean by specifying.

(1) The limitations of the analysis I have developed as regards stationary equilibrium in general are twofold:

   (a) I have assumed free competition. I have not treated the case of monopoly or monopolistic competition.

   This is a mere matter of time and the division of study. An analysis of monopolistic competition can be developed. As we realized when we discussed barter, this introduces elements of indeterminateness which are not present when competition is relatively free.

   (b) I have assumed divisibility of productive factors and a wide possibility of substitution at the margin. This is akin in some ways to the assumption of competition. It facilitates exposition and there are reasons for believing that it is most suitable as a first approximation.

(2) The limitations of *any* analysis of stationary equilibrium are much more serious. Clearly we exclude from our consideration many changes which as independent variables are continually altering the conditions of equilibrium.

   (a) We exclude exhaustion of mineral deposits.
   (b) We exclude variations in population.

2 [*An Inquiry into the Nature and Causes of the Wealth of Nations* ed. E. Cannan (1904) Chapter X].
3 [H.J. Davenport, *The Economics of Enterprise* (1913); Ricardo, *Notes on Malthus' "Principles of Political Economy"* eds. J.H. Hollander and T.E. Gregory (1928)]

(c) We exclude changes of consumers demands.

(d) We exclude inventions etc.

(e) We exclude all those changes due to "monetary causes".

It is the task of a wider synthesis, the theory of moving equilibrium and the theory of fluctuations, to show how these combine with the tendencies we exhibit. Usually it is not difficult to do this for single causes of variation, provided the variation is small. You may find specimens of this sort of analysis in Marshall's Chapters on Progress[4] and in his discussion of changes of demand and supply etc etc. I have tried to apply this analysis of variations in two articles – Hours and the Consequences of the coming of a stationary population.[5] The difficulties arise when you consider several variables all functioning at once. Little work has as yet been done here. It is the great task of the future.

Nevertheless in spite of these deficiencies the analysis of equilibrium which we have achieved up to date does indicate forces which are continually at work in the economic system as we know it. The dominating conception of the equilibrating forces of the market is not likely to be displaced by further refinements. In any given situation the tendencies discussed in the analysis of stationary equilibrium are active, just as in any condition of the sea the forces making for a condition of rest are present. In neither case can you ignore these tendencies.[6]

Moreover – and with this I have finished – you must not overrate the frictions which prevent them showing themselves within short periods.

No doubt we must not forget the existence of frictions – we are not likely to – anyone can see frictions. It takes an economist to see underlying tendencies – we all know that markets are not perfect, that labour and capital do not move instantly etc etc. These things are dinned in our ears by people who do not understand what we are trying to do. The danger I think is that we forget what an amazing degree of flexibility there is in the economic system – that we may overlook the power of rapid readjustment within periods that are comparatively short that arises from the facts of wastage and depreciation at one end of the system and renewal and recruitment at the other. If it were not for the fact of free recruitment at one end of the labour force and free capital at one end of the material equipment, we might regard our analysis of equilibrium as abstract and wooden. The danger, I think, is that we may often let the short period dislocation blind us to the ubiquity of the forces tending to reestablish balance between the fundamental facts of choice and obstacles. But these are matters of first year analysis

---

4 [*Principles of Economics* (1920) Chapters XII and III].

5 ['The economic effects of variations of hours of labour' *Economic Journal* 39 (March 1929) pp. 25–40; 'Notes on some probable consequences of the advent of a stationary population in Great Britain' *Economica* 9 (April 1929) pp. 71–82].

6 Illustrate by reference to Wage Theory.

Read

Gustav Cassell, *The Nature and Necessity of Interest* (1903) Vol. I

Alfred Marshall, *Principles of Economics* (1920) Book VI Chapters 1 & 2

H.J. Davenport, *The Economics of Enterprise* (1913)

L.C. Robbins, 'The economic effects of variations of hours of labour' *Economic Journal* (March 1929)

'Notes on some probable consequences of the advent of a stationary population in Great Britain' *Economica* (April 1929)

Frank H. Knight, 'A suggestion for simplifying the general theory of price' *Journal of Political Economy* (June 1928)

Note: *The notes for the following lecture were found in the 1939–40 Notebook but appear to have been written much earlier though not in 1929/31. Since the course syllabus in the LSE Calendar for 1931/32 added 'Inter-spatial and inter-temporal Price Relationships' to the topic 'General View of Economic Equilibrium', the lecture has been included here.*

15* Price relationships in the economic equilibrium

For the time being I have finished all I wish to say about Interest and the equilibrium of supply of material factors. I shall be coming back to Interest in another connection later.

At present I want to examine more closely certain price relationships in the economic equilibrium. Hitherto we have been content to speak of prices in general and their general relationship to demand and the technical conditions of supply. I now want to examine certain relationships between particular groups of prices – examination of which will I believe throw light on certain very much disputed questions of economic analysis.

The first group of price relationships I want to examine are the price relations of goods of the same technical kind in different geographical locations – *interspatial* price relationships.

Now in itself this is an easy problem. I deal with it in the first year lectures.[1] The fundamentally important thing to remember is that goods of like technical (physical) quality existing at different places are different goods. Sugar in Cuba is the same the same commodity as sugar in London from our point of view. From the point of view of the London demand sugar in Cuba is *not* a consumption good – not a good of the first order. Before from the point of view of the London demand it can be regarded as a consumption good it must be combined with the producers' good transport and brought to this locality.

Hence, we should expect to find in a state of final equilibrium of the competitive order a simple relationship between the prices of goods of similar physical qualities which are capable of being moved the price differences would not be greater than the cost of transport through space – the cost of "producing" the consumption good at the place at which was consumed. In the real world, leaving monopolistic complications on one side, we should also have to take account of the effects of taxation. The effects of an import duty are of course in this respect exactly similar to an increase in the cost of transport.

All this is well known and very simple. The underlying principle however – the principle that goods of like physical qualities in different places are not the same

---

1 [Robbins lectured on Elements of Economics in the years 1929/30–1934/35.]

goods from the economic point of view throws light upon certain problems which are not so generally understood.

I take first the problem of retail price maintenance. Goods of like physical quality in different places are different goods. In a competitive system therefore we should not expect to find goods of like physical qualities in different places with similar prices – unless costs of transport from centres of production and costs of marketing were similar. That is to say we should not expect to find coals in London as cheap as coals in Newcastle. Nor should we expect to find petrol in the highlands of Scotland as cheap as petrol in London. If, therefore, we do find similar prices when the costs of production are obviously dissimilar we know that competition is not perfect. We know too that what is happening is that the consumers in the places where the cost of marketing is small are being made to subsidize consumption in the places where cost of production is high.

Now I am not arguing that this is bad. That is not my business.

I am not arguing even that it is inconceivable that there are productive economies associated with *some* practices of this sort – e.g. if I send a letter to Hampstead it costs as much as if I send a letter to Yorkshire. In fact it doesn't. But the post office might incur greater expense of sorting if it attempted nicer adjustments of prices and costs. I am not clear even here. But it is obviously conceivable that standard prices may be associated with productive economies in some cases.

But I do want to emphasise that where there do exist these uniformities of price where costs are not uniform, there also exist concealed subsidies and that, in certain cases at any rate if consumers demand is the criterion, they do lead to a definitely uneconomical use of factors of production. In the case of retail price maintenance agreements e.g. the fact that the retailer is not allowed to change the price means that the only service he can render to the consumer by economizing is by way of extra services. Any economies which may result from better use of situation and labour cannot be passed on in price.

The second point I want to mention in connection with this conception of interspatial price equilibrium arises in regard to money. It is sometimes said that at any given time the value of money at different places is different – that it is higher in one place than in another. Now as we shall see in a minute, there is a sense in which this statement has meaning. But if we recollect our fundamental principle that goods of like physical qualities in different places are *not* the same commodities, we can see that taken literally of a state of equilibrium it is patently fallacious.

Suppose we are considering the value of money in terms of the prices of goods in a hotel in a valley. It would be absurd to say that the value of money was different in the valley from what it was higher up because the same goods in a higher chalet were higher by the cost of transport. The goods higher up would be different goods and it would be as silly to say that the value of money was different because e.g. bread at an altitude of 1000 feet was cheaper than the commodity bread at 10,000 feet as it would be to say that the value of money was different in two adjacent shops because in one you could buy boots and in another clothes.

The same holds when we are considering differences not of altitude but of latitude and longitude. The collection of commodities available may be physically the same in different countries. But in regard to spatial position they are different. Because coffee and sugar are dearer in London than in Brazil, that is no reason for saying that the value of money is different. It would only be different if sugar and coffee were the only things on which money could be spent and it would pay to send money to Brazil to get sugar and coffee rather than buy them in London. But that would not be a state of equilibrium. In a state of equilibrium, coffee in Brazil and coffee in London would command different prices, but the value of money would not for that reason be different.

But if this is so what meaning are we to attach to the statement that living in one place is dearer than living in another? The thing is quite simple. We mean that our needs are less amply satisfied in one place than another. This can happen for two reasons:

(1) Needs in one place may be different from needs in another.

    (a) Thus, the amount of clothing one needs at the North Pole is different from the amount of clothing one needs at the equator. That is a question of needs changing with changing physical environment.

    (b) Or the amount of conventional necessities may change with a changing social milieu – e.g. a don living at Oxford to give more lunches to people he doesn't particularly want to meet than a professor living in London.

(2) The possibility of satisfying given needs may be different.

    (a) This may happen for technical reasons. It is easier to satisfy the need for bananas in Africa than in Kew.

    (b) Or for reasons of a social nature – e.g. if many people want to live within two miles of Piccadilly Circus that drives up the price of land.

For any of these reasons, living may be dearer in one place than another. And it is quite intelligent to say that it is so.

The confusion arises because the value of money – that is its relationship to all commodities in the circle of exchange – is confused with its power to purchase certain collections of physically similar commodities defined out of relation to their spatial relations. The fact that coffee in Brazil is cheaper than coffee in London may make living cheaper in Brazil than in London. But it does not entitle us to say that the value of money is different in different places.

One further point in this connection. I have said that the price relationship between goods of like physical qualities which are capable of being moved is a simple one. It is important to realize that many goods are not capable of being moved (houses e.g.), and if this is important in connection with consumers goods it is still more important when you consider factors of production.

Lands of different sorts cannot be moved. Labour may be disinclined to move – in which case it will command a higher price in the parts where it is relatively scarce. Or it may be unable to move owing to national restrictions of various sorts. This means that various factors, although of like technical efficiency, will be worked in different combinations in different parts of the world. (Of course the factors may not be of like technical efficiency.) And this means that their relative prices incomes will be different.

Of course this falls outside general equilibrium theory. It is part of the theory of international trade and to develop all its implications would take many lectures. But it is easy enough to see how it follows on equilibrium theory, and how in essence the theory of international trade is just on all fours with the theory of distribution between heterogeneous factors. Factors of like physical qualities in different places are as different from the economic point of view as factors of different technical qualities in the same place. There is no reason to expect that in equilibrium their remuneration will be equal. It depends on the general conditions of supply and demand *cet par* – their marginal productivity properly interpreted – *where they are*.

This has a bearing on the matter we have just been discussing. One of the main influences on the cost of living in different places is of course the price of factors – efficiency prices. In countries where services are plentiful the cost of living to people who come from elsewhere will seem low. When English people go to America the cost of living seems high. One of the main reasons is that services are relatively scarce. When Americans come here or – better still – to France or Italy, the cost of living seems low. From their point of view they are right. But that is no reason to say that the value of money is different. The fact is that services here and services in America are different "goods" from an economic point of view.

Now I want to turn to a second kind of price relationship – the relation of prices in *time – intertemporal price equilibria*. This is more difficult, but in the end it is not dissimilar.

Now so far – save in our consideration of interest – we have neglected the time element in our discussion of equilibrium. Our price equilibria have been conceived as existing *simultaneously* or as persisting unchanged over any period of time whatsoever. Now as a methodological device this was quite justified. It would be perfectly intolerable to handle all the complexities of the situation at once. If at the very outset of our discussions, I had been obliged to insert all the qualifications and elucidations I am now introducing; our analysis would never have gotten started (that's why Marshall is so difficult). But it should be clear that even in analysing stationary equilibrium, it is not necessary to assume that at all times different goods have the same prices, or are produced in the same quantities.

In a community in which year in year out the same processes repeated themselves with complete regularity, it is improbable that at all times of the year the same commodities would be forthcoming with similar ease – that is, it is improbable that the conditions of supply would be constant throughout the year. It would obviously be more difficult to produce strawberries in November than in July. Yet in any given year we might conceive that in an equable climate the total supply forthcoming would be the same.

In exactly the same way on the demand side, we can conceive regular fluctuations in time which do not fall outside the scope of our conception of stationary equilibrium. It is clearly as easy to erect a bathing tent in December as in the middle of summer. Yet in conceiving the equilibrium of a stationary community there is no reason for us to assume that the demand for the services of bathing machine attendants will be the same in the midwinter as in the summer holidays.

All that is necessary is to assume that within the unit period – the year the week or whatever – it may be the same processes and prices appear at the same times as in preceding unit periods. Now in order that such regularity may appear it should be clear that certain definite price relationships must exist not merely *at a moment* of time, but also *through* time.

We may therefore consider not merely an interspatial but an *intertemporal* equilibrium, and indeed if our conception of equilibrium is to be at all realistic it is most important that we should do so.

At this point it is desirable to formulate a principle similar to the principle we formulated in considering interspatial price relationships. In the case of interspatial price relationships we decided that it was useful to recollect that commodities of like physical qualities at different points of space were not similar commodities from the point of view of equilibrium analysis. So now, in considering intertemporal price relationships, we may lay it down that *commodities of like physical and spatial qualities at different points of time (in the unit period) are not similar commodities*.

• Strawberries in November are not the same as strawberries in June. Taxi rides at midnight are not the same as taxi rides at midday. That being understood, we may proceed to more detailed investigation.

Let us start first with the case of a foodstuff such as wheat, which is produced only at one season of the year *but which is capable of being stored*. In equilibrium conditions there should be a simple relationship between the price of wheat at different times of the year.

The prices of the different commodities wheat at harvest time and wheat six months after harvest should differ by the cost of transport through time – the cost of holding – that is to say the rate of interest on the money invested for the period of holding. If this relationship does not hold then there is not equilibrium. There is an incentive to change the distribution of sales through time until it does.

Thus supposing a certain quantity of wheat now is selling at £100 and supposing that wheat six months hence is selling at £100. Suppose that the rate of interest is 10% – (that is 5% per six months). There is a clear incentive to buy spot wheat and sell forward wheat until the rise in spot wheat and the fall in forward wheat wipes out the difference between the interest charge and the price margin.

This is a well-known case familiar to you from first year economics. I shall be coming back to deal with it in another connection in the next lecture.

Now let us consider the case of a commodity which can be produced at all times during the unit period but whose production at times is cheaper than it is at others. The simplest example I can think of is the production of eggs. The rate at which hens will lay will vary at different times of the year. It follows therefore that the price relationship between eggs at one season of the year will vary. That is to say it is not necessarily a one-to-one relationship, even in equilibrium conditions.

Now the next thing to observe is that these intertemporal price differences will not be without influence on other elements in the equilibrium. Revert for a moment to the case of strawberries. When strawberries are in season, labour and capital which at other times is devoted to the cultivation and production of other things are devoted to picking strawberries. It follows that the number of other things which can be produced with given supplies of capital and labour is curtailed. Unless production takes place under conditions of constant cost this will lead to price differences between the price of these other things in strawberry season and at other times. Not only the numbers produced but also the prices will be different at different points in the unit period.

Now let us suppose that the price differences are now allowed to emerge. Suppose the price of strawberries is held midway between the price of strawberries in November and the price of strawberries in June. Two things follow:

(a) On the supply side, the number of strawberries coming forward in November is curtailed. The demand for strawberries in November is increased. There is disequilibrium.
(b) At the same time the supply of strawberries in June is greater and the demand for strawberries is less.

So that:
(a) demand is not so adequately supplied; and (b) the factors of production concerned are not put to such profitable uses in time.

Finally, let us notice how these periodic changes in productive conditions may affect the so-called purchasing power of money as measured in index numbers recording the price changes of certain commodities.

Suppose to take an example of Hayek's, the inhabitants of a community in equilibrium take out substantial proportions (though changing ones) of their real incomes in a certain kind of fruit procurable all the year round at greatly differing costs.[2] (Suppose also to simplify matters that the amount of labour etc. available throughout the year does not vary.) Then it should be clear that at some periods of the year the price of the fruit will be much higher than at others. At the same time more factors of production will be devoted to its use and the prices of other products may be affected some one way some another according to cost conditions. It is fairly clear that an index number recording these price changes would vary even though the system was in equilibrium throughout the period. (Note in passing that the quantities of other commodities produced would vary – there would be trouble with the weighting.)

Suppose it were attempted to put purchasing power into the system in such a way as to keep this index constant. Would it not necessarily disturb the equilibrium?

2 Incapable of storage.

You can see this in two ways:

(a) Think first of the effect *via* incomes.

 If the money supply were undisturbed, money incomes would be determined by the usual distributive apparatus. Each factor would be "rewarded" according to its marginal productivity.

 If it were disturbed then this would mean that at one stage when money was being injected into the system some spender was in possession of money not released by the sale of a product, at another stage some of the money released by the sale of a product would be withdrawn from the system. A new disturbing element would have come in and the equilibrium would be disrupted.

(b) Or second, look at the effect on prices.

 If the supply of money was undisturbed producers would look to securing prices different at one point of time from what they would be at another.

 The injection or withdrawal of money would not necessarily keep relative prices constant. Hence it is difficult to see what use it would be.

 But it would certainly make relative prices different from what they would have been. Hence producers would make different arrangements. Again there would be a disturbance of the equilibrium.

 But more on this later.

 Finally, notice that just as in the case of interspatial price relationships we were driven to admit that the existence of different prices for commodities of like physical qualities at different places did not justify us in stating that therefore the value of money was different in different places, so in dealing with *intertemporal price relationships* recognition of the fact that commodities of like physical quantities at different points of time are different commodities should lead us logically to the conclusion that in a system of equilibrium over time the fact that at different points of time different commodities have prices different from what they have at other times does not justify the view that for that reason the value of money is different at different points of the unit period. This is perhaps a startling conclusion, and it certainly has very revolutionary significance for general monetary theory. Whether it is all that can be said, it is worth thinking about.

See

Ludwig von Mises, *Theorie des Geldes und der Umlaufsmittel* (1912)

F.A. Hayek, 'Das intemporale Gleichgewichtsystem der Preise und die Bewegungen des "Geldwertes"' *Weltwirtschaftliches Archiv* (July 1928)

Frank A. Fetter, *Economic Principles* (1915)

Special topics

16 Consumers surplus

I now come to the series of special lectures which I promised in my last lecture.

I want today to direct your attention to certain matters relating to the interpretation of the phenomenon of "demand". In particular, I want to direct your attention to the theory of consumer surplus. My conclusion, I am afraid, will be largely negative, but I hope in the course of arriving there I shall be able to throw oblique light on certain positive features of theory. In any case this is an enquiry which must be undertaken. For good or bad, many of the constructions and propositions of modern theory are not intelligible save against a background of this discussion.

Our problem relates to the interpretation of the demand curve and the schedule behind it. You will remember – it is the most familiar feature of first year theory – that in examining the theory of demand we found that for certain purposes it was convenient to express the conditions of demand for a commodity in terms of a table showing the various amounts which would be bought – at various prices – a demand schedule – or if we assumed variation to be continuous – in terms of a downward sloping curve.

There are certain inaccuracies about this conception. It suggests that demand is a function of one variable – the price of the commodity concerned, when in fact it is a function of many. It assumes a kind of continuity which is dubious. And there are other crudities in the conception which are known to those who use it. But as a first approximation no one denies that it is a useful and powerful instrument. The main use of the demand curve is to enable us to tell the effect on price and amount demanded of variations of supply. It enables us to examine with expedition problems of taxation and monopoly. If we were able to obtain statistical measures of the demand functions for different staple commodities the rational conduct of policy would be very greatly facilitated. These are the main uses, and about these things there is no serious disagreement.

Certain economists, however, of the utility school have sought to extend the sphere of its usefulness. They have attempted to make it the measure of the ultimate satisfactions derived from the consumption of any commodity. It is admitted by all to be the main analytical instrument of "price economics". They have attempted to make it also the main analytical instrument of "welfare economics" – whatever that may mean. They have done this by means of the doctrine of total utility and consumers surplus.

The main outlines of these doctrines are extremely simple. They arise as supposed corollaries of the old hedonistic theory of utility. Let us examine them as they are stated in terms of geometry. (The verbal explanation of the demand schedule and its significance is best read in Marshall in private.) We have the justification that historically it was unquestionably as a result of this construction that the conceptions of the surplus arose.

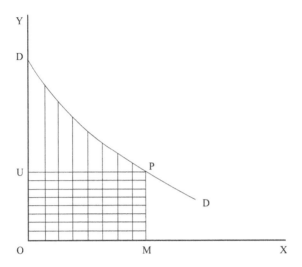

The demand curve DD, which expresses the functional connection between price and amount demanded is also conceived to express the functional connection between final degree of utility and amount conceived to be possessed. That is to say OY is supposed to measure rates of final utility. As OM increases final degree of utility falls. That being the case, it seems natural to me – and they do assume – that total utility will be the integral area behind the curve. If the amount bought be OM then DPMO is conceived to express the total utility arising from it.

But it does not express the net utility enjoyed – so it is proceeded to argue. For in order to procure OM units at the price PM, OMPU money has to be expended. The utility thus sacrificed is said to be measured by this area, so that the utility enjoyed is expressed by the area DPU the consumers rent or by surplus.

The earlier units, it is said, are acquired at the same cost as the later units, but they are valued more highly; therefore there is a surplus of utility.

Such in very broad outline is the theory we have to examine.

Now I may say at once that I disagree with this theory. I find it illogical and misleading. I do not find in it anything that I want to incorporate into the main body of economic theory. But some versions of it are more open to criticism than others and it is therefore very necessary to conduct the criticism by stages.

Let me start by disposing of the most vulnerable version.

The demand curve I have drawn might stand for the demand of an individual or for the demand of the whole market. Now certain exponents of the theory have attempted to discover a consumers surplus not only behind the demand curve of the individual but also behind the demand curve of the market. In this way, indeed, the doctrine is used by Marshall in his celebrated chapter on the doctrine of maximum satisfaction. In this form, I do not think there is anything at all to be said for the theory. It assumes comparability of different satisfactions experienced by different people. And as I have tried to emphasize already, there is nothing to justify such an assumption. Bread, e.g., is bought by rich and poor, old and young, sick and healthy, and their demands taken collectively are exhibited in the demand schedule for bread. I know no method whereby the satisfactions experienced by these different people can be reduced to a common denominator and exhibited as a geometrical area.

Marshall is aware of this difficulty and makes the explicit assumption that the commodity is bought by people of approximately equal incomes. But this does not help at all. It simply makes the thing look more plausible. It *seems* easier to compare the satisfactions of a man with £1000 a year with those of a man enjoying a similar income than to compare them with those of a man enjoying a larger or a smaller income. But in fact it is not. Bread to me may be a means of exquisite pleasure. To you it may be a mere defensive product. To another it may be positively distasteful. How are we justified in assuming that there is anything similar about our attitudes save our willingness to pay 6d a loaf for it at certain margins?

It is fairly clear then that if the concept of consumers surplus is to mean anything at all it must be related not to the market demand curve but to the individual demand curve. The area behind the market demand curve no more expresses surplus utility to the community than the curve itself expresses marginal degrees of utility. We have to split the demand curve up into its component parts before the analysis is ever complete.

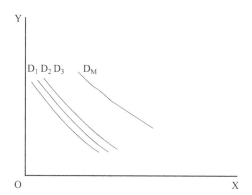

Consumer's surplus therefore must be understood as having the apostrophe *before* not *after* the s. It is the surplus of *a* consumer not the surplus of *the* consumers. This in itself deprives the notion of most of its practical applications.

But now before proceeding to the analysis and criticism of this more plausible concept let me pause to remove two minor variants.

(1) The doctrine of consumer's surplus is sometimes said to be justified because in a market a consumer gets his goods for less than he would be prepared to pay for them. That there is a surplus of marginal as well as on inframarginal purchases. Now stated thus the doctrine is entirely unacceptable. It is of course true that as Marshall suggests you can buy certain essential items in your budget cheaper in England, say, than on the West Coast of Africa. That is true. But it is not a matter of consumers surplus; it is a matter of different costs. Of course, on the West Coast of Africa some things are more expensive than they are in this country, but that is not to say that when you buy them in this country you get your marginal purchases for less than they are worth to you; of course you do not. We have seen already that if the terms on which you can get commodities are less than your marginal estimation of those commodities there is an incentive to rearrange your expenditure until at the different margins marginal significance and price are proportionate to one another. Marshall's illustration only seems plausible because he is contrasting different states of equilibrium.[1]

(2) Another version of this theory of the good luck of inframarginal purchasers derives from the contemplation [of] cases of lumpy or imperfectly divisible commodities. I buy a bottle of ink e.g. for 2d. Rather than do without it I would pay six pence. Therefore I reap a consumer's surplus "equivalent" to 4d.

This is much more plausible, and indeed *if I only bought one bottle of ink all my life* I might indeed thank whatever gods may be for a consumer's surplus. But the plausibility disappears when we reflect that the diagrams refer *not to simple purchases* but to *rates of purchase*. The bottle of ink may not be divisible here and now but I can vary the number I buy within a given period. If at my present rate of consumption the 2d bottle of ink is worth 6d obviously I quicken up my rate of purchase of ink. The surplus in this sense disappears.[2]

The two versions of the doctrine of individual consumer's surplus which we have contemplated up to date have suggested a surplus *at* the margin of individual purchase. The main theory however does not do this. It concerns a surplus on *inframarginal* units. It does not suppose that the OMth unit is worth than PM. It is to this theory that I now wish to return.

The consumer's surplus is to be measured in money, and the demand curve is taken as providing one edge of the area. This is the point on which to concentrate. Surely this suggests at once an important criticism.

Is it really correct to regard the demand curve as an absolute utility curve – as indicating absolute degrees of utility measured in money? Surely the answer must

---

1 The point is not whether you get your marginal purchase in England for less than it would be worth in Africa, but whether it is worth more than you pay for it in England, and if it is why don't you buy more?

2 N.B. The case of indivisibility contemplated is of course rarer than is commonly supposed. Qualitative variations are possible. See J.B. Clark.

be no. Because, unless the demand curve is of the constant outlay order, as you go down the curve the amount of money expended varies. And as the amount of money expended varies, so (according to the hedonistic law) must *its* marginal utility vary.

Marshall recognized that this objection might be made and he attempted to meet it by saying that he assumed that the marginal utility of money to be constant. This assumption was legitimate, he thought, because the variation in the marginal utility of money could be treated as being of the second order of smalls.

But at this point it is necessary to join issue with Marshall. The question is: *Can you* treat the variations in the marginal utility of money as being of the second order of smalls compared with the variation in the marginal utility of the thing bought? And the answer is that, surely, you cannot.

If you spend less on a commodity then you have that much more to spend on other commodities. If you spend more you have that much less and as you measure (according to Marshall) the utility of those other commodities in terms of money your gain or loss is surely of comparable magnitude.

Marshall's assumption that the effects on the marginal utility of money may be disregarded seems ultimately to derive from a curious concentration on single lines of expenditure. He thought that if, say, you had to spend ten shillings more on tea there was no need to vary your expenditure much on other single commodities – that the variation at *each* margin would be negligible.

It is conceivable that this might be so – though the general assumption is disputable. But it is not what happens to expenditure on *each other commodity* which matter. It is what happens to expenditure on *all* other commodities. For on Marshall's plan the utility of all commodities is measured in terms of money. If therefore your expenditure on x increases and your income remains constant, it does not matter how you rearrange your expenditure on b, c, d, e, f, g, h, i etc. What does matter is that your valuation of b, c, d, e, f, g, h, i, etc. *must* change because the quantity of general purchasing power in which you measure their utility has undergone just that shrinkage.

That comes out most clearly if you revert to our original example of the exchange of *two* commodities. Corn is being exchanged for gold. It is valued at one stage as being worth 2 units of gold at another as being worth 1 unit of gold at the margin. It is surely clear that the change in the relative significance of corn in terms of gold from 2 to 1 implies a change in the relative significance of gold in terms of corn from 1/2 to 1. Or if we use the apparatus of scales:

	Gold		*Corn*
(1) corn	2		
(2) corn	1		
		(2) gold	1
		(1) gold	1/2

When corn moves down on the gold scale gold moves up on the corn scale.

All of which suggests that the idea of a demand curve which shall measure rates of decline of utility in some constant unit is profoundly unsatisfactory. It is as though you were using a measuring rod which changed with changes in the things measured, yet you insisted in using the number of times it fitted any over any given length as the indication of the true measure of that length. The price units on your axis are constant but the money in which you measure utility is itself continually varying.

It is clear I think that the idea of measurement of this sort sprang from the assumption that utility was something absolute which could be measured exactly. It is another byproduct of the intrusion into economics of the old hedonistic psychology.

Well I do not wish to deny the hedonistic psychology. There may be such a thing as absolute utility. But if there is we have clearly not yet learned to measure it. It is not measured at any rate by the downward sloping demand curve. You cannot jump from subjective values to subjective worth in this way.

But what then does the curve measure? The answer is that it measures nothing save price and amount taken. But it *expresses* relative utilities, at different margins of expenditure.

It indicates that at the price P the significance at the margin of the good a is equal to the significance at the margin of PM units of money. That at the price P_1 the significance is equivalent P_1M_1. But if P_1M_1 is twice as long as PM, it does not indicate that the marginal utility of a is twice as great at that margin. The marginal utility of money has changed in the meantime.

Once this is grasped consumers surplus vanishes. The demand curve is seen to *exhibit a series of hypotheses each of which is incompatible with the coexistence of the others*. If coal were 24/- I would buy one ton. If it were 20/- I would buy 2 tons. But it does not follow at all that I would be prepared to pay 24/- & 20/- for two tons. Not at all. How could I without disturbing my other expenditures? Here you have, I think, perhaps the most conspicuous case of the breakdown of the "one thing at a time" analysis.

You can see most clearly if you take the most extreme food examples affected by the textbooks. To get one loaf of bread I would be prepared (in a desert) to give almost the whole of my income. (*Not* as Jevons suggested an infinite amount – I have not got an infinite income.) To get a glass of water I should be prepared to give almost the whole of my income. But it is absurd to argue as if I would be prepared both to give almost all of my income for bread and almost the whole of my income for water simultaneously. For clearly this assumes that I have almost twice my income to dispose of.

Consumer's surplus that is to say only looks plausible if you examine things one at a time. If you look to expenditure on all commodities it simply disappears. It is wiped out. It amounts to zero.

This leads me to the final reflection that with the realization of the true significance of the demand curve as an expression of relative utilities at different margins the old theory of marginal utility completely stands on its head.

On the old theory marginal degree of utility was regarded as a derivative. It was the rate at which some ultimate total utility was decreasing. On our theory relative utility per unit is itself an ultimate fact. Total utility is a pseudo-concept. The integral area means nothing. Economic analysis says nothing on the great question whether economic activity yields a surplus of pleasure or pain. *The theory of maximum satisfaction becomes simply the theory of minimum resistance.* All that we learn from the theory of exchange is that there is a tendency for costs and prices to become equal.

Note This treatment intentionally omits discussion of:

(a) philosophical distinctions between satisfactions utilities ophelmities, etc.;
(b) units of estimation (Wicksteed);
(c) stunt[?] cases (Pigou Hats and Diamonds)[3]; and
(d) (This is more important) applications of the theory. Taxation. International Trade etc. etc.

Read

Alfred Marshall, *Principles of Economics* (1920) Book III
Frank H. Knight, *Risk, Uncertainty and Profit* (1921) Book II Chapter I
Philip H. Wicksteed, *The Common Sense of Political Economy* (1910) Book II Chapters I–III
Edwin Cannan, ' "Total utility" and "Consumer's surplus" ' *Economica* (February 1924)
D.H. Macgregor, 'Consumer's surplus: A reply' *Economica* (June 1924)
A.C. Pigou, 'Some remarks on utility' *Economic Journal* (March 1903)
Allyn A. Young, 'Marshall on consumers' surplus in international trade' *Quarterly Journal of Economics* (November 1924)

---

3 [Mentioned by A.C. Pigou in 'Some remarks on utility' *Economic Journal* Vol. 13 (March 1903) pp. 60–1].

17 The laws of returns

Last week I was discussing consumer's surplus and the Theory of Demand. This week I want to turn to the other side of my problem and to examine certain matters relating to supply. Today I want to discuss the so-called "Laws of Return". I have alluded to these already in connection with the marginal productivity theory of distribution. Now I want to return and review them in more detail.

The conception of non-proportional returns is one which is ubiquitous in Economic Theory. We find it in the theory of Production in regard to population and land. We find it in the Theory of Distribution in regard to relative factor prices. We find it in the general theory of equilibrium explaining the technical combination of factors. And it has so many shades of meaning that it is often very difficult to decide exactly which variant is relevant to the situation contemplated. This is a case I think where a very mild dose of history of theory can prove to be very illuminating. Accordingly, in spite of the unpopularity of this branch of the subject I propose to indulge a little in exegesis.

The Law of Diminishing Returns in its original form is essentially a product of the English Corn Law Controversy. An anterior statement by Turgot on the margin of a prize essay has been made much of, but it had no influence on thought and is merely an historical curiosity. The real origin of the "Law" comes from those days when under the stress of war and a growing population the margin of cultivation was pushed outward and downwards, and the price of corn was higher than it had been for centuries.

The discoverer of the Law – if the man can be said to have discovered it - was one Sir Edward West, a fellow of University College Oxford, who in 1814 published a tract entitled An Essay on the Application of Capital to Land in which he tried to show firstly that the high price of corn was due to high costs of production consequent upon resort to inferior soils and, secondly, that therefore corn duties, which prevented the purchase of wheat produced on richer soils, were undesirable.[1]

---

1 [Sir Edward West, *An Essay on the Application of Capital to Land* (1815)].

In the body of that Essay you will find the Law stated as follows:

> Each equal additional quantity of work bestowed on agriculture yields an
> actually diminished return and of course if each equal additional quantity of
> work yields an actually diminished return the whole of the work bestowed on
> agriculture yields an actually diminished return whereas it is obvious that an
> equal quantity of work will always fabricate the same quantity of manufac-
> tures (p 6–7 Essay)

A very similar statement is to be found in Ricardo's Essay on the Influence of
a Low Price of Corn on the Profits of Stock. He imagines the peopling of a new
colony.[2] He also shows how the growth of population tends to lead to the cultivation of poorer and poorer soils, and so for the price of food to rise – the cost of
producing the socially necessary corn – as Marx would have called it – having for
this reason risen. In this form, the "Law" as it came to be called was made one of
the foundational stones of the main classical system. There is no need (I hope) for
me to explain its bearing on the Classical theory of Rent and Interest or to dwell
upon the more complicated propositions of the Ricardian theory of taxation.

Now there are certain features about this classical law which are quite well
worth noting.

(1) It was an agricultural law – a law of diminishing returns in Agriculture. You
    see this in West's title, An Essay on the Application of Capital to Land. You
    will notice too that he explicitly denies that it can apply elsewhere than in
    agriculture.

The effect of this has been twofold:

(a) In the first place, it tended to blind economists for nearly a century to the
    inherent reversibility of the proposition. When I stated the law to you a lit-
    tle while back I stated it in terms of x and y – a generalization concerning the
    results of varying the proportions in which two factors are combined. It is
    now quite clear that the law is quite general, that it applies to the application
    of land to capital just as much as capital to land – and so on.

But this was not always the case. And if you ask why it is that even in good textbooks the thing is nearly always stated in terms of men in a field instead of fields
to a group of men or supervisors to groups of manual labourers or coals to a grate
or any other of the thousand and one combinations which are vivid and conceivable, it is because the idea of the reversibility of the generalization propounded

---

2 [*An Essay on the Influence of a Low Price of Corn on the Profits of Stock* (1815)].

by West is only (broadly speaking) about 40 years old and we still tend to think in terms of the more familiar examples.

(b)   Second – still as a consequence of this agricultural emphasis – not only was the "law" not thought to apply to industry, it was, on the contrary, definitely asserted that in industry another law was working – the law of increasing returns. You find this very clearly stated by Senior (Fourth Elementary Proposition): "Additional labour when employed in Manufacture is more, when employed in Agriculture is less efficient in proportion" (Political Economy p 11)[3].

Now of course there is a sense in which this contrast is important and significant. It is true that the benefits attendant upon the increase of division of labour are always as it were working against the disadvantages of limited land space and mineral resources. It is this opposition of tendencies which we study in the theory of population and the theory of progress, and there can be little doubt from the context of the passages I have read you that it was this opposition that the classics had in mind. (I emphasize this, for I think in my essay on the Optimum Theory of Population I have rather overstated the case against the classics.)[4]

But when this has been admitted, it must still be held to be unfortunate that the terminology employed should have suggested that the tendency discerned and described in agriculture was on all fours was *technically symmetrical* with the tendency discussed and described in industry, so that in due course people should have come to think of diminishing returns as especially prevalent in Agriculture and increasing returns as being specially characteristic in Industry.

In fact of course there is no symmetry in the conceptions. The Law of Diminishing Returns refer to what happens when one factor varies other things remaining constant. The Law of Increasing Returns, supposed to refer to industry, refers to what happens when all factors vary in suitable relationships. It is another name for the doctrine of the advantages of the division of labour. The two "laws" are thus not in opposition. They both apply to agriculture and industry. But more of this hereafter.

(2)   I return to the critique of the classical conception.

I have said it was an agricultural law. The second feature was that it was a dynamic law. That is to say it was conceived to refer not only to what would happen if the labour and capital were applied to land in different proportions and nothing else were allowed to vary but also to what had happened in the course of history as the world's population had increased and the margin of cultivation has pushed from the Garden of Eden outward. It was not only a law of diminishing returns

---

3 [*An Outline of the Science of Political Economy* (1836)].
4 ['The optimum theory of population' in *London Essays in Economics* eds. H. Dalton and T. Gregory (1927) pp. 103–34].

in history. West and Ricardo actually thought that throughout the course of history returns to agricultural effort had diminished. They claimed that improvements might take place which could arrest this process. But they thought that what improvements had taken place had not succeeded, and they explained the historical fall in the rate of interest in terms of this bogus theory.

Now of course this was bad history and worse theory. Returns to Agriculture have not diminished and there is no general presumption that for very long periods of time they need diminish. Of course if the world's population went on increasing forever presumably – eventually – things would get uncomfortable in this respect. No doubt a good case can be made for the view that this pressure has been considerable at various times in the past. It may be so now. But certainly it cannot be upheld for a moment that such a state of affairs *through time* can necessarily be inferred from the mere statement of the law of diminishing returns by hypothesis.

(3) Third, and finally, notice that the formulation of the Law by West which I have read you treats the two versions which I gave earlier as if they were one. You remember that when I was dictating the modern version of the Law I provided two versions – one relating to average returns and one relating to marginal returns. West does this too. He speaks of each equal additional quantity of work yielding an actually diminished return – diminishing marginal returns – and of the whole of the work bestowed yielding an actually diminished proportionate return – average returns.

So far so good. But it is fairly clear that West thought that the point of diminishing marginal returns and the point of diminishing average return were coincident. This is not so. And for certain work it is essential to realize that it is not so.

You can see this quite easily by aid of an arithmetical example used by Edgeworth.[5] (Arithmetical induction is not out of place here. You only want to prove *one* exception.)

Labour	Product	Marginal Product	Average product
A	B	C	D
13	220		
14	244	24	17.43
15	270	*26*	18
16	294	24	18.38
17	317	23	18.65
18	339	22	18.83
19	360	21	18.95
20	380	20	*19*
21	396	16	18.86

5 ['The laws of increasing and diminishing returns' *Papers Relating to Political Economy* (1925) Vol. I p. 68].

Column C is obtained by subtracting the appropriate total in B from the one preceding. Column D is simply B/A. It is clear from this that the Average Product may go on increasing while the marginal product is diminishing.

The same difference may be represented graphically. OX represents quantity of varying factors; OY quantity of product.

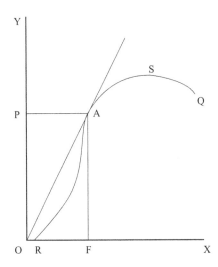

It is clear that average returns begin to diminish at A where the curve is tangent to a straight line from the origin. For beyond that PA/AF will obviously be *less* than it is at that point. But the *rate of increase* of product will have begun to decline somewhere around M where the curve RQ ceases to be concave.

So much for the Classical theory. Its history since that time has been varied. There are two main fields in which it has been developed:

(1) In the first place, it has been used in what may be roughly called population theory, that part of Economic Analysis which seeks to show in what way variations in the number of people affect the volume of production per head. There is no need for me to elaborate this part of the history of theory. I have done so at length elsewhere.

Broadly speaking, it has two main features:

(a) Firstly the theory has been deprived of what I have called its dynamic or historical implications. Ricardo and West thought that Returns actually diminished. This was clearly wrong, and it was not long before it was refuted. In the hands of Mill and his successors, it became merely a statement of what might happen if population were to increase and no improvements or further accumulations to accompany it.

(b) Second, the theory has been generalized so as to cover not merely agriculture but the returns to labour as a whole. The advantages of division of labour are balanced against the disadvantages of limited space, and it is held that at some point or another (which point may of course shift) returns per head are a maximum. After this they diminish.

But notice that in becoming so generalized the law has subtly changed its nature. The returns to which it refers in this form are not homogeneous physical units of product – so many tons of coal or so many quarters of corn. They are parcels of a heterogeneous aggregate, returns to labour in general. No doubt this change is necessary if the theory is to be used in this connection, but it cannot be denied that it introduces new complications.

(i) In the first place you have the difficulty present whenever it is necessary to discuss heterogeneous aggregates of devising some measure of returns in general. How are you to lump together all the constituents of real income and measure their movements without invoking the aid of money values which in any case such as the one here contemplated are bound themselves to be treacherous and shifting.
(ii) And secondly it is not at all clear that we may jump lightheartedly from generalizations which are true of the variations in one factor in one combination to generalizations, which shall be true of variations of a group of factors (the working population) in combinations which *by hypothesis* are necessarily changing. I think in the past this extension of the Law of Diminishing Returns has been made too lightheartedly.

What I mean is this. When we are thinking of the original "law" – the law dimly discerned by West – more accurately formulated by modern economists, we are just thinking of simple variations: x varying; y constant. We can assert quite simply that returns here reach a maximum and then diminish. But in population theory we are not thinking of anything so simple. We are not thinking of increasing returns in the sense of the returns before the simple maximum is reached in single combination for *in that sense* increasing returns are not normally to be contemplated (I shall explain this later). We are rather balancing the increased returns – in Senior's sense the advantages of division of labour – against the general disadvantage of limited natural resources – and although no doubt there is a certain broad symmetry about the idea of diminishing returns past the optimum point and diminishing returns in the more limited sense, the one generalization does not follow from the other. It has to be proved separately.

(2) The second broad line of development has been in what roughly be called distribution theory. Here developments have been simpler and, I think, less unsatisfactory. The original law of diminishing returns was from the outset used to support one branch of distribution theory – the theory of rent. Rent

was held to arise because successive applications of labour and capital to the same land would yield diminishing returns. Gradually you get extension of this mode of analysis. Longfield the much neglected Irish economist uses the idea of diminishing returns to the investment of capital in general in the thirties. Von Thunen the German economist had worked out a marginal product theory of distribution by the fifties.[6] Marshall under the influence of Von Thunen surreptitiously introduces the idea of the diminishing productivity of factors other than labour in connection with the idea of substitution at the margin.

Then suddenly at the beginning of the 1890s it seems explicitly to have dawned on a number of economists working separately – J.B. Clark in America, Wicksteed and Thompson[7] here, that the old law could be reversed, that you could just as well do labour with land as land with labour – that in fact such a conception was just as apposite to the imaginary history of a new colony as the idea of the reverse process – as the island fills up it is true you may think of dosing the island with labour. But when the colonists first arrive, when they contemplate the agricultural programme for the first year, surely they think rather of a fixed labour force and variable land resources. The question "how much shall we cultivate" is a mere variant of this notion. Once this had happened the generalization of the law was inevitable. Clark and Wicksteed extended it to Land and Capital (in the old sense), Carver and Bullock made it clear that it applied equally to managerial ability. Nowadays when the law is stated, e.g. by Taylor or Edgeworth, it is therefore just a matter of xs and ys. The thing is recognized to be just a general law of technical variation.

One final note on this law of variation. I have referred to it throughout as the law of diminishing returns. Yet in my statement of it in my earlier lecture, and indeed in my treatment today I made it clear that it is only after a point that returns (either average or marginal) are conceived to diminish. Why then have I not followed the suggestion of some modern economists and substituted the wider title, the law of nonproportional variation or the laws of increasing and diminishing returns? It is clear that there is something to be said for this procedure. It is true that in considering variations of this order we do consider increasing returns *of a sort*. Yet it is clear, I think, as I have already tried to show that the increasing returns that were contemplated by the ancients were due to a different kind of variation – that kind of variation we have in mind when we think of the advantages of division of labour, and I do think it is desirable to keep the two conceptions apart.

---

6 [M. Longfield, *Lectures on Political Economy* (1834); J.H. von Thunen, *Der Isolierte Staat* Vol. 2 (1850)].

7 [J.B. Clark, *The Distribution of Wealth* (1899); Wicksteed, *The Common Sense of Political Economy* (1910); H.M. Thompson, *The Theory of Wages* (1892)].

Moreover it should be clear, I think, that although increasing returns in the sense of variations of product more than proportional to variations in the factors are conceivable and do of course occur in some cases, yet for the most part they relate to a kind of combination which is not to be conceived as occurring if the factors of production are divisible. This may sound obscure, but in fact it is very simple: increasing returns in this sense means that one factor is being negatively productive. No producer in his sense dealing with divisible agents only would ever carry out such a combination.

Consider the old case of the farmer in the field:

L	P	L/P
1	1	1
2	4	2
3	9	3
4	16	4
7	21	3

He only has two men, and for that field the point of maximum average return is achieved only when four men are cultivating it. When two cultivate it output per head is only 2 – the total product being 4. Clearly unless he has to work the field as a whole it will pay him to throw half of it out of cultivation for two men on 1/2 field are equivalent, so far as proportionality of factors are concerned, to four men on a whole one. Therefore production per head will be 4 and the total product will be 16. It is only if the field is indivisible that the increasing returns combination is conceivable.

If this all sounds odd, think of it in terms of labour. You would not crowd more men into the field than could give you the maximum produce even if you got your labour for nothing. You would throw the men that got in the way out of work. But if you were to do so the returns measured as an average of the land would clearly be in an increasing returns stage. *If you had more land returns per head would be greater*.

Hence, although I do not underrate the importance of other conceptions of increasing returns, I do think this variant is of sufficient importance to warrant the displacement of the term diminishing in the designation of the main generalization. It is unfortunate that the term "increasing returns" should have been used in other connections, but we must recognize that this is established usage, and if we do not wish to make ourselves unintelligible we must either abide by it or invent *new* terms – not try to make the old one bear yet further meanings.[8]

8 [Robbins later added: 'Knight: Essay on Scientific Method in Economics' *Trend of Economics*, p 258. "In a universe governed by a general law of increasing returns the output of goods would be increased by decreasing the amount of resources devoted to their production." The essay is 'The limitations of scientific method in economics' in *The Trend of Economics* ed. R.G. Tugwell (New York: Knopf, 1924) pp. 229–67].

Read

C.J. Bullock, 'The variation of productive forces' *Quarterly Journal of Economics* (August 1902)

E. Cannan, *A History of the Theories of Production and Distribution in English Political Economy* (1917) Chapter IV *A Review of Economic Theory* (1929)

F.M. Taylor, *Principles of Economics* (1924) Chapters 9–12

F.Y. Edgeworth, 'The laws of increasing and diminishing returns' *Papers Relating to Political Economy* (1925) Vol. I pp. 61–99

J.M. Clark, *Studies in the Economics of Overhead Costs* (1923)

L.C. Robbins, 'The optimum theory of population' in T. Gregory and H. Dalton eds. *London Essays in Economics: In Honour of Edwin Cannan* (1927)

P.H. Wicksteed, *The Common Sense of Political Economy* (1910)

T.N. Carver, *The Distribution of Wealth* (1904) Chapter IV

18 Returns and costs

I was talking to you last time about the laws of returns. Today I want to talk about the connection between returns and costs. And here my treatment will – if possible – be more superficial and inaccurate than ever. It is not possible in less than half a dozen lectures to deal at all thoroughly with the issues that have been raised in this connection by recent discussion.

Now the first thing which we have to recognize is the *difference* between the topics we are to discuss today and those which we discussed last time.

The Law of diminishing returns relates to variations of physical product when one of the factors employed in production is varied. In the last resort, it is a technical "law" It relates to "objective" properties of the factors.

The "laws of cost" – the term law is more ludicrously out of place here than in connection with returns for by law here we mean merely concept[1] – the idea of costs clearly involves valuations – a psychological element – in the particular context in which we are to discuss it today money valuation – prices of the factors of production.

Moreover, and this is an even more significant point of difference, when we are thinking of costs we are measuring in terms of the product – so much per 100 units produced – total costs average costs marginal costs it is all the same – the cost concept is conceived in relation to a determinate amount of *product*. Whereas when we are thinking of returns we are thinking of factors as the variable – so much per unit of labour etc.

- What is even more important – we are thinking in terms of the variation of one factor. Whereas when we are thinking of costs we consider *all* the factors to be suitably varied.

Such reflections should make us very suspicious of the traditional terminology, which suggests that the terms costs and returns are reversible – that we may speak indifferently of increasing costs and diminishing returns or increasing returns and diminishing costs.

---

1 See Edgeworth ['The laws of increasing and diminishing returns' *Papers Relating to Political Economy* (1925) Vol. I pp. 61–99].

It is true that we may so redefine returns as to make this procedure permissible if we think of returns of being simply money returns per unit of money expenses. Then no doubt there is this symmetry between the two conceptions. Diminishing returns will be identical with increasing cost per unit and vice versa.

But to do this, I suggest, is to conceal the very real complications which arise when we try to relate the conception of costs in the usual sense to that of returns in the sense of variation of physical product. *If* it were true that variations of returns in the sense of physical variations in the product in response to variations in *one* factor were merely the converse of variations in costs in the sense of expenses of producing the product the world would be a much simpler place than it actually is.

In point of fact, it can be shown quite easily that they are seldom if ever identical, that the point at which costs are a minimum – i.e. the point beyond which they will commence to increase is seldom if ever the point at which returns to one of the factors are a maximum – i.e. the point beyond which returns diminish.

Let us look into this a little more closely. Let us operate with average returns and average costs since the demonstration here is simpler.

Suppose our old case of the farmer operating in a single field with a variable labour force. We know that as the labour force varies returns measured as an average of the number of labourers will first increase, reach a maximum and then diminish. Now suppose the farmer gets the field free. It is clear, is it not, that *in this case* when his costs which are only labour costs are a minimum his returns will be a maximum. For by hypothesis he only expends money on labourers (at a constant rate). When the labourers are producing most *per head* the cost of what they produce per unit will be at a maximum.

Suppose e.g. he pays his labourers £50 per head. And suppose that each labourer produces most when 10 labourers are employed – say 100 bushels a head. Then the cost per bushel will be £- 10 0 (£50/100). But suppose he had employed 15 and average returns had been 75. Then the cost per bushel would have been £50/75 = 2/3 = £13 4 –.

But now notice how we have reached this conclusion. We have assumed that the farmer gets the land for nothing. Once we assume that he has *pay for it* this identity of movements of costs and returns vanishes. For now he has to consider not merely the use of the labour but also the use of the land; he has to consider the costs incurred in regard to *two* factors. In such a case his costs will increase *after the point at which returns measured as an average of the labour diminishes*.

Suppose e.g he pays £500 for the field. Then if 10 men produce 1000 bushels (100 per head) at £50 a year his costs per bushel are £1 (i.e. (£500 + 500)/1000). Now suppose if he increases his labour force by 1 returns drop to 99 per head or aggregate returns rise to 1089. Then his costs per unit drop from £1 to £(500 + 550)/1089 = £1050/1089, which is manifestly less. His costs are still diminishing.

You can see roughly [how] the thing works if you contemplate the other extreme case. Suppose he got his labour for nothing – a peasant farmer with a prolific wife – but paid for his field. Then clearly it would pay him to go on dosing the land with labour until *aggregate returns* began to diminish. For the constant cost of the field would up to that point be spread over an ever increasing number of units.

Thus when the constant factor land was free, the point of least cost per unit was the point of maximum *average* returns measured in labour. When the variable labour was free, the point of least cost was the point of maximum *aggregate returns*.

When prices have to be paid for both *the point of least cost lies in between.* It will be nearer the maximum average return combination the less paid for the constant land, nearer the maximum aggregate return combination the less paid per unit of labour. That is why intensive cultivation pays much more in an old country than in a new one. The relative scarcity and hence the relative prices of labour and land are in favour of labour in the latter, in favour of land in the former. You can get land almost for nothing in a new country. Hence you cultivate lightly. You can get labour for very little in a country which is overpopulated while land is scarce, hence you cultivate intensively.

Notice *en passant* how this example bears out my remark about increasing returns in the narrow sense last time. When land is free it is used at its point of maximum aggregate productivity. (The labourers are producing their maximum average returns; more land would mean less returns per labourer.) When labour is free it is employed to its point of maximum aggregate productivity. (The land is producing its maximum average product; more land would mean less per unit of land).

So much for the distinction between increasing costs and diminishing returns. Unless we redefine returns so as to mean money returns per unit of expense, the two conceptions are not symmetrical.

Now so far for the sake of simplicity, I have been talking in terms of average returns and the least cost combination.

We know already that the better way of approach to this idea of least cost is by way of the marginal productivity analysis. In an earlier lecture I tried to show you how the entrepreneur tried to organize his production so that each factor was employed in just such relations to the others as to make its marginal net product equal to the price paid for it. Now in connection with that discussion we ran into a problem, the solution of which I was only able to mention to you. We found ourselves asking why the size of the business of the single entrepreneur should ever stop increasing. He buys his factors at constant prices, he sells his products at constant prices; why then should he not continue to buy more factors, combine them in suitable proportions and sell more products thus continually increasing his *total* profits?

The answer, I suggested, was to be found in the fact that returns to managerial ability also diminished – that there comes a point at which the taking on of more factors to supervise so diminishes the efficiency of supervision as to make the extension not worthwhile. That was the rough answer I suggested in the earlier lecture. In the light of our recent more extensive analysis of the idea of variation, this notion should now be very much clearer.

The appropriate analogy is the dosing of land with labour. The entrepreneur was before considered to administer varying doses to a fixed field. He is now considered to administer varying doses of the other factors *to a fixed self.* At first returns, measured as an average of the varying size of the business (the quantity of other factors suitably considered) increase. They reach a maximum and then diminish.

Now if of course when returns measured as an average of the other factors[2] are a maximum costs per unit are a minimum. That is, the profit margin, if there is a fixed price, is a maximum. Beyond that point costs will rise and the profit margin will diminish. But it must not be thought that the entrepreneur will necessarily expand up to this objectively optimal size. That will clearly depend on whether he thinks it is worth the candle. Clearly he will not work beyond the point at which the rate of return is equal to the rate of sacrifice of those things he has to surrender in order to get the increase. That is to say, if supply is flexible – unless his elasticity of demand for income in terms of effort is equal to unity – the equilibrium point will depend not only on technical productivity and its value but also on willingness to work. But that is a result which we have reached already.

The same thing can be put another way. So far I have approached things from the point of view of the entrepreneur. Let us look at it from the point of view of society. If entrepreneurs were free goods – if they were so plentiful that they had no specific productivity obviously they would be used like the free land in the new colony. Only the productivity of the other factors would be considered. So far as the combination of "other factors taken together" with the entrepreneurs was concerned, the dosing would not go beyond the point of maximum returns, that is of minimum cost. That was what happened with land when it was a free good. That is the general rule when a factor is a free good. *Being a free good it has specific productivity. It can be ignored.* Attention can be focussed on the productivity of other factors only.

But managerial ability is not free. It is scarce. It is commands a price. It is therefore worthwhile to push its use beyond the maximum return stage. When land had to be paid for it was expedient to push investment in it beyond this point. When managerial ability has to be paid for it is worthwhile pushing investment *on* it beyond this point. How far it is worth going depends on its price – its relative scarcity. If there are only few men capable of managing business concerns, undertakings will tend to be bigger than they would be if there were many – of course this is not the whole story about the size of undertakings but it is true of the very limited universe of discourse I am discussing. It is thus clearly possible to speak of a size which is optimal for a firm producing for a given market with access to given factors of production with a given managerial equipment.

But – and this is a point I want to emphasize – it is a mistake to speak as if one size were optimal for all concerns in the given industry. This is not so. It would only be true if all entrepreneurs were of one grade of ability and this I think is an assumption which it is totally unreal and totally unnecessary to make. We have no difficulty in adapting our analysis to cover land of various grades. There is no reason, I submit, to suppose that all managerial ability is uniform. And if we reject this assumption we must necessarily reject with it the notion that in any given

---

2 These can only be measured if the other factors are homogeneous.

industry any one size is optimal. On the contrary we must realize that there are as many different "best" sizes as there are different grades of entrepreneurial ability.

This is one of my main reasons for declaring the Marshallian concept of the representative firm to be an unnecessary instrument of analysis. I do not contend that in certain circumstances the Representative Firm analysis is definitely wrong, though I do think that its sphere of application is much more limited than supposed either by Marshall or Mr Robertson. But I do argue that it introduces an unreal and misleading simplification.[3] It is one step from the Representative firm to the idea of an optimal size of business establishments. That view, I hope, I have succeeded in thoroughly discrediting.

In a state of equilibrium therefore there is no reason to suppose that the costs other than entrepreneurs earnings (or profits if you will) in different undertakings will be similar. But the differences will be at least such that at a constant price the managerial ability in the different concerns will have no temptation to go elsewhere.[45]

---

3 [Robbins, 'The representative firm' *Economic Journal* 38 (September 1928) pp. 387–404; D.H. Robertson, 'Increasing returns and the representative firm' *Economic Journal* 40 (March 1930) pp. 79–89 and 92–3].

4 This should be the starting point of the lecture on profits.

5 [The notes for the rest of this lecture were crossed through. They read:

   'Now this brings me to the final matter on which I want to touch on in this lecture.

   Throughout these lectures I have not yet attempted to draw a cost curve save in quite subordinate constructions relating to the rate of interest. I have simply tried to show the way in which the existence of fixed prices for the factors of production influenced the demands of entrepreneurs and how these demands affected the prices and how finally in this way you got an equilibrium distribution of factors.

   This omission is no accident – I have not forgotten to lecture on this branch of the subject. I have omitted the cost curve because I do not think it is useful or convenient to introduce it into this kind of equilibrium analysis.'].

19 Costs

Definitions and the conditions of equilibrium

Today I want to return to the question of costs.

Now we have already (in the lectures on general equilibrium theory) had occasion continually to dwell upon the notion of costs as displaced alternatives. The cost of fish, fruit, etc. That is the fundamental conception, which in all interpretations of economic equilibrium it is fatal to forget. But today I want to concentrate on the narrower conception of money costs of production and its various aspects. I want, in particular, to discuss the very difficult problem of the variation of costs of production with various volumes of output.[1]

A. Let us first of all elaborate certain definitions.

Three different conceptions need to be kept in mind:

(1) Aggregate costs of production
(2) Marginal costs of production
(3) Average costs of production.

Aggregate costs are simple: they are the fundamental conception $F(x)$. Marginal costs are the difference between the costs of one output and another infinitesimally larger or smaller, more accurately the rate at which aggregate costs are changing $F^1(x)$. Average costs are the aggregate costs divided by the output $F(x)/x$.

This can be illustrated diagrammatically.

The aggregate cost of OM units of output is OC. The average cost is OC/OM or tan P0M. The marginal cost is the rate at which OC is changing i.e. the trigonometrical tangent of the slope at $P(M)$.

(Those of you who find this hard should think not of the rate of change at M but of the cost of increasing OLM by a finite amount.

Q_1R is the increase in cost. $QR = MM_1$. If this is a unit the *rate* of increase is $Q_1R/QR = \tan Q_1Q$. Now think of the unit getting smaller and smaller until M and M_1 become identical. Then you get the rate of change at that point).

___
1 Long period discussion this time. Short period later on.

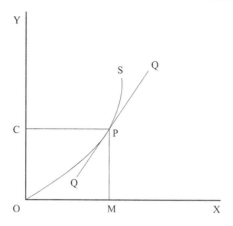

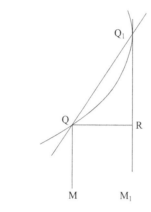

From this we can deduce the geometrical representation of certain other conceptions.

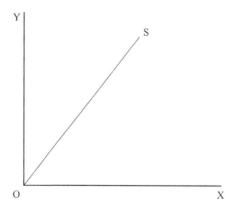

A straight line (as above) represents constant average and constant marginal cost.

If you have a curve such as OS then the points of diminishing marginal and diminishing average costs are identical.

Up to OM_m under B (the point of inflection) in OS *marginal costs* diminish. After that point they increase. Average costs are least when the straight line from the origin OR is tangent to OS. That is average costs diminish until output OM_a and then increase. Of course average and marginal costs are coincident at A. But this is not inconsistent with what I have just said. At A average costs commence to diminish. Marginal costs have been diminishing since B. Note also that before this point marginal costs are *less* than average costs. After it they are *greater*.

All this can be translated into the more familiar language of unit costs curves.

On OY measure either (a) average costs of different output or (b) marginal costs. SS_a and SS_m are curves representing these magnitudes.

Total costs of OM units are represented either

(a) By rectangle RPM0 (representing output *times* average costs)
(b) By area SRMO (representing the costs of each unit added together).

   (The relationship of S_a and S_m is to be defined in this way that RPMO = S = SQMO).

One further distinction: Marginal *additive* and Marginal *substitute* costs. What does this mean? When a firm expands it may *add* to output of industry. Or it may

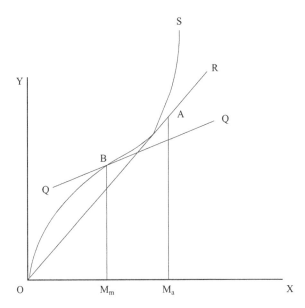

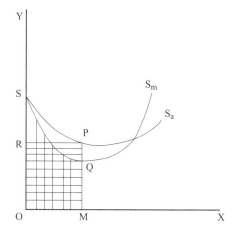

take the place of output previously contributed by others. Now it may be that the cost of expanding to new market different from cost of taking markets of others. Not important in *pure* competition. Very important when competition impure. To bring out this distinction, Pigou coined terms "marginal additive cost" and "marginal substitute cost". For the moment, I intend to overlook this definition and to speak of marginal cost pure and simple.

B.   Now let us proceed to analysis.

Let us first of all describe the conditions of equilibrium (competitive). This [is] very simple. Take any firm. Disregard complications of changes of efficiency over time.

   If price of product is less than *marginal* cost, there is incentive to expand. Gain on margin between price and cost. If below marginal cost incentive to contract. Hence price must be equivalent to marginal cost. But if price below *average* cost the firm would be making loss. It would contract. On the other hand if the price is above the average cost, there is opening for outsiders to come in and bring it down. Hence in a state of final equilibrium the output of the firm is at the point where average and marginal costs are both equal to the price.

   To revert to the diagram:

   (Demand a straight line – single firm)

   Such are the conditions of equilibrium so far as single firms are concerned. Costs conceived in this sense of course include the remuneration of management. All the factors of production used. They include rent also.

   Important to bear this in mind otherwise confusion with other doctrines. This [is] especially important in reconciling doctrine with Marshall's particular expenses curve. Marshall in habit of excluding rent and other payments for differential advantages from cost. From this point of view even in state of perfect

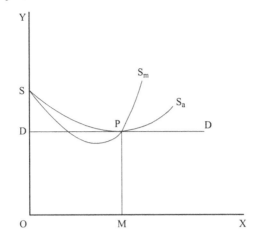

equilibrium some units produced at lower cost than others – e.g. wheat on good land costs less of the factors other than land etc.

To show this Marshall devised particular expenses curve:[2]

Total output in industry OH^1. Then units arranged in order of their cost in things

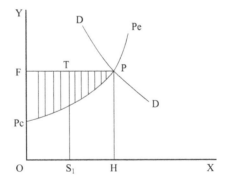

other than land from left to right (OH the unit on margin). E.g. OS_1 costs OS_1 in "labour and capital" – Price is S_1T therefore Rent is TQ. Hence rent or producers surplus FPP_2.

Now we have already seen that not very much in this. From point of view of producer of OS_1th unit nothing. Has to *pay* rent. Or if he owns land should keep book entry and charge it against produce. Hence if you count rent into expenses the particular expenses curve in equilibrium becomes a straight line parallel with

---

2 [*Principles of Economics* (1920) Appendix II Limitations of the use of statical assumptions in regard to increasing return].

the x axis. *It is the function of rents to even out cost disparities.* This applies just as much to payments for other. differential advantages. Superior entrepreneurs. Hence our description of conditions of equilibrium holds good. – Price = marginal costs = average costs different firms involved.

Before I proceed excursion on Henderson Supply and Demand Chapter III. What I have just said has bearing on this.

Henderson [is] talking about importance of looking at margin for costs [on] pp 55–56:

> If the mines were nationalized the deliberate policy might be pursued of sell-
> ing coal at a price which left the industry no more than self supporting as a
> whole. Some coal might thus be sold at less than its cost price and the selling
> price would thus conform roughly to the *average* cost. Such a policy could
> not applied widely without the most serious results.[3]

Now what he means is clear. He means a bad thing to pool – to use rents of bet-ter mines to subsidize working of poorer. This [is] perfectly sound. But wrong way to put it to contrast average and marginal cost in this way. For in a state of equilibrium all costs of production equal if rents counted in. Better mines get coal cheaper but pay more in royalty. (Of course in practice there is never this nice adjustment – but a tendency that way). Mr Henderson only gets his contrast by imagining rents left out – as in Marshall's particular expenses curve.

Which is odd since at end of his book he says leaving rents out leads to "bog of unreality".

But this is not to say that his view unsound. A very "uneconomical" thing to use rents of better mines to subsidize weaker mines. Simply dissipating "the bounty of nature".

How to put this. Simply that price of any factor reflects in competitive condi-tions its specific productivity. If price of labour and capital such that will not pay in poorer mines, this [is] a sign that they are better used elsewhere. It is absurd to subsidize uneconomical working.

Finally, distinguish what is said here about Marshall's particular expenses curve etc. from American accounting cost curves. War Price fixing experience. Different costs in different firms. The bulk line producer. These essentially cross sections of changing conditions. Not a picture of long period equilibrium. A fundamental error to identify with Marshall's particular expenses curve. (Schultz)

Read

Frank H. Knight, *Risk, Uncertainty and Profit* (1921) Part II Chapter IV
Philip H. Wicksteed, *The Common Sense of Political Economy* (1910) Chapter IX

---

3 [H.D. Henderson, *Supply and Demand* (1922)].

Alfred Marshall, *Principles of Economics* (1920) Book V Chapter VI and Book VI Chapters 1 and 2

J.B. Clark, *The Distribution of Wealth* (1899)

T.N. Carver, *The Distribution of Wealth* (1904)

H. Schultz, 'Marginal productivity and the general pricing process' *Journal of Political Economy* (1929)

Fred M. Taylor, *Principles of Economics* (1924) Chapters 9–12

F.Y. Edgeworth, 'The laws of increasing and diminishing returns' *Papers Relating to Political Economy* (1925) Vol. I pp. 61–99

'The application of the differential calculus to economics' *Papers Relating to Political Economy* (1925) Vol. II pp. 367–86

20 Costs

The supply curve and variations in demand

Recapitulate. Definitions. Description of equilibrium. The particular expenses curve. Today I want to discuss the supply curve and its relation to all this discussion. In doing this I shall be compelled to impinge upon certain phases of contemporary controversy. Hence in all probability much of what I shall say will be wrong.

Let us first be clear what supply curve we are to talk about. We have already had many occasions to observe that different curves have different implications according to the initial assumptions concerning the "given" conditions.

It is clear that the recent controversy has not been concerned with the *market* supply curve. We have discussed this already in an earlier lecture and we have seen that it is simply a disguised demand curve.

Recall Wicksteed's Theorem. Supply prices [are] reservation demands of the sellers. Can be redrawn as demand curves. (Bear this in mind – has bearing on what we're saying later on.)

The supply curve as we find it in Marshall – inventor of this kind of analysis – relates not to *market* price problems but *normal* price problems (long period normal) – not to buying and selling so much as to production and consumption.

This means more complicated implications.

In market conditions, it is pretty clear that higher price will elicit more offers. (Wicksteed shows why). When considering production, then the question is ultimately varying cost of different quantities. This clearly involves considerations of technical productivity. An obvious example is getting more wheat out of fixed land factor, or the mass production of motorcars. Laws of Returns are involved.

• The question is at what price can amount in question ultimately be profitably supplied? Clear that in short run (market conditions) higher price needed to evoke more offer in most cases. Question is whether that will persist.

Now at first sight three possibilities:

(1) Increasing costs   )
(2) Constant costs   ) as amount produced increases
(3) Diminishing costs   ).

This is how we find it set out in Marshall. (Treatment gradually built up through 19th century. Classics constant or increasing costs. With modern production methods diminishing costs more apparent.) (In Germany and Austria never very popular – see Morgenstern's bibliography.)[1]

Then in 1926, Piero Sraffa[2] published article "Laws of return under competitive conditions", which called whole apparatus in question, raised controversy second only in importance to monetary controversy of postwar period. Pigou Shove etc.

(Note on "Cost Controversy" as it has developed has involved two distinct questions.

(1) Supply curve. This is what I shall be dealing with.
(2) Theory of maximum satisfaction. As it has developed it has linked up to earlier controversy which developed out of Pigou's attempt in Wealth and Welfare (published 1913) to develop Marshall's theorem that tax on increasing cost industries and bounties on diminishing cost industries helpful. Knight Robertson etc.

– This last highly difficult problem of advanced economics which I shall leave untouched here. (No need to worry examinations.) Very interesting for specialists. Not very important practically. But cost curve dispute very fundamental.

Sraffa's attack twofold. I[ncreasing] C[ost] and D[ecreasing] C[ost].

(a) Increasing cost. Urged most unusual circumstances demanded to make actual. Considered to be usual by concentrating only upon cases of widespread change in demand for a whole group of products (e.g. food) when price of land factor (rent) rises, and more normal case change in demand for *one* commodity. Here extra factors necessary probably obtained at constant price. It is rare for one commodity to demand for production a large proportion of any one factor. (There was another point relating to demand changes. This an attack more on method of particular equilibrium analysis than increasing cost. Come back to this later).

Same point (or much the same point) put the same way by Pigou a little later in E[conomic] J[ournal]. (The laws of increasing and diminishing costs).

Assuming factors hired at constant prices – *note this assumption* proportionate to efficiency how can an increase in supply lead to an increase in cost. Because relative values of factors are unaltered, there is no reason why producers should not meet increased demand by increasing the quantities of *all* factors employed

---

1 [O. Morgenstern, 'Offene Probleme der Kosten- und Ertragstheorie' *Zeitschrift für Nationalökonomie* 2 (March 1931) pp. 481–522].
2 Knight earlier in America.

in exactly equal proportions. Hence, increasing costs are impossible with such classes of commodity.

(b) Diminishing Cost. Here Sraffa suggested confusion arose out of confusing industry and firm. An increase in size of firm might lead DC. But while this is so, equilibrium conditions are not attained. For industry to be in equilibrium firms must be at optimal point – the internal economies must be exhausted.

Marshall's external economies not at all plausible. Trifling importance. Only practicable way of explaining DC resort to the theory of local monopoly for each firm. Hence he concluded that *if* competitive conditions to be discussed, constant costs are the only sensible hypothesis.

Great sensation caused by Sraffa's work. Pigou's article admitting point as regards IC (in fact it did not admit as much as it appears to do – see note as to assumptions earlier) came as another shock. Whole theory of costs in jeopardy from Cambridge point of view, i.e. partial equilibrium.

At same time further confusion caused by infiltration [of] Austrian ideas and Wicksteed. Wicksteed had never drawn normal supply curve. He denied its existence.

Austrian opportunity costs theory suggested costs must be increasing at point of equilibrium. (Schumpeter's lecture at School.[3] My consternation as a teacher.)

Here then is our problem. Sraffa urging constant costs only for competitive hypothesis. Equilibrium theory suggests increasing costs only and the awful problems of diminishing costs. How to reconcile all these?

Let us go back to fundamentals. In equilibrium theory, as we have seen, displacement costs is the fundamental concept. (These can be measured in money terms). Now clear that if *at* a point of equilibrium it is attempted to increase supply – *demand remaining unaltered* – costs will increase. Why? Because the pull of demand elsewhere will be undiminished; therefore there will be increasing resistance to securing more factors in this particular line of production. Factors are more valuable in other uses. Thus at a point of equilibrium costs must be increasing. *If* supply were increased, it would encounter increasing resistance. The fundamental Austrian theory is vindicated. (It is merely an extension of Wicksteed's theorem. Costs merely reservation prices of *factors*.)

But how do we reconcile this with Sraffa or Cambridge School – the whole body of supply analysis? Look carefully at what we have just established. *If* demand remaining unchanged supply increased costs increase. But notice the supply curve of partial equilibrium theory "cuts" into problem from different point of view. It says rather *if* the amount produced changes then the cost changes in this way. It helps us to answer questions concerning what happens when demand

3 [Schumpeter gave two lectures on 'The present position of economics' at LSE in February 1927: R.L. Allen, *Opening Doors: The Life and Work of Joseph Schumpeter Volume I: Europe* (1991) p. 230].

changes. That is to say it is not concerned with the *description* of final equilibrium. It is concerned rather with the effects of variation. It is a concept proper to the theory of variations rather than the theory of equilibrium. If demand changes, then clearly the consequences rigidly implied (so far as costs are concerned) by the theory of equilibrium which assumes demand unchanged are not inevitable. If e.g. demand increases then the same change may release factors elsewhere which may be transferred at constant cost. Hence, the two conceptions are not mutually destructive. The Austrian theory refers to general equilibrium theory. The Cambridge theory relates to variations. To use a distinction employed by Schumpeter: One relates to the conditions of final equilibrium. The other relates to the path by which equilibrium is reached.

Recognition of this enables us to sidestep another of Sraffa's objections. Sraffa had urged that in considering IC, it was illegitimate to assume demand conditions unchanged. Imagine an increase in supply of wheat, e.g. This may affect price of wheat land and hence price of land used for other food. This change will in turn affect price of other food. This will again affect demand for wheat. All of which is very true. But since in the analysis of variation we are simply asking what happens to prices if a change in demand occurs it does not matter much. We assume the change to be given. The problem then is: simply how will the price be affected by the change in amount demanded, and the supply curve enables us to explore possibilities. The question of substitution is *another* complication. Sraffa's objection would be weighty if it were attempted to push the analysis very far. As we shall see later, it has its relevance in so far as it shows how the particular equilibrium analysis conceals perhaps the most important case of diminishing cost. But it does not rule out the analysis of variation of this sort altogether.

So much for the apparent conflict between equilibrium theory and the supply curve analysis. Now, having recognized the nature of supply curve analysis, let us go on to examine in greater detail the possibilities of the curve itself.

I.　Let us take, first of all, the case of increasing costs.

　　(a)　Suppose to begin with that the factors of production can be hired at constant prices. Are IC conceivable?

Here you should recollect the Pigovian argument I have already explained. If demand increases the supplies of the factors will be increased proportionately. There is no reason at first sight to suppose that costs will increase. That expansion will take the form of an increase in the number of firms. Any firm attempting to increase will meet with increasing costs because by hypothesis it is already at its optimal size. But new firms can come in and work at the least cost combination.

The argument is convincing granted the assumptions. But there is one possibility which would allow IC to appear: the possibility of (external) *diseconomies*.

Suppose the increase in the size of the industry involved – let us say congestion at loading stations used by the firms concerned – the setting up of frictions outside the productive units – then costs per unit might rise although internally nothing had happened to bring about the increase.

How practically important this is I don't know. But it is clearly a theoretical possibility. Otherwise *when factor prices are constant*, constant costs must prevail.

(b) But *if factor prices are free to vary*, then clearly increasing costs are conceivable.

If when an industry increases in size, the consequent increase in demand for some of the factors it uses drives up their price, then clearly costs per unit will rise.

This was the case contemplated in the old textbooks when changes in the demand for "food" were supposed.

There is no ground for theoretical dispute here. The only question is how often does this sort of thing occur in practice in circumstances suitable to be conceived in this way. Sraffa urges that so far as individual commodities are concerned, e.g. *wheat* not food, not usual.

This may be so. Clearly when we use the apparatus we usually contemplate increases in demand for group products. E.g. effects of food taxes. (Wheat oats and barley etc.). But no doubt, our results are only first approximations.

II.   Now turn to Diminishing Costs.

Here Sraffa's attack has been responsible for great improvement. This is due chiefly to Shove and Allyn Young.

Start with Shove – twofold contribution: (1) internal and external economies (2) DC theory proper.

(1)   Economies [of] large scale production.

Marshall had distinguished between internal and external economies.

Internal economies: best size of plant etc.

External economies subsidiary industry: lowering of costs external to plant. This suggests that internal economies *independent of size of industry*. But not so necessarily. Different prices of external factors influence internal arrangements.[4]

Hence, it is important to distinguish between:

(a)   Changes in efficiency of a single firm consequent on increase or diminution of output while industry as a whole unchanged; and
(b)   Effect, which the expansion of industry as a whole has upon productive capacity of resources employed in it.

   –   Economies of individual expansion. Economies of large industry.

These are to be distinguished from economies of concentration, the redistribution of given output between firms.

---

4 Marshall recognized this.

(2) Now turn to DC theory proper.

Shove argues that in equilibrium economies of concentration excluded. But diminishing costs are not impossible. How does he do it?

Two solutions:

(1) involve resort to theory of impure competition. Each firm is a certain local connection. (Goodwill etc.). It may be that if expanded output while industry remained constant, economies of individual expansion offset by diseconomies of increased advertising etc. But if the market is extended then these are not necessary: hence economies are present without diseconomies (internal).

That is to say, using our terminology of the last lecture, marginal *substitute* costs for firms are increasing but marginal *additive* costs are diminishing.

(2) involves resort to hypothesis of changing skill etc. on part of entrepreneurs. Expansion involves time. Smith & Co might be better off if could expand *instantaneously*. But they can't. And by the time [they] have expanded, their special advantages of skill etc. used up.

One way of putting this point is to say that the additional cost which a firm would incur by expanding its output would be less than the price if its ability luck and so on remained constant, but yet it would not be less if we allow for the probable change in its circumstances over the time interval required for expansion.

How then can an increase in demand help matters? By increasing the speed at which the business may grow if it is growing. 'The larger volume of business increases the change of obtaining trade for new young or fortunate businesses, and therefore increases the rate at which they may grow'.

Shove's points important because they save particular equilibrium analysis. There is no appeal to wider external economies, *but* they involve in one way or another frictional influences. Does not deal with a wider kind of economies of large industry – economies outside firms. What about these?

Sraffa questioned importance of these when one industry only concerned. Probably correct when single industry being considered. External economies of this sort important when industry as a whole is growing.

This [was] Young's contribution. Pointed out that diminishing costs arise through time as capital accumulates and as the roundabout process and division of labour extended. Extensions of the Roundabout Process *are* External Economies. (Links up Marshall with Böhm-Bawerk).

At any point of time it may be true that costs increase from the equilibrium position. But *over time* costs diminish, although competition persists because of increase of efficiency due to greater roundaboutness. This links up with Shove's *speed* of increase, but it is much more important.[5]

---

5 [At this point Robbins crossed through 'Thus diminishing costs figure chiefly as phenomenon of *moving* equilibrium. The others aspects not nearly so important' and replaced it with 'But cost curve no longer appropriate.'].

Recapitulate.

(1) The supply curve proper to a theory of variations rather than the theory of equilibrium;
(2) Increasing cost possible either diseconomies or increasing factor price;
(3) Decreasing cost conceivable either in impure competition a la Shove or as part of moving equilibrium a la Young. But here particular equilibrium analysis is out of place.

How does "particular equilibrium analysis" come out of this? Clearly the other things equal assumption wears very thin. Much less logically satisfying than general theory. Still for studying certain changes e.g. effects of taxes etc a useful first approximation. And very difficult to dispense with it for practical work. Tariffs etc.

Read

Fred M. Taylor, *Principles of Economics* (1924) Chapters IX–XIII
Frank H. Knight, 'A suggestion for simplifying the general theory of price' *Journal of Political Economy* (June 1928)
'Cost of production and price over long and short periods' *Journal of Political Economy* (1921)
Piero Sraffa, 'The laws of returns under competitive conditions' *Economic Journal* (December 1926)
L.C. Robbins, 'The representative firm' *Economic Journal* (September 1928)
D.H. Robertson, P. Sraffa and G.F. Shove, 'Increasing returns and the representative firm' *Economic Journal* (1930)
Allyn A. Young, 'Increasing returns and economic progress' *Economic Journal* (December 1928)

21 Rent, quasi rent and costs

Today I want to discuss the traditional theory of Rent and its relation to the modern theory of Economic Equilibrium. I have dealt with certain aspects of this theory already in my lectures on Returns and on the equilibrium of stationary production. Now I want to gather together the various problems involved and discuss them in relation to each other.

The first thing to do is to be sure what it is we are to talk about. The traditional theory of Rent – the theory expounded by Ricardo – was concerned, not with the annual income from house property, pianos, hired motor cars and land of various descriptions, but with the return to Ricardian land – to the indestructible powers of the soil. There were variants of this definition with which we need not trouble ourselves. Broadly speaking it is clear that Rent was regarded by Ricardo as it was regarded by Marshall as the return to a factor of production whose supply was fixed – that factor being chiefly these powers of the soil described by Ricardo. I have explained already that I regard this nomenclature as unfortunate. I do not want to go into that again. The question I want to discuss rather is what theories were deduced from this definition and what bearing had these theories on the modern theory of equilibrium?

The Ricardian Theory of Rent is often spoken of as if it were a simple generalization. In fact, it included at least four different inquiries.

(1) There was a theory of why rent was paid.
(2) There was a theory of the determination of differences in the rent paid for the use of different acres.
(3) There was a theory of changes in rent over time: the dynamic theory.
(4) Finally, there was a theory of the relation of rent to cost of production.

I have discussed already in an earlier set of lectures the main outlines of the first three of these theories. It is the fourth of these theories and the developments which have been built upon it with which I want to concern myself in this lecture.

The doctrine that rent does not enter into cost of production was an integral part of the Ricardian theory of value. Ricardo was out to demonstrate that the main underlying regulator of value was the quantity of labour expended in production. To do this he had to show that the use of capital – in the sense of capital goods – and land either made no difference or could be introduced into the theory without modifying its main outlines.

As you know, so far as capital was concerned, he attempted the second of these alternatives. He tried – unsuccessfully as he admitted – to provide a theory which should take proper account of the use in production of varying amounts of capital.

So far as land was concerned he adopted the former expedient. He tried to show that the use of land made no difference to his theory. The labour cost relevant to the labour theory of value was the labour expended at the margin of cultivation on land that paid no rent. Hence rent did not enter into cost of production and the use of land did not necessitate any modification of his theory.

Such was the origin of the theory that Rent does not enter into cost of production. It was an impressive feat of argument. It contained an important germ of truth and although it has always been repugnant to plain men in some form or another it has persisted down to the present day.

What then are we to say about it. Are we to side with the plain men or the economists? This is a bad way of putting the question. For even if the plain man's attitude is similar to our own, we can be sure he has not reached it by right reasons.

Broadly speaking my answer is that there is a fundamental truth behind the Ricardian doctrine unrecognized by the plain man but that to state this truth by saying that rent does not enter into cost of production is about as misleading and question-begging a way of putting this matter as could well be imagined.

But let us analyse the matter a little further.

The proposition that rent does not enter into cost of production is usually upheld by appeal to one of two main arguments.

(1) The first refers to money costs and is substantially the same as the Ricardian argument I have already outlined. Rent is a surplus over the cost at the margin. It does not therefore enter into cost of production. The "surplus" aspect.

(2) The second refers to real costs and argues that as Ricardian land requires no efforts or sacrifices to bring it into existence, the payment for its use, rent, can have no counterpart in real cost. Rent therefore "measures" nothing that enters into the real cost of production.

No doubt this is a crude statement of the position. It would require a couple of lectures to exhibit all the ramifications of this curious and fascinating doctrine. For our purposes, however, it will do. Now let us proceed to examine each argument more closely.

(1) Take first the surplus argument – the Ricardian theorem I have explained to you.

First of all, let me remove a possible misapprehension. It is sometimes thought that the form of the argument depends on the existence of no-rent land. Critics of the doctrine therefore have attempted to disprove it by denying the existence of such land; superficial defenders have tried to suggest its existence. All this is completely beside the point.

It is true that the Ricardian theory is expounded from time to time in terms of the extensive margin. Rent a surplus on the better lands. But it does not depend upon this assumption. As Ricardo himself saw quite clearly the important conception is the intensive margin. It is not the question whether there exist lands which pay no rent. It is the question whether there are made investments of capital – last doses – which yield no surplus and that is not open to question.

We may leave aside then as irrelevant to the main issue the futile disputes with regard to the existence of no-rent land and no-wage labourers etc. and concentrate on the main issue of whether rent is a surplus over costs.

(a) Let us look at this from the point of view of the individual entrepreneur. We have started from this point of view in our studies of equilibrium. Clearly it is appropriate to do so in this instance.

Now from the point of view of the entrepreneur, there is clearly very little in the theory. That is why it is so repugnant to the common sense of the plain man. He knows if he is a business man that he must pay rent for the "land" he uses. He knows that it enters into his calculations of cost of production. He knows that if the price does not cover the rent he pays he must go bankrupt or change the scale or nature of his business. From his point of view rent is a cost equally with wages, interest, raw material charges and so on.

This is true whether we regard rent arising behind the extensive or intensive margin.

(i) The infra-extensive marginal farmer knows that he pays rent just because his land is that much better than his neighbours. The rent payment "evens out" costs in this respect. It makes it impossible for one man to bring his goods to market more cheaply than another just because he has a better piece of "Ricardian land".

(ii) But if all land is of the same fertility, rent is a cost just as much as anything else – infra-intensive marginal rent payments.

The idea that rent is a surplus over wage and other costs arises simply because we look at the rentless margin. But if we look at the wageless margin – we are perfectly entitled to do so – we have seen that it is just as legitimate to regard the farmer as dosing labour with land as it is to regard him as dosing land with labour. If we look at the wageless margin we find rent a final cost and wages a differential surplus. It is clear that the analysis proves too much.

In fact of course the idea of this infra-marginal "surplus" only persists because of certain geometrical ways of exhibition the production analysis. If we take the time honoured figure for wages and marginal productivity[1], rent emerges as a surplus thus:

---

1 [Wicksteed in *The Common Sense of Political Economy* (1910) Book II Chapter VI refers to it as the 'ordinary diagram' and the results illustrated by it as 'very familiar to all students of Political Economy'].

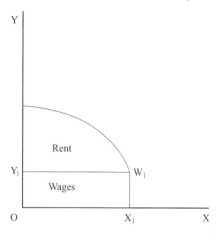

OY output OX labour

But if we apply exactly the same analysis to the analysis of what the farmer spends on land, wages emerge as a surplus:

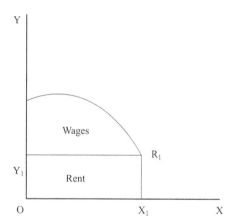

OY output OX rent

In the last resort, that is to say as Wicksteed and Clark have abundantly shown, the productivity analysis and the rent analysis are only two modes of exhibiting one and the same fundamental set of facts – the varying specific significance of the factors themselves.

And thus considerations of a highly theoretical nature bear out the verdict of experience that for the single entrepreneur, as Marshall says somewhere, it is equally important for him to consider whether to buy more ploughs or more land, more labour or more advantageously situated fields.

(b) But what about the point of view of society? Are land in the Ricardian sense and the other factors of production on all fours here? It is here that our plan of sorting out into classes the various kinds of equilibrium enables us in five minutes to dispose quite simply of a century of controversy.

The answer is that it all depends on the ultimate assumptions with regard to the conditions of equilibrium. If we examine carefully the implicit assumptions of the contesting parties we perceive that all were right and all should have prizes – at least all except the plain men and one or two writers of the Historical School.

If we are contemplating an equilibrium in which the ultimate supplies of the factors of production are fixed by hypothesis, then rent wages interest and all the other payments are on precisely the same footing with regard to cost. It is just as legitimate to exhibit the one as surplus as the other. All costs are transfer expenses.

Thus in J.B. Clark's static state, rent is on the same footing as all the other payments. You cannot say it is more or less price determining or price determined than other factor payments. For of course all are simultaneously determined by the general supply and demand equilibrium.

But when we turn to the stationary state – the equilibrium in which the supply of factors of some kinds is free to vary, then there is more to be said for regarding the other factors as the variables and exhibiting the return to "land" (and the fixed factors generally) as the surplus. For as we have seen in the stationary state there are equilibrium supply prices for different kinds of labour and renewable material agents, whereas by definition the supply of Ricardian land is rigid. We must assume that if prices were different the supply of "capital and labour" – in the classic sense – would be different, but we need not make any such assumption about the factors in fixed supply.

In the sense therefore that cost is to be interpreted as the price of keeping supply constant, there is significance of a sort in the argument that Rent in the Ricardian sense does not "enter into" this conception.

But it is nevertheless decidedly inconvenient to express this by saying that Rent does not enter into cost of production. For (a) after all the fixed land factors are used by more than one concern and for more than one purpose. *And as soon as there is competition for a factor between different producers whether in the same industry or in different industries a price has to be paid for its use* and this price will enter into cost in the usual sense of the term; and (b) although ultimately the supply of the flexible agents is flexible and the supply of the fixed agents is fixed yet *at any moment*, the supply of each is given. The price depends on the play of demand. These were not altogether clear to Ricardo[2], but Marshall perceived them fully although he hesitated to break with tradition. They are set out quite clearly in

2 There are traces of a theory of quasi rent in the Chapter on Taxes on Houses [David Ricardo, *On the Principles of Political Economy and Taxation* in *The Works of David Ricardo* ed. J.R. McCulloch (1846) Chapter XIV].

his discussion of the margin of building on the one hand and his doctrine of quasi rent on the other.[3]

So that in the last resort the "important truth" concealed in the doctrine that Rent does not enter into cost of production in so far as the argument is supported by discussion by money cost boils down to the statement that the money costs of securing the use of Ricardian land and the fixed factors have no coincident supply price in the structure of stationary equilibrium.

(2) The same is true, I think, of the real cost argument.

This side of the argument comes from Senior rather than Ricardo, and of course it has led to all sorts of obscure extensions of the rent concept – any gain not involving a commensurate sacrifice being regarded as a rent.

It is clear, I think, that once the classical conception of real cost as a sum of efforts and sacrifices is thrown overboard this argument becomes unimportant. Real costs are simply the alternatives sacrificed, and land which is in fixed supply may have alternate applications equally with tools and labour.

But it is still true that land in the Ricardian sense has no supply price, while the flexible factors have. Payment for Ricardian land is a "transfer expense" but payment "capital and labour for" . . .

---

3 Cf Marshall's letter to Edgeworth quoted later [sic].
   [The letter, dated 28 July 1902, is in *Memorials of Alfred Marshall* ed. A.C. Pigou (London: Macmillan, 1925) pp. 435–8.]

22 Profits

Today I want to discuss profits and the place of profit in the theory of equilibrium. I am afraid this is bound to be a little sterile. So much of the dispute about the theory of profit is a mere dispute about words. But it is necessary that the survey should be undertaken. It is difficult to read on this topic unless you have some notion of the intentions of the various writers.

Let us first examine the notion of profits as we find it in business usage. What does the word "profit" mean to an accountant?

Its main significance clearly is that of an excess of receipts over expenditure – a residue left over out of the proceeds of sales after all expenses have been met. No doubt the detailed interpretation of the term expenses is often very difficult. It is one of the main difficulties of accounting how much to allow for depreciation for instance. But these are technical difficulties. The broad conception of the reside of receipts is simple.

Now let us go a step further. Let us take a few cases of profit in this sense and see what kinds of income the term may be conceived to cover. Let us take three specimen cases.

(1) The excess of receipts over expenditure of a joint stock company employing salaried managers. That is to say profit here corresponds to the dividends of ordinary shareholders and reserve.
(2) The excess of receipts over expenditure of a tenant farmer working on borrowed capital. What is left over after rent interest charges and his other business expenses have been met?
(3) The excess of receipts over expenses of a farmer working with his own capital.

Now look at these carefully. In the first case the income is derived from the ownership of property. In the second it is derived from the performance of work. In the third case both work and property are involved. Now this does *not* mean that the business use of the term is illegitimate. All the incomes involved are *residual*. They are what is left over when expenses have been met. From the point of view of the people concerned, they are profits.

But of course it is fatal to the hope of any *single* theory of profit. Very frequently, people complain of the lack of a single theory of profits. So long as economists are unable to agree about profits they urge, so long must their whole basis of analysis be suspect. In part this complaint is justified. As we shall be seeing in a minute economists have been more than usually perverse in their use of the *term* profits.

But in part, as you see, the confusion is due not to ambiguity of thought of the part of economists but to the multiplicity of meanings on the part of the word itself. Outside the broadest generalizations you have no single theory to explain: profits per cent – earnings per entrepreneur – profits and earnings as a lump sum. They are different things and need different explanations.

But instead of recognizing this and settling down to coin new terms which should elucidate these ambiguities, economists have tried to impose more restricted meanings on the term. They have even made confusion worse by attempting to give it new meanings!

It is to the somewhat arid elucidation of these confusions and arguments at cross purposes that I want to direct your attention in this lecture.

A. The first thing we have to do is to examine the restriction which economists have attempted to impose. The new meanings will be clearer when we have satisfied ourselves on this point. I have explained already that the profit in business usage may be held to cover any of three classes of residue

(1) income from property
(2) income from work
(3) income from both work and property.

If you survey the history of economic thought from Smith to Marshall, you will find it used in each of these ways.

(1) Adam Smith used profit as that part of income which was derived from the ownership of *stock*. By this he meant property other than land. He goes out of his way to warn us not to confound profit with rent or with wages. Common farmers he thinks are apt to call their whole gains profits, whereas it is obvious that part of these gains are wages.

Profits in this sense are equivalent to interest, and the theory of profit concerns the determination of the rate of profit, so much percent of the capital invested. It is in this sense that you get the Ricardians discussing the tendency of profits to a minimum in the stationary state: the rate of profit is such as to call forth no new accumulation.

(2) But the classics on the whole used the term in a looser sense. They used it as equivalent to yield of property and return to managerial services. They regarded profits simply as the "leavings of wages" (and rent) as De Quincey called them. They recognized – or at least Mill recognized – that there was an

element of labour income in this residue but they never made an attempt to explain this element. This was only natural. They were so preoccupied with the Wage Fund theory and the Iron Law as explanations of wages, that the idea of a possible unification of the theory of labour incomes was not likely to occur to them.

You couldn't explain that element in profits due to superintendence in terms of a fixed determinate "profit fund", for profits were clearly a residue.

(3) Finally we get a group of economists who use the term profits as equivalent to the entrepreneurs earnings, to the excess of receipts over expenditure of the farmer working on borrowed capital.

Here we find J.B. Say, the American Walker and Marshall with his "earnings of management".[1] Say and Walker were downright on this point. Profits were just the earnings to entrepreneurs. They reproach the classics for failing to make the distinction earlier. Marshall is more ambiguous. He saw that "profits" was used in a wider sense and he did the right thing therefore in trying to coin a new term to separate out the element of earnings – though of course the term he coined was confusing and ill chosen – earnings of management suggest contract earnings – but in his Principles he does not separate of it his treatment of Earnings of Management and Profits in the wider sense, and the effect is confusing.

B. So much for attempted restrictions. We can now proceed to deal with innovations. The best way I think to explain these without letting the lecture degenerate into a mere technical dictionary is to proceed by way of examination of the celebrated doctrine that in a state of equilibrium there is no such thing as profit – a doctrine which springs on the one side from Walras and the mathematicians and on the other from J.B. Clark and his American followers. Let us start by enquiring how far this proposition can be held to be true of profits in the senses in which we have encountered the term so far.

(i) Take first "profits" in the Smithian sense of return on invested capital. Is it true that in a state of stationary equilibrium profits in this sense would be nonexistent?

Obviously not. We have seen in our discussion of interest that if everything else is supposed to be given, it is the equilibrium rate of interest which keeps the stationary state stationary. I have already discussed with you Schumpeter's dynamic theory of interest, and we have found that there is no reason to suppose it to be valid. If there were no rate of interest there would be no incentive to maintain

---

1 [J.B. Say, *Traité d'economie politique* (1803); F.A. Walker, *The Wages Question: A Treatise on Wages and the Wage System* (1906); Marshall, *Principles of Economics* (1920) Book II Chapter IV].

capital intact, the consumption of capital would begin, and the stationary state would cease to be stationary.

(ii) But what about profits in the sense of Marshall's earnings of management? Is there any reason to suppose that managerial functions would go unpaid in stationary equilibrium?

Surely not. So long as we assume that such services are productive in the economic sense, so long as we assume that the factor of production management is *scarce* – has specific productivity – so long as we are entitled to assume that it will have to be paid for. This, I think, should be quite obvious. After all the noncontractual residual nature of the income is only, so to speak, an accident of the organization of production. No one would suggest that if the independent tenant farmer who forms the stock type of recipient of this kind of income were employed on contract by the capitalist whose capital he borrows, he would not be paid. Clearly he would be paid just as any other workman. The mere fact that he employs himself is not likely to disqualify him from drawing anything out of the social dividend. On the contrary, since the risks and responsibilities are greater, the probability is that (because such things limit supply) his remuneration will be greater.

Profits in this sense, therefore, are simply a sort of labour income, and there is no reason whatever to suppose them absent from the stationary equilibrium or to suppose that their mode of determination in a competitive economy is any different from the mode of determination of other labour incomes. The one thing to remember here is that of course in the world of practice the entrance to this kind of activity is much more restricted than entrance to contract income occupations – at least so far as large undertakings go. It is more necessary to keep in mind the doctrine of non-competing groups. Moreover of course the competitive hypothesis is not infrequently inappropriate even within these groups. There is much more friction and indivisibility knocking about this part of the economic system.

But these are matters of applications rather than pure theory. The general conclusion stands that for profit in any of the senses in which we have encountered it up to date, there is ample room in the hypothesis of stationary equilibrium.

But this is not seriously denied by those who urge the doctrine we are examining. They do not deny that interest or earnings are present in stationary equilibrium.

What they deny rather is the appropriateness of the term profit to cover either of these two branches of income. In stationary equilibrium they urge these incomes are certainly present and properly understood they cover all static incomes. (For J.B. Clark interest included land income). But when conditions are changing then a new kind of income emerges – the dynamic surplus. In stationary equilibrium all incomes are in another sense costs and costs and prices are coincident. But when you introduce change then costs and prices diverge until equilibrium is restored. Out of this disparity profit, pure profit, emerges. When the equilibrium is restored it is obliterated. In static equilibrium therefore you can contemplate employers' wages *unternehmen lohn* but not employers' profits *unternehmen gewinn*.

Side by side with this separating out of the dynamic element in profits normally so-called goes an attempt to refine the conception of the entrepreneur. The entrepreneur in pre-Clarkian theory is just a loose name for the organizers of complex production. The entrepreneur may be a person or it may be a group of persons – a directorate of a joint stock company. The term is usually left deliberately ambiguous in order that it may be variously employed in very general analysis. But this school of writers takes the concept more seriously. The entrepreneur becomes a highly specialized fiction. It is not enough to be the head of a business organization, discharging functions of routine management. To be entitled to this status you must make *new* decisions, initiate *new* combinations of the factors of production. For the performance of these functions, and these functions only, you receive the reward of pure profit. Hence the motto for those who want pure profit is obviously to keep moving.

Now in judging such theories there are two distinct issues to be decided. Firstly there is the issue of fact. Do such gains occur? And do they go to the entrepreneur thus defined?

Second, there is the issue of terminology. Is it convenient to use the term profit in this connection?

(I) Take first the issue of fact. Undoubtedly such surpluses do occur. Economic activity is not in a state of stationary equilibrium. He who is first on the spot tends to get the biggest haul.

But it is not only the entrepreneur who reaps such surpluses. Surplus gains of this sort occur to other agents. Suppose there is a great increase in demand for munitions. The price of munitions rises. There is a great gap between price and cost. Unquestionably the entrepreneur be he man or fictional person gets something. But munitions workers who are on the spot tend to gain too. In order to get more labour more material instruments, the entrepreneur is willing to offer better terms. Wages rise as well as profits. There are dynamics gains for other factors. No doubt if the labour market were perfectly competitive this would not happen. At once the disparity would be corrected. But that after all applies to profit also. If there were no friction – if it took no time to change the direction of production – the dynamic surplus would not arise *anywhere*.

(II) The second question – the question of terminology – therefore answers itself automatically. It does not seem in the least convenient to label these "surpluses" profits. If we do we have to speak of a pure profit element in wages, in interest on capital – even in rent – which is surely very confusing. If we want to discuss such phenomena, and no doubt it is of the very highest importance that the thing should be done, let us devise suitable terms which have no ambiguity about them. Let us say, if we like, that there is no dynamic surplus in the stationary state. It is one way of *defining* stationary equilibrium. But let us avoid the suggestion that in the stationary state we find a set of entrepreneurs who make neither loss nor profit. The stationary state is not so dull as all that for the wretched profit maker.

But now I come to a more fundamental topic. In representing these surpluses as due in the last analysis to the fact of change, are we not concentrating attention on the wrong aspect of the situation? Is it change which is responsible for the surplus or the absence of knowledge?

What is it that the surplus implies? Surely that in the new conditions there is a disparity between the valuation of resources in different lines of production. There is not an equilibrium of production. The machinery is out of adjustment.

But supposing the change had been *foreseen* a sufficiently long time ahead. Is there any reason to suppose that in these circumstances the maladjustment would have arisen? Surely not. Steps would have been taken to anticipate the new situation. There would be no surplus because there would be no maladjustment.

Hence it may be argued that it is not change which is responsible for the dynamic surplus, but *change which is unforeseen*. Anticipated results are frustrated by unexpected happenings. Some factors get less than expected;others more.

Reflections of this sort have led to the development of yet another theory of the entrepreneur and his remuneration, the Risk theory. The essential function of the entrepreneur according to this theory is the assumption of risks and responsibility. In a world in which so many things are changing, production is always a speculation. No doubt some risks can be insured against. They are not born, they are destroyed. The device of pooling enables the individual producer to contract out of these altogether. What is a risk for an individual is a certainty for the community in these cases. Insurance obviates the necessity of risks being born at all. But there are many risks which are not predictable in this way. You can predict with some certainty the average number of fires in a large area (leaving out of account widespread conflagrations). But you cannot e.g. predict the vagaries of consumers demand, the weather, the success of a search for oil and so on. These are risks which have to be born, somebody has to assume them, and according to the theory we are discussing the assumption of such risks constitutes the essence of entrepreneurship, and the reward the payment for the discharge of this function is profit.

Such is the Risk Theory of Profit. As in case of the dynamic theory two questions arise. First the question of analysis. Is it a correct statement of the facts of the case?

Second is the question of terminology. Is Profit a convenient name for the reward of payment for uncertainty bearing?

Here again I can see nothing in favour of the procedure and many reasons against it. Quite apart from the question of analysis whether you can identify a payment for risk, I think it is supremely inconvenient whenever you discover a new aspect of economic life to attempt to give a new meaning to a term with an already established usage. But let the old terms retain their old significance.

But that brings me to the question of analysis. How far is the theory a convenient way of expressing the facts? How far is it useful to think of uncertainty as a separate factor of production? Here I have two comments to make.

In the first place, I do not think it is correct to speak as if risks of the sort we are discussing were only born by entrepreneurs in the ordinary sense of the word, or even by ordinary shareholders. Professions and other occupations are risky – not merely risky to life and limb which in this connection is perhaps irrelevant – but risky as regards prospects. It is surely twisting words a good deal to suggest that in so far as entering these occupations involves risk, it involves becoming an entrepreneur. And second. if risk-bearing is to be regarded as a factor of production, how are we to count up the factors? What is the unit of supply? By definition the risks assumed are unknown. How then can we speak definitely of a supply (or supplies) of this factor?

But if we reject this approach how are we to deal with uncertainty? Clearly the assumption of uncertainties is an important aspect of economic activities in a changing world. How are we to work it into our theoretical analysis?

The answer, I think, is very simple. *We must regard the uncertainty of an occupation or an investment as one of the "other advantages or disadvantages"* of work and investment which we have already discussed in dealing with the distribution of factors in stationary production. That is to say, we must regard it as one of the influences which tend to regulate supply.

If we do these two things, that which the other theories obscure become clear.

(1) The influence of risk on supply is *via* a subjective estimate. It is not the mathematical expectation of loss which influences people. Very often the thing is not susceptible of mathematical computation. It is what they believe the risk to be and how they behave vis-a-vis such a possibility.

(2) And second, we can see clearly that not all risks need be regarded as unpleasant. People may positively prefer risky jobs or risky investment. If we approach this from the theory which regards risk-bearing as connected with a definite remuneration we have to say that the payment for risk-bearing is negative. It is surely more elegant and less artificial to say that the risk is attractive. Hence that the supply to that line of work or investment is augmented.

Announce for non-specialists:

(1) Benham's lectures next term
(2) Mine

    Announce for specialists:
    Hicks on Risk and Profit[2]

2 [Frederick Benham's 'lectures next term' were Problems of Monopoly and State Control, given in the Summer Term of 1930; Robbins's in the same term were The Nature of Economics and its Significance in relation to the kindred social sciences; Hicks' were Theory of Risk and Profit. Hicks gave this course only once; out of it came his article, 'The theory of uncertainty and profit' *Economica* Vol. 11 (May 1931) pp. 170–89].

Read

Edwin Cannan, 'Profit' in *Palgrave's Dictionary of Political Economy* (1926)

Frank H. Knight, *Risk, Uncertainty and Profit* (1921)

J.B. Clark, *The Distribution of Wealth* (1899)

M.H. Dobb, *Capitalist Enterprise and Social Progress* (1925)

[ADDED IN PENCIL:] J.R. Hicks, 'The theory of uncertainty and profit' *Economica* (May 1931)

Part II 1932/33–1934/35

Introduction

Principles (1932–33)

Editorial Note: *The lecture notes in this part come from the second of the Principles notebooks and are labelled on the cover as 'Transitional Notes 1932–34'. The first five are clearly stated to have been given in 1932/33. The second five lectures, on Production, correspond to that section of the course syllabus in the 1935/36 LSE* Calendar, *but they were probably prepared for and given in the second half of 1934/35, since the 1935/36* Calendar *would have gone to press before the start of the academic year.*

1   Preliminary injunctions

What course is about. Title – syllabus – Look at contents table of books in Library. Broad outlines of main principles. Not to say *same* as books. (1) Possible to synthesise some results of recent discussion. Clearer view of whole area. I shall try to do this. (2) Where subjects are adequately treated in easily accessible books, it shall go very quickly.

Moral: Lectures are no substitute for reading.

Essential

Philip H. Wicksteed, *The Common Sense of Political Economy* (1910) Book I
[ADDED LATER:] Knut Wicksell, *Lectures on Political Economy* trans. E. Classen and
    ed. L. Robbins (1934–5)
Frank H. Knight, *Risk, Uncertainty and Profit* (1921)
F W. Taussig, *Wages and Capital* (1896) Chapters I-VI Alfred Marshall, *Principles of Economics* (1920)
J.R. Hicks, *The Theory of Wages* (1932)
Ludwig von Mises, *Theorie des Geldes und der Umlaufsmittel* (1924) translated as *The Theory of Money and Credit* trans. H. Batson (1934)[1]

Those who can read German:-

Knut Wicksell, *Vorlesungen uber Nationalokonomie* (1913)
Enrico Barone, *Grundzuge der theoretischen Nationalokonomie* trans. Hans Staehle (1927)
Eugen von Böhm-Bawerk, *Kapital und Kapitalzins Erste Abteilung: Geschichte und Kritik der Kapitalzins-Theorien* 4th edition (1921)
Eugen von Böhm-Bawerk, *Kapital und Kapitalzins Zweite Abteilung: Positive Theorie des Kapitales* 4th edition (1921)
Other works recommended as lectures proceed.
Classes Look on boards.
Importance of all this. Background to everything else on Economics side. This applies to B.Com as to B.Sc.

---

1   [Robbins wrote: 'Mises Money (when translated)'].

2 The nature of economic analysis

Ground already covered. Establishment of fundamental conceptions.

    The nature of the task of the Economist. Given the data (Ends [and] Means) how are means disposed of?

    General terms. Particular complexes unpredictable – depend on data – E.g. Individual Valuation

    Exchange

    Production one factor

    To deal with such problems "equilibrium analysis". That is to say we take the various quantities of relations involved in different hypothetical situations and enquire concerning conditions under which no tendency to change.

    E.g. Valuation

    Exchange

    Production

    Further elucidations

(1) Meaning of equilibrium

    (a) Not merely constancy. False equilibrium. Fixed Prices. Supplies.

        A certain freedom assumed. Constancy not because of force. Exchange. Production.

    (b) But freedom within limits. Not free to kill coal merchant. Framework of law. (Strigl's organization)

(2) Implications of generalizations.

    No suggestion equilibrium ever reached.

    Or that in all circumstances the forces operative would secure equilibrium if left to themselves. (Money Rosenstein).[1]

    Significance by way of contrast. We know when situation not in equilibrium and what way it might move.

---

1 [P Rosenstein-Rodan, 'Das Zeitmoment in der mathematischen Theorie des wirtschaftlichen Gleichgewichtes' *Zeitschrift für Nationalökonomie* Vol. 1 (1930) pp. 129–42].

(3) Logical Method.

   (a) Isolation. Examples.

      (This method of all science; difference economics and experimental science. Indeed method of all thought. If thought needed it is because we cannot grasp total situation.)

   (b) Successive approximations.

Examples
  Difference between most complex model and reality. The data.

Read

L.C. Robbins, *An Essay on the Nature and Significance of Economic Science* (1932)
Hans Mayer, 'Untersuchungen zu dem Grundgesetze der wirtschaftlichen Wertrechnung' *Zeitschrift für Volkswirtschaft und Sozialpolitik* 1 (1921)
Ludwig von Mises, *Die Gemeinwirtschaft* (1922)
Alfred Ammon, *Objekt und Grundbegriffe der theoretisches Nationalokonomie* (1927)
Richard Strigl, *Die ökonomischen Kategorien und die Organisation der Wirtschaft* (1923)

3 The divisions of equilibrium analysis

The nature of the successive approximations.

Two broad divisions

(1) Theory of Equilibrium. Conditions of Equilibrium described.
(2) Investigation of Change. Variations.

Two points here:

(a) Comparison of different equilibria. Examples. Labour supply etc.
(b) Analysis of actual effects of change. Uncertainty. Money etc.

   Now look more closely at theory of equilibrium.

Two ways of dividing:

(a) According to assumptions as to means. Given goods Given factors etc.
(b) According to assumptions as to social conditions. Individual. Society.

   Both to be employed. First to be major division.
   Two main divisions:

(1) Given Goods. Value and Exchange
(2) Given Factors. Production.

   Now look more closely.

(1) Value and Exchange.

   (a) Individual Economy
   (b) Exchange Economy.

      (i) Two persons two commodities
      (ii) Market. Indirect Exchange.

(2) Production. Flows of goods free to vary.

But within what limits?: a very complex set of influences here. Factors may be given or not given. The static state and the stationary state.

(1) The static state.

  Within this another division as important as last. Does production take time or not? Is there capital? Hence,

  (a) Hand to mouth production; and
  (b) Capitalistic production.

  Within each of these there may be one or more than one original factor of production.

  Throughout, individual and social distinction useful.

(2) Stationary state. Labour land and capital free to vary.[1]

  Spatial and Temporal Equilibrium.

Variations

Less settled content.

A. Particular demand and supply changes. Elasticity and costs. Taxes.

  Changes in labour supply
  Changes in capital supply
  Invention. Spatial I]International T[rade]

B. Dynamics. Profits.

  Money

Comparison with other systems

(1) *Classical system*. Production Distribution analysis.

  Disadvantages of this. Nothing precise. (see N & S.)[2]

In fact, all significant in classics equilibrium analysis.

  Ricardian system essentially a study of the stationary state. Natural Value. Wages. Profits. Rents

(2) *Marshall* Greater similarity.

---

1 Here deal with rent and cost.
2 [L.C. Robbins, *An Essay on the Nature and Significance of Economic Science* (1932)].

But (1) no clear distinction between Theory of Equilibrium and Theory of Variations. The Statical Method. (2) Marshall focusses attention on prices and incomes. Divides Value and Distribution. Meaning of these.

Thus you get price with production treated separately from incomes. Books V and VI.[3] Whereas we deal with Exchange without production and Production including Exchange. Discuss prices and incomes simultaneously.

Within his two divisions divides according to length of period under consideration. (Curious mixture of equilibrium theory and variation theory)

In theory of price or value four problems:

(1) Market price.
(2) Short period normal. Period short enough to prevent influx of factors.
(3) Long period normal.
(4) Secular changes.

You remember he illustrates this in terms of the fishing industry.[4] Day today (M[arket] P[rice]) Year S[hort] Period Period during which new boats etc. Long Period Normal. Changing population etc. Secular change. Distribution. Short and long. Almost all long in Marshall.

(3) Marshall and particular equilibrium. Possible to exaggerate this. But significant in theory of value.

(We deal with particular equilibrium under variation.)

Connection between Marshall and the scheme adopted here.

Market price   = Exchange
Short & long Value   = Production (factors fixed)
Also distribution   = Production (factors fixed)
Long distribution   = (Flexible factors)
Secular price change = (Flexible factors)

Equilibrium	*Value*	*Dist[ribution]*
Exchange		M[arket] P[rice]
Production (static)	N[ormal] P[rice]	Short Dist
Production Stationary	Secular P[rice]	Long Dist
Variations	Secular Price change etc etc	

So much for Marshall.

(3) *Clark* Deals only with our Production factors fixed.

---

3 [*Principles of Economics* 8th edition (1920) Book V General Relations of Demand, Supply and Value Book VI The Distribution of National Income].
4 [*Principles of Economics* (1920) pp. 369–70].

Importance of distinguishing all this. Theories true on some assumptions, false on others.

E.g. Wages and M.P. theory
Rent and cost of production, etc.

L.C. Robbins, 'On a certain ambiguity in the conception of Stationary Equilibrium' *Economic Journal* (June 1930)
Alfred Marshall, *Principles of Economics* (1920) Book V Chapter V
J.A. Schumpeter, *Die Theorie der wirtschaftslichten Entwicklung* (1911) Chapters I and II
    FrankH. Knight, *Risk, Uncertainty and Profit* (1921)
Knut Wicksell, *Vorlesungen uber Nationalokonomie* (1913)

General outline of equilibrium analysis

4   Valuation and exchange

Individual disposition of goods

First problem. Individual. Given wants etc. Given goods. What is equilibrium disposition of goods?

Fundamental assumption that different possibilities can be ranged in order of importance. Recollect corn example. 1 sack hunger, 1 sack comfort in food, 1 sack animals chickens etc.

A	B	C	D
IV			
III	III		
II	II	II	
I	I	I	I
0	0	0	0

Notes on this:

(1) It gives an order:

A_{IV} greater than $A_{III} = B_{III}$ greater than $A_{II} = B_{II} = C_{II}$

(2) But it does not imply possibility of measuring:

1 unit serving A_{IV} greater than A_{III} or B_{III}.
We do not say *how much* greater. It is impossible to say.
Why? Measurement involves third point of reference. No point of reference here. Simply an *order*. A_{IV} is preferred to A_{III}.

(3) No suggestion that it is an ethically right order. Whisky to feeding the chickens. We assume merely that the man would behave in this way.

(4) It is a descending order. Dim[inishing]. S[ignificance].

Relation of this to Gossen's Law.[1]

---

1 Many laws of Gossen. See J. Neubauer, 'Die Gossenschen Gesetze' *Zeitschrift fur Nationalokonomie* Vol. 2 (October 1931) pp. 733–53.

Additional quantities of a good applied to satisfaction of one class of need yield diminishing satisfaction. – (Roughly)

That is to say A_{IV} greater than A_{III} greater than A_{II} greater than A_{I}

But our scale applies to A B C. A wider concept. A more formal concept. Not dependent on psychology at all. Immune from disputes about satisfaction upward sloping curves etc.

Now look at actual distribution of goods.

Suppose three units:

A	B	C
IV		
III	III	
II	II	II

Distributed in such a way that impossible by withdrawing one to fill higher place on scale.

So far illustration crude. A sack of corn. A pail of water.

Suppose finer divisions.

Same grading possible.

What limit of division (*minimum sensible*).

Distributed so that significance in one unoccupied no higher than in the other.

Knight's diagram[2] Significance of units:

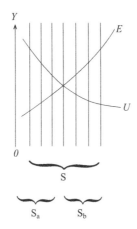

2 [F.H. Knight, *Risk, Uncertainty and Profit* (1921) p. 68].

Or fluid in flasks:

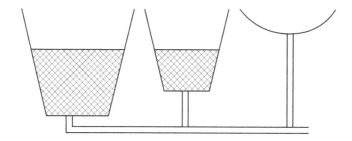

Disadvantage of this suggests measurement.[3]

Treatment hitherto timeless.
But of course, ends arise *through time.*
Same principle applies.

Difficulty how long a period? Necessary to assume arbitrary period. This a difficult problem. More work to be done here. (Rosenstein)[4]

Note shifting goods through time in a sense transcends our assumption of given goods. Production? – One of the cases where loose ends permissible.

Carl Menger, *Grundsatze der Volkwirtschaftslehre* (1923)
Johann von Komorzynski, *Der Wert in der isolierte Wirtschaft* (1889)
Hans Mayer, 'Gut' in *Handworterbuch der Staatswissenschaften* (1927) Vol. 4 pp. 1272–80
Frank A. Fetter, *Economic Principles* (1915)
Irving Fisher, *The Nature of Capital and Income* (1906)
Friedrich Wieser, *Social Economics* (1927) pp. 39–49

3 I doubt utility of this diagrammatic analysis here.
4 ['Grenznutzen', *Handwörterbuch der Staatswissenschaften* Vol. 4 (Jena, 1927) pp. 1190–213].

5   Valuation and exchange

Simple exchange

That concludes individual.

Same applies to society if acting as a whole. Socialism. Social. scale. (Unitary) Need not enquire how established. General election.

But suppose individual free to exchange goods? To dispose by exchange. New problems. First 2 Ind[ustries] 2 Com[modities]. Two main questions:

(1) Conditions of Exchange
(2) Conditions of Equilibrium.

> Clear no exchange unless each party has use for thing to be acquired. This is not enough.
> Extend idea of scheme of uses.
> A has uses for corn which he has and uses for the wine which he hasn't.
> B vice versa.
> They can compare.

Thus A (who has corn) can judge whether a unit of corn is more or less important to him than a unit of wine, given quantity of corn he possesses.

- The marginal use (significance): He can judge what quantity of wine he would regard as equivalent to 1 unit of corn. So [can] B.

E.g. A 1 C = 1/2 W;
B 1 C = 2 W.

We can exhibit these valuations diagrammatically. Relative scales.

Wine

	A	B
3		
2		corn -
1		
	- corn	
0		

Notice about this four points:

(1) Unit or *marginal* valuations. A may reflect on use to him of all. But not here.
(2) Assume given supply. Varying (as we shall see) with variations in supply – as dependent uses change.
(3) Valuations relative. Corn = so much wine. No measurement implied at all.
(4) No interpersonal comparisons.

Now look at data we have postulated
A   values 1 C as 1/2 W
B   values 1 C as 2 W

A values corn in terms of wine less than B. A has corn, B has wine. Conditions of exchange are present. For supposing they exchange at 1:1. A will give 1 corn which he values at 1/2 wine and get 1 wine. B will get 1 corn which he values at 2 corn for 1 wine.

Now suppose different data.
A   values 1 corn as 2 W
B   values 1 corn as 1/2 W

A values corn in terms of wine more than B. A has corn B wine. Conditions of exchange not present. For suppose exchange 1:1. A gives that values at 2 and gets only 1. B gets 1 corn which values at 1/2 for 1 W.

Now let us generalize.
In the first case, A valued corn less than B (in terms of wine).
   In the second case more. So with B.
   In the first case it stood *lower* on his relative scale than on B's, in the second case higher.
   We may conclude, therefore, that exchange is possible when the possessor of a commodity values it *less* than he who might acquire it.
   Very important to be clear about this. Condition of exchange that corn lower on A's scale than on B's. Not that A values 1 unit of corn at less than a unit of wine and B more. Though this is true in this case, it *need* not be so. E.g. A values 1 corn at 2 W B values 1 corn at 4 W. Exchange is clearly possible *although each counts 1 corn more valuable than 1 wine*. For if they exchange at say 1:3 A gives what values at 2 W for 3 W, B gets what values at 4 W for 3 W. The important thing is not whether A (or B) values the thing he has more or less than a unit of the thing he might get but whether he values at less than B in terms of the thing in terms of which they are both valuing.[1]
   But now we have to describe the conditions of equilibrium. At what point will exchange cease? Note the obvious fact every exchange made has effect of diminishing stock of thing given and increasing stock of thing received. What effect on

---

1 I used to use Barone's diagram here. Does it suggest measurability?

relative valuations? Remember Law of D[iminishing]. M[arginal]. S[ignificance]. Uses ranged in order of importance. Hence as stock of corn diminishes   wine increases relationship between uses of corn sacrificed and uses of wine secured changes. That is A's valuation in terms of wine changes in favour of corn. So with B. Thus A may start valuing 1 C = 1/2 W. As he exchanges he may come to value at 1 C = 1 W and later 1 C = W. Similarly with B. Reverse direction.

Sooner or later difference between A's valuation and B's must cease. At that point exchange must cease. If A values C and W as 1–1 1/2 and B likewise no incentive to change.

Diagrammatically:

A   B

           I
           II
III   III
II
I

Exchange ceases when position on relative scales the same.

Notice how this brings out the point I was making about comparative valuation. We start with A valuing corn less than wine (units). But exchange does not cease when it is equivalent. The equilibrium position has A and B both valuing corn more than wine.

Note on equilibrium conception.

(1) No assumption about rates of changes of relative valuation.

A moves from 1 = 1/2 to 1 = 1 1/2 while B moves from 1 = 2 to 1 = 1 1/2.

(2) No suggestion that exchange ceases when commodities exchanged have equivalent unit significance. Exchange does not cease when 1 C = 1 W.

This is important. In certain textbooks condition of equilibrium is said to be that marginal significance of *different* commodities *equal*. This a fallacy. What is equal is marginal significance of same commodities to the exchangers. In our example when in terms for A and B m[arginal] s[ignificance of] corn was of the order II.[2]

(3) Assumption of divisibility.

If units not divisible perfect equilibrium ruled out. A may be at a stage when values two commodities as 1–1 and B as 1–3, yet when they change one

---

2 Take this up in next lecture Gesetze der Grenznutzen niveau.

more unit A may value as 1–3 and B as 1–1. In this case it has to stop before relative scales are equal.

(4) Rate of exchange not determinate.

Look again at data.

A   values 1 C = 1/2 W

B   values 1 C = 2 W

Many rates possible. A satisfied anything more than 1–1/2, B anything less than 1–2.

Initial rate indeterminate.

But if this is so final, the rate is indeterminate too, for valuations are marginal relative to quantity possessed.

6 Production
Introduction[1]

Production distinguished from exchange. General characteristic. Supply of *products* variable.

Two fold basis of further division

(a) Factor supply (free or fixed)
(b) Presence or absence of capitalistic methods.

    Thus
    A   Static state

        (i) Acapitalistic

       (ii) Capitalistic

    B   Stationary state

    Labour and Land supply
    Capital supply

---

1 Next year bring preliminary lecture here? This involves duplication.

7 Introduction

Factors fixed (acapitalistic)

Further distinction

    i   Simple
   ii Joint

Definition of these. Why not "Labour" and "Land"?
Excursus on "material" laws. Greater generality of our terminology.

8 Capitalistic production

Roundabout production more productive.

In what sense?

(a) More same
(b) Products not possible otherwise but *preferred*.

D[iminishing] R[eturns] here as elsewhere.
(How much roundaboutness. This a problem for later on. Flexible supplies)
For moment assume willingness to wait given (supply [of] capital). What conditions e.g.?
This involves interest. What is this?
Essential price difference present future. Surplus on investment.
In our example here interest excluded.
Hence *productive* interest only. Examples of this. Sale and hire.
(Assume only labour).
Then present labour one value (m[arginal] p[roduct]). And as we have seen labour of past another – greater. But dec[lining] m[arginal] p[roductivity]. Some used replacing.
Therefore Int[erest] essentially different m[arginal] p[roductivity] [of] present and past "Labour" and "*Land*" (resources)
(Price differences).
But why does this not disappear?

9   The theory of interest

Problem. How capitalist production organized.
  Conditions of stationary equilibrium.
  This leads to Interest Problem.

Two fold nature

(a) Why price?
(b) What determines? Pareto's strictures.[1]

  The Problem stated.

Alternative solutions:

(1) Exploitation
(2) Productivity
(3) Time Preference.

Positive Solution

  Interest a difference.
  M[arginal] P[roductivity] present and past labour.
  Why does this not disappear?
  Exchange between two years. Not constant rate.
  But why does this not go on?
  Possibility of decumulation. Another choice.
  The market an intermediary. Demand for producers goods and consumers
    goods.
  The replacement fund. The role of the rate of interest.

---

1 [V. Pareto, *Manuel d'economie politique* (Paris, 1927) Chapter V].

10   The theory of capital

Nature of investigation. Relation to general equilibrium theory. Difficulty. An area where finality not reached. Nature of hesitancy. Best in such circumstances to have recourse to history.

Broad Division

(a)   Nature of capital
(b)   Nature of capitalistic production
(c)   Capital in ordinary speech. Two senses

    (i)   Money invested in past
    (ii)   Money realizable in present.

This the "accountancy concept". Thus to be found in pre-Smithian literature. Thus in modern business use.
Clearly, in this *sense*, not on all fours with other factors of production e.g. land. Combination of £s sterling and acres of land.

Moreover Capital in this sense invested in "other factors". A business man spends his capital hiring labour, buying use of land etc.

Clear that use in E[conomic] T[heory] has special significance. Means not property rights valuations etc. but things. Real capital.

Trace history of acquisition of this meaning.

(1)   Interest and Ethics. Aristotle and Schoolmen. Barren money. Prohibition.

Anomalies of this. Purchase of land not prohibited. Nor hire. Nor purchase of things like wine and trees whose final price tended to leave surplus over cost.

Gradual revolt against all this. Business practice. Apologists come to emphasize interest paid not for barren money but for use of *things* barren money would buy.

(Did this solve problem? "Use" bought in original price put a surplus over this price. Constituted interest. Böhm-Bawerk's objection.)[1]

---

1   [E. von Böhm-Bawerk, *Capital and Interest* (1890) Chapter III].

(2) Monetary Theory. Locke, and view that interest depended on quantity of money.[2]

Where is this theory wrong? Interest a relation between yield and principal.

Where are they right? Transition periods.
Not seen clearly for many years.
Hume and Cantillon protest against crude version.[3]
Emphasize that interest price not for money but on goods.

Both streams of thought point to real capital.

Actual change comes with Adam Smith. Capital is that part of stock which yields a revenue, i.e. stock (land + consumption goods).
Nature of this distinction. Classification.
Capital one of factors of production.
The division has not proved helpful. Endless discussion of what is land and what capital.
Land? Indestructible. Where to find it? Gradual restriction to urban sites.
Capital. Original powers of soil excluded. But permanent improvements excluded too.

At same time business usage kept creeping in. Difficult in Economics not to talk of capital of a firm. Absurd to say capital of a firm excludes the land it owns or the goods it holds ready for sale to consumers.
Thus, a widening and a narrowing tendency.
With work of Cannan and Fisher and Fetter[4] there is a reversion to old use.
Capital not a part of wealth but an aspect of wealth. Wealth at a point of time.
Compared with income, a stream of services of wealth over a period of time.

(This incomplete unless human beings counted in. Fisher does this).
Thus parallelism between business usage and economic usage restored.
Real capital = all wealth.
Money capital = Value of all wealth.
(Extreme ingenuity of Fisher's synthesis).
One other distinction changed in emphasis. Rent and interest.
Yield to two different factors?

2 [J. Locke, *Some Considerations of the Consequences of the Lowering of Interest, and Raising the Value of Money* (1691)].

3 [D. Hume, 'Of interest' in *Essays Moral, Political and Literary* eds. T.H. Green and T.H. Grose (1931) Vol. I pp. 320–9; R. Cantillon, *Essai sur la nature du commerce en général* ed. H. Higgs (1931)].

4 [E. Cannan, *A History of the Theories of Production and Distribution in English Political Economy* (1893); F.A. Fetter, 'Recent discussion of the capital concept' *Quarterly Journal of Economics* 15 (November 1900) pp. 1–45; I. Fisher, *The Nature of Capital and Income* (1906)].

This is very thin. Hire of a piano, interest on land.

All yield rents. (quasi rents)

But interest. Net yield over cost.

Rate of Interest relationships between net yield and present value,

so that Rent and Interest become two different problems (Fetter).[5]

(3) But all this, save the last, not very fruitful in analytical interest.

Not interesting to classify, and abolition of classification seems to leave problems unsolved.

Emergence of distinction between capitalistic and noncapitalistic production.

Return to classificatory discussion. Three original factors?

At any moment Land (Nature) Labour Produced means of production.

But "produced means of production" derivative.

"Stored up" land and "stored up" labour.

(Problem of interest again. Why do land and labour not get all yield?)

This does suggest a distinction which may be useful.

Direct production – Hand to Mouth and Indirect.

Using factors of production in roundabout ways. Capitalistic production.
   (Involves "waiting" – unless some willing to postpone consumption cannot
   be done). More of that later.

Cross section in time.

Not merely consumption goods of first order.

Also a series of production goods at different stages.

Some on point of becoming consumer goods. Some a year behind. Some two
   years.

Take e.g. a forest. Suppose stationary equilibrium.

Sets of rows for cutting this year, next year and so on until you come to a set
   just planted.
   –

Suppose life of the tree is 20 years. 20 sets of rows of equal numbers making
   allowance for decay etc.

In stationary equilibrium as many trees planted as cut. Total number = number
   cut each year x length of production period.

Dangers of this example. A tree one year old a different commodity from tree
   two years old.

Remember goods of higher temporal orders change as they come down through
   time.

E.g. steel plates in hull of liner. Ore – steel – rolled – part of hull.

5 [F.A. Fetter, 'The relations between rent and interest' *American Economic Association Papers and Proceedings* 5 (February 1904)].

B.B.'s circles.[6]
Useful terminology.
Goods maturing at once; *present* goods maturing later than *future* goods.
Look back at cross section.
Factors of production applied at different points in series.
Labour which will mature five years hence – Land.

Remember for later. This paid for now. All outlays subject to discount process.

Productivity of roundaboutness.

   (a) More of same sort. B.B. and water.[7]
   (b) Thing inaccessible. Spectacles.

Durability.

---

6 [E. von Böhm-Bawerk, *The Positive Theory of Capital* (1891) Book II Chapter V The Theory of the Formation of Capital].

7 [E. von Böhm-Bawerk, *The Positive Theory of Capital* (1891) Book I Chapter II The Nature of Capital].

Part III 1935/36–1939/40

Introduction

Part III sections A & B

Editorial Note: All the lecture notes in this part come from Robbins's 1939–40 notebook. According to the syllabuses in the LSE Calendars and the student notes for 1938/39 (Urquidi) and 1939/40 (Ungphakorn), the first two lectures were given in 1938/39 and 1939/40. Lecture 3 'The subject matter of economics' is clearly dated 1934–35 but is included here because Robbins filed it in the 1939–40 notebook; there are traces of it in Urquidi's notes under the same title. The 1939–40 notebook also contains the notes for lectures on 'Production: Factors Flexible: Labour Supply', 'Price relationships in the Economic Equilibrium', 'Rent, Quasi Rent and Costs' and 'Profits', which were written in 1929/32 and are therefore in Part I above (Lectures 8, 15*. 21 and 22). The file opens with an outline of the course which is reproduced here.

Principles

[ADDED: History] *Introduction*

I Subject Matter
  II Ends and Means
  III Problems. Programme

Equilibrium
(a) Exchange
  IV Introduction to Theory of Exchange
  V The Individual
  VI Isolated Exchange
  VII Markets
(b) Production
  VIII Simple Production. The Labour Theory of Value
  IX Simple Production. Comparative Costs
  X Joint Production. The Laws of Returns
  XI Joint Production. The Firm
  XII Joint Production. Marginal Productivity
  XIII Capitalist Production

1 The development of scientific economics

The twofold root in philosophy and practice.

(1) [a] Plato and Aristotle. Part of enquiry concerning justice.

   Not important in itself. The slave state.
   But important as starting tradition.
   (b) The Schoolmen. The Just Price. Interest.
   Aquinas.

(2) Practice. (a) The Civil Servants and money. Kameralism.

   (b) The merchants and trade. Mercantilism.

(3) The reaction and the beginning of Economics.

   [a] The Physiocrats. *Naturrechtlich*. (Cantillon)[1]
   (b) The Scotch Philosophers.

The accident of enquiry and the philosophic tradition produces science.
   The Smithian system.

(4) The Classical System. Value and distribution.

   The Labour Theory
   The Ricardian Theory of Rent
   Malthus.

(5) The deficiencies of the classical system as a general system.

   The Jevonian Revolution

1 [R. Cantillon, *Essai sur la Nature du Commerce en général* trans. and ed. H. Higgs (London: Macmillan, 1931)].

[ADDED:](6) Historismus

> Good aspect
> Bad Denial of Laws Relativisim

(7) Socialism

> Classical Economics

Sociology

2 19th century economics

Rise of Classical School.
    Historical background. Population. War. Inflation
    War and extension cultivation. Ricardo's pamphlet.

Ricardo's Principles

    Ricardian doctrine

        Labour theory of value
        Comparative costs
        Rent
        Wages. Short and long
        Profits

Malthus. Population.
Other Ricardians Senior Mill etc.
Net effect. Value and Distribution the centre of picture.
Smithian Production in background
Influence. England chiefly. Smithianismus elsewhere.

Critics

1)   Socialism. Sismondi.

    Utopian.
    Marxian.

Directed attention to institutions.
Central theory classical.
(Theory of Capital and Fluctuation original)
Brought out disharmonies –
But *not* new principles.

2)   Historical School

    Chiefly German;
    Historical Method everywhere;

Twofold aspect.

    (1) Justified protest against overlooking of institutions – the provisional element.

    (2) Denial of fixed laws. This is one of the origins of present state of affairs.

Two phases. Roscher Hildebrand Knies. The sturdy and independent.
Schmoller etc. – the sycophantic.
(See Eucken)[1]

Deficiencies of Classical School not exposed. This must come from *with our* abstract method.

Attack on wage fund – Not really important.
Consciousness deficiencies – theory of value.
Labour Theory lacked generality.
Jevons – His letter.
The essence of the change Value and Utility.
Significance:

    (1) Individual
    (2) Conception subject matter
    (3) Causation.

Cost theories of value – Value of factors of production prior
Utility – reverse. Demand and factors of production.

    (4) System Walras and Marshall.

Since then, difficult to summarize.
Carrying over of marginal theory to money and interest.
Fluctuations.

---

1 [W. Eucken, 'Die Uberwindung des Historismus' *Schmollers Jahrbuch für Gesetzgebung, Verwaltung und Volkwirtschaft* (1938) pp. 191–214].

3 The subject matter of economics (1934–35)

This is one of the subjects dealt with in books (!). Hence rapid survey.

I. Definition

Economics is the science which studies human behaviour as a relationship between ends and scarce means which have alternative uses. More briefly – the disposal of scarce means (Disposal implies possibility of alternative uses).

Look at this.

(1) Economics a science. That is concerned with what exists or what might exist. Its function to explain. It is not concerned with the value of what exists. It does not say this is better or worse in ultimate sense. Good and bad alien terms. Of course this [is] not to say of immense help in this sort of judgment. If you want to know whether a certain course of conduct to be regarded as good or bad you need to know two things: objective effects of course of conduct [and] what judgment to be passed on this. Economics can't help with last – it can with first.

But what [is the] subject matter of [the] science? Examine conditions under which phenomena studied arise from:

(1) Multiplicity of ends
(2) Scarcity means
(3) Means with alternative uses
(4) Scales of valuation.
(5) Multiplicity of Ends.

Easy to see. If only one end – if only one thing wanted to do – no economizing possible – no economic aspect. Means used no alternative significance. Action involves no sacrifice. In fact of course the state one end a rare occurrence. If to die tomorrow – But in a continuous existence even if you want to do only one *kind* of thing you want to do it at different times. Thus *if time index appended different ends*. Greater or lesser achievement of these.[1]

The idea of one end mainly useful for contrast. But note this enables us to distinguish economic from technical questions. When we consider ways of achieving ends without considering other uses of means we are considering problems from technical point of view. Doing things regardless of money. Easy to see that technical and economic considerations may clash. The technical optimum. The economic optimum. Indeed they must clash, unless no scarcity and then no economic problem at all.

(2) Multiplicity of ends therefore essential.

But this [is] not enough. Suppose more than one end but enough means to satisfy all. No economizing – no sacrificing this for that – no "pull" of activities. The means must be limited in relation to ends i.e. be scarce. Something left unsatisfied.

(3) But scarcity of means not enough. Supposing means only capable of *one* use. Then there might exist multiplicity of means and ends without action with [an] economic aspect. In order that may have economic aspect there must be possibility of alternative uses. In practice, difficult to find illustration here. Scarce means may be specialized to one *kind* of use but yet possibility of using them at different times gives alternative uses and possibility of economizing. Best thing: isolated man finds some sort of food which must be eaten at once or go bad. May be scarce in regard to wants but not yet to be economized.

In the world we live in, we find all these conditions. People do have multiplicity of ends. Means are scarce and capable of alternative application. Hence, most acts of conduct have economic aspect. This is the subject matter of economics.

(3) [sic] Difference between this definition and others. Other definitions often fence off specific *kinds* of conduct and say this economic activity, e.g. Cannan – material welfare. I've argued inconvenience of this at great length. Nothing to add. Here note only that our definition does not do this. Any kind of behaviour can have economic aspect. We don't say some *ends* are economic and others are not, hence some behaviour is economic and others noneconomic.

Our criterion is a relation between any ends and any means. Scarcity with alternative uses. No economic ends as such.

You can put this another way. Different kinds of action may have an economic aspect at one time and not at others. Thus, procuring a drink of water in a place

---

1 In Book footnote on difference between *sparsamkeit* [thrift] and economy. Therefore, using resources specialized to one kind of case at different points of time.

where water is scarce has economic aspect. But getting drink beside a stream when nothing better to do at the time has not.

(4) [sic] Definition covers human behaviour in all sorts of social arrangements. Some definitions have tried to limit Economics to Exchange Economy. This is not so here. Covers actions of isolated man. Man in exchange society – complication can rearrange means by exchange and cooperative production. Behaviour of collective groups. Municipalities. Trusts. Collectivism.
(5) The definition studies a relationship. We don't study ends or means as such. Not ends – in sense of evolution of wants – psychology etc. etc.

Not means – technical properties technology or natural science.

Only relationships between ends and means as expressed in various ways.

But notice we do study certain relationships between particular ends and particular means. For they have bearing on means-ends relationship: e.g. complementarity of wants; complementarity of goods

But what [is] meant by behaviour as a relationship?

Essence of economizing that involves choice – surrender of one thing for another. Isolated man gives an hour's labour for a fish. Man in society gives a fish for two oranges or a shilling for two fish. Man in society gives an hours labour for the price of two fish. Thus we see the means-ends relationship seems to show itself as exchange – or can be conceived as such.

This important later on.

Next: closer examination of Ends and Means.

4   Ends and means

Ends

An end in Economics means a terminus of a particular end of conduct. An activity valued for its own sake as distinct from activity merely instrumental to something else. Thus I pick [an] apple – that is action to get apple into possession. I eat the apple. That is final consumption. Eating the apple there and then is an "end".

Now of course eating the apple may be regarded as merely the means to a larger "end" of sustaining life. That is legitimate enough, but not what we want. We want not ultimate ends in this sense but proximate ends. The larger ends, if you will, as translated into possibilities of particular acts of conduct.

This involves exact definition in regard to place and time.

Place obvious. Time ought to be equally so. Breakfast today and Breakfast tomorrow. In this sense can speak of a time structure of ends.

Note in this connection only in so far as needs are foreseen do they influence system of ends. Time structure a function of foresight. Actually, in history a series of end systems manifest themselves in action. But what actually happens is not necessarily at all a consistent end system. The ends can change from moment to moment.

Note a difficulty. The distinction clear cut in conception (activity which is end in itself and means to end) but blurred in practice. Thus I pick the apple in order to be in a position to eat it. But I also like picking apples. Life is full of this kind of thing. Does not disturb validity of distinction between means and ends. In this case, *two* ends are served by picking an apple. Procuring apple. Enjoyment of action. That's all.

(We shall notice similar difficulties with goods).

Finally, notice the Ends which are at one end of the Economic relationship neither individual or collective. Individual ends are simple.

Collective (Political Science, to say whose) Difficulty when they collide.

Means

Means of three kinds:

(1) One's own time[1]
(2) Other people's services
(3) Material goods.

If these are scarce in relation to ends they can be described as economic goods. Let us examine this concept more carefully.

(1) Note first scarce in relation to *given* ends. Relation to end the title to being an economic good. Not technical quality. A thing can be any economic good at one time and not at another. (Wells's story of man who could work miracles or lady who smashed the whisky.) Difficulty thus created for statistics. Physical computations meaningless. Bear this in mind judging statistics of five year plan.
(2) Second, note not what good will actually do that constitutes its relation to end. What it is believed to do – e.g. opium, patent medicine, doctors. This not always realized. Menger e.g.[2] Menger thought to be a good, following conditions had to be satisfied.

(a) Need
(b) Technical capacity to supply (a)
(c) Knowledge of this
(d) Ability to get hold of good in question on part of someone.

But this raises intolerable difficulties. Need for whisky? Judgments about other people's judgment of what is good for them etc. Nonscientific judgments. Must take ends as given. And ends must be defined in relation to actual objects of *verkehr* [trade].[3]

Note that goods must be defined not merely by reference [to] tech[nical] qualities but also [by] reference [to] space and time. Two important rules. Goods of like kind in different places are not the same class of economic good.

Coffee in London. Coffee in Brazil.
Coal in the valley. Coal in the hotel at top of mountain.
(This provides important clue to price relationships).
Goods of like technical kind at different times not same good.
Strawberries in June. Strawberries in November.
(This again important for price relationships).[4]

---

1 Note (to come in lecture) Time thus on both sides:
   The structure of ends
   The system of means – Time as complementary good.
2 [C. Menger, *Grundsätze der Volkwirtschaftslehre* (1871)].
3 Relation of this to Liberalism (footnote).
4 Examples. Applied Ec. Resale price maintenance.

So much for conception of goods. Now for *relationships*.

(1) As regards purposes served:

    (a) Goods may be related as regards substitutability.
        Coffee – tea (Consumption)
        Unskilled labour – machines (Production)

Notice – degrees of substitutability – this to be studied later on.

But in meantime – collections which are perfect substitutes -same price. This fundamental.

Also notice conception of substitution enable us to define "same good".

Goods of similar technical properties etc. which are perfect substitutes.

Easy to see how this involves similar place index. Similar time index.

    (b) Goods may be related as *complements*.
        E.g. Bread and Butter. Knives and Forks etc. (Consumption)
        Machine Minder (Production)
        This enables us to see the position of time as a complementary good.

I want to eat and I want to read within the period of 9–9.30. Operations cannot be done at same time. Each involves use of time. Time has to be economized even if food and books are free goods.

    (c) Specific and nonspecific.[5]

(2) So much as regards purposes served. Now for relationship in production.

    (a) Some goods joint products – i.e. the production of one necessarily involves production of others. Gas and Coke. Wool and mutton etc. Note – only when second good an economic [good] that [it is] relevant to our discussion. Useless bye products.
    (b) Much more important. Direct and indirect relation to consumption. E.g. Bread on plate satisfies directly. Flour etc. indirectly. Barber Iron founder. Significance *derived* from direct. This gives rise todistinction between consumption goods and production goods.

Note *not merely* difference of technical kind. E.g. Bread on plate and Bread in larder. Bread in larder – or at any rate in Baker's shop a production good. Always remember space and time indices.

Moreover same technical good may be both consumption good and production good. The train which carries men and milk. The fire which bakes bread and warms kitchen. Marshall on this account objected to division. This is absurd.

Note finally that production goods enjoy status not merely in relation to consumption but in relation to other production goods.

---

5 Classification *at* a point of time.
    Seldom absolute. Degrees of specificity.

E.g. pig iron no good unless coal blast furnace etc.

Supposing these disappear – strike etc – cease to be economic good.

Distinction prod[uction] and con[sumption] good useful enough for some purposes.

But on any refined view insufficient.

Different degrees of indirectness.

Bread on plate – Bread in larder – Bread in Baker's shop – Flour – Wheat – Seed.

Necessary to study relationships between these.

To do this, Menger invented terms goods of "first" and "higher" orders.

"First" means:

Higher remoter from consumption use.

Plant's objection. Can't start at other end. Processes of different complexity.

But if you like earlier and later stages.

This brings me to another point. At any moment goods of first and higher orders coexisting. But at a later moment things will have moved on; higher will have become lower. Present goods – future goods (Note: this is not only a meaning of future goods). Better think of each good with label showing when yielding consumption use.

Thus we may speak of a time structure of means a *time structure of production*. E.g. forest. Ready for cutting next year – saplings.

This to be studied most minutely later on.

Meanwhile, yet another distinction within production goods. Some made, some given by nature. Everything [that] comes [from] Nature and Labour can be analysed back. Therefore divide into original means of production, intermediate products, produced means of production. This again is very important later on.

Read

F.H. Knight, *Risk, Uncertainty and Profit* (1921)

Richard Strigl, *Die ökonomischen Kategorien und die Organisation der Wirtschaft* (1923)

P.H. Wicksteed, ' "Elementary mathematical economics", "political economy and psychology" and "final utility" ' *Palgrave's Dictionary of Political Economy* (1926) Vol. I pp. 583–5, Vol. II pp. 140–2 and 857–9 [all of which Robbins included in Vol. 2 of his edition of Wicksteed's *Common Sense of Political Economy* (1933)]

Hans Mayer, 'Bedürfnis' in *Handwörterbuch der Staatswissenschaften* Vol. 2 (1924) pp. 450–6

Franz Cuhel, *Zur Lehre von den Bedürfnissen* (1907)

Leo Schönfeld, *Grenznutzen und Wirtschaftsrechnung* (1924)

Programme

Aim explanation economic phenomena.

What this means. Reduction to terms of data.

E.g. price changes. Explained when show how this arises from change in conditions of demand, change in conditions of supply etc.

Now this complex. Must be solved in stages. Arbitrary nature arrangements. Propose here three divisions.

(1) Statics. Describe conditions constancy. Example.
(2) Comparative Statics. Compare different states equilibrium. Examples.
(3) Dynamics. Describe change conditions. Examples.

Contrast Production and Distribution.

Statics

5   Valuation and exchange

Introduction

First main division of work. Disposal of goods.

Clear that this implies value. Exchange depends on value. Disposal of goods of individual.

But look at assumptions – goods given. No production. Obvious therefore all expl[anations of] value which invoke productive process out of place. Labour Theory of Value. Our goods may have been produced or may have fallen like manna. They are given. Clear that there is a value problem here. This admitted even by those who believed Labour Theory. Old masters, rare wines etc. Value clearly out of relation to effort of production. We here take this case as general. Ask how value arises. Our assumptions cut us off from explanation in terms of supply. Demand side invoked.

This done fairly early. Say.[1] German Economists. Value in exchange depended on value in use. But what [is] "value in use". Depended on *class* of need. Needs arising from demands of life higher than comforts; comforts higher than luxuries. E.g. Bread which sustains life more useful than butter etc. etc. Not difficult to see that this out of touch with reality. But examine the theory more closely. Deficiencies very illuminating.

(1) Value in use to *whom*? We have seen already nothing an economic good but thinking makes it so. Now some prefer tea others whisky. What has causal significance? Pretty clear the conception of an abstract value in use presupposes an absolute scale of values. But this an ethical not a scientific idea. No reason to suppose helpful in explaining what is.
(2) Value depends on *class* of use. But surely improbable that class without number significant. Presumption is that value varies with supply.
(3) Value depends on class of use. But same class of good serves different classes of need. Corn to feed man make whisky and feed parrots.

---

1 [J.B. Say, *Traité d'Economie Politique* (1804)].

Nor is this exception. When we think of goods of higher orders we can see that this is not exception but rule. How determine their value on *Gebrauchswerttheorie* ["use value theory"].

(4) Value depends on use. But in fact value of an object does not always depend on concrete use it serves. I have six sacks of corn one sack makes my bread another feeds my horse another makes whisky another feeds my chickens. The value to me of the sack which makes my bread [is] not the utility of having bread. But utility of feeding chickens. If lost it would be chickens go short not I.

(5) Value depends on use. How explain case of free goods. Water is useful, supremely so. Little or no value. Adam Smith so impressed that made pretext for abandoning any attempt to explain connection value in use and value in exchange at all.

The things which have the greatest value in use have frequently little or no value in exchange, and on the contrary those which have the greatest value in exchange have frequently little or no value in use. Nothing is more useful than water but it will purchase scarce anything: scarce anything can be had in exchange for it. A diamond on the contrary has scarce any value in use: but a very great quantity of other goods may frequently be had in exchange for it. W.N. I p 30[2]

Contrast the *Paradox of Value* and the *Gebrauchswert* ["use value"] theory breaks down.

But is there nothing in idea?

Clearly in an exchange between two men what obtained thought more of than what given. A comparison here.

Something in idea. De Quincey[3] others.

In 1871 Jevons Menger Walras.[4] Gossen[5] before etc etc. The subjective theory of value.

Contrast with *Gebrauchswert* theory.

(1) Individual valuations – social value not in it. Alcohol opium etc. etc.

(2) Not a class valued but concrete goods. This clears up Smith's difficulty. Water and diamonds. A drop of water and a diamond. Is there a paradox here.

(3) Value of concrete good. Thus number of concrete goods available will count. Value a relation between number and need. Scarcity.

2 [A. Smith, *An Inquiry into the Nature and Causes of the Wealth of Nations* ed. E. Cannan (1904)].

3 [T. De Quincey, *Logic of Political Economy* (1844)].

4 [W. Stanley Jevons, *The Theory of Political Economy* (London: Macmillan, 1871); C. Menger, *Grundsätze der Volkswirtschaftslehre* (1871); L. Walras, *Elements d'economie politique pure ou theorie de la richesse sociale* (Lausanne, 1874)].

5 [H.H. Gossen, *Entwicklung der Gesetze des menschlichen Verkehrs und der daraus fliessenden Regeln für menschliches Handeln* (1854)].

(4) Not actual use that thing serves but *dependent* use (*Abhangignutzen*). The sacks of corn.

(5) This clears up difficulty free goods. Water so much no specific use dependent on particular bucket.[6]

So much for a general outline. As we shall see development of the theory underlying the whole theory of equilibrium. But detailed application needed.
[ADDED IN PENCIL:]

History Marginal Utility
Jevons[7]
Austrians
Pareto
Wicksteed[8]
Hicks-Allen.[9]

6 On all this Komorzynski useful [J. von Komorzynski, *Der Wert in der isolierte Wirtschaft* (Vienna: Manz, 1889)].

7 [W. Stanley Jevons, *The Theory of Political Economy* (1871)].

8 [V. Pareto, *Manuel d'economie politique* (1927); P.H. Wicksteed, *The Common Sense of Political Economy* (1910)].

9 [R.G.D. Allen and J.R. Hicks, 'A reconsideration of the theory of value' *Economica new series* Vol. 1 (February and May 1934) pp. 52–76 and 196–219)].

6 Individual valuation

Now to more detailed analysis. First individual disposing stock of goods. Consider first individual [in] isolation. Stock of one kind of good.

Recollect Böhm-Bawerk's example sacks of corn.[1]

Table of wants satisfied by such a commodity:

A	B	C	D
IV			
III	III		
II	II	II	
I	I	I	I
0	0	0	0

Fundamental assumption here an order of wants.

Clear that if three units distributed

A	B	C
IV		
III	III	
II	II	II

distribution in such a way that impossible rearrangement to fill higher place in scale. If stock reduced least important use relinquished.

Now consider complication. Individual confronted by market *fixed ratios* of exchange – i.e. by surrendering some of what he has he can acquire another commodity. Problem – how in equilibrium will his holding of *both*be distributed between each?

Extend idea of scheme of uses. Individual can judge – given holding – what quantity of second commodity equivalent to one unit of that he has.

1 [*The Positive Theory of Capital*, Book III Part A Chapter III].

Thus given 20 units of corn one unit corn equal significance two units of coal.

Scale		Corn	units
		|	4
		|	3
	coal	|	2
		|	1
		|	0

Note(1) a marginal valuation – might ask total – how much coal all corn. Not usual. Yet if so, not necessarily same as marginal.

(2) Clearly changes with changes in supply of each commodity. Dependent use changes.
(3) Relative valuation.
(4) No measurement of utility. 1 corn = 2 coal. Only an order implied. 1 corn greater than 1 coal less than 3 coal.

Now look at market. It too expresses a ratio – an objective ratio. These can be compared in a scale. Suppose individual values corn and coal as 1:1 and market as 1:4.

Individual		*Market*	
	|	|	corn
	|	|	
corn	|	|	

Clearly an incentive to change corn into coal. Gets what values as 1 for 1/7. No equilibrium. Exchanges some. As this happens valuation changes. Will stop when own valuation and market are together.

Individual		*Market*	
	|	|	
	|	|	
corn	|	|	corn
	|	|	

Won't go beyond – for would be giving something valued more for something valued less.

Description of Equilibrium. When M[arginal] S[ignificance]. Relative utility equal ratio of exchange. Same position on individual scale as market scale.

Set this out more elaborately by indifference curve method.

We can suppose individual in possession of all manner of combination of commodities 1 W 10 C 10 W 1 C etc. These can be mapped on coordinates.

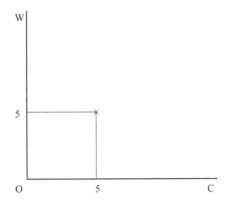

Some combinations he will prefer to others.
Some will be of equivalent significance.
Thus e.g. we can conceive a series:

C	7½	6	5	4	3
W	3	4	5	6	7½

etc.

These can be plotted

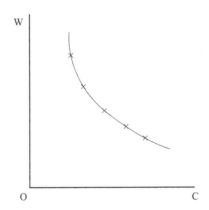

and joined by a smooth curve if we assume continuous variation. This is an indifference curve. The whole thing can be covered by curves of this sort.

Look at meaning of curves. Each curve an indifferent set of combinations. But clearly each set of indifferent combinations different as regards choice. E.g. 10:10 is greater than 9:9 i.e. is preferred. Clearly curves near origin less preferred than curves further away 10:10 9:9. Until point when one or other commodity or both becomes objectionable. (This applies only to the positive segment).

Now if we could measure satisfactions could erect axis – indifference lines as contours – Hill of pleasure. But this illegitimate – and unnecessary. Measurement ordinal not cardinal. Pictures. Hence simply indices I II III – This is all we want. Many Hills.

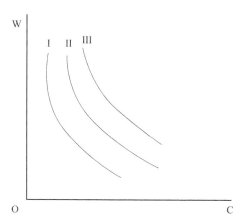

It follows that no indifference curve can cut another.
Why? Suppose contrary.

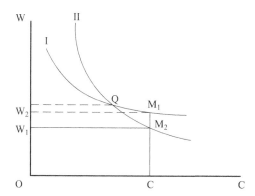

Intersect at O. It follows that combination at 1 = combination at 2 because both equal combination at Q. But this is absurd. M_2 is composed of OC corn + OW_1 wine and M_1 OC + OW_2. That difference is OW_2 – OW_1 wine. But such a pair cannot be indifference unless wine has no significance.

Now look at single curves. Convex to origin. Why?

Express diminishing relative utility. Look closer. Imagine it magnified so that the short stretch of curve is a straight line.

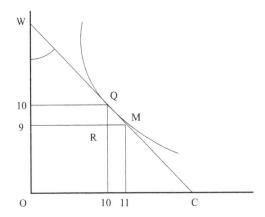

This means when 10:10 if W by 1 C has to increase by 1 to maintain equivalence. Therefore marginal significance of wine in terms of corn 1:1 (This our old friend.) (Subjective *price* of corn in wine terms QR/RM (or tan triangle OCW) or wine in terms of corn RM/QR (or tan triangle OWC OR cot triangle OCW))[2] Thus we can express m[arginal] s[ignificance] in terms of slopes.

Back to original diagram:

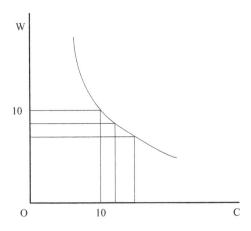

When 10:10 m.s. of corn 1 wine. But 9:11 less wine more corn perhaps only 3/4 – certainly not 1. Means while base of triangle same perpendicular less, therefore tan triangle less. Therefore curve convex.

2 tan = Perp/Base   cot = Base/Perp.

This is "law of diminishing utility". More of C and less of W the less C in terms of W *or* (this increasing marginal substitution) the more W in terms of C. No reason to suppose any exception to this.

Suppose corn ceases to have use. Then curve flattens out.

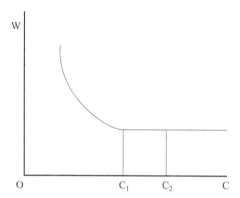

Addition from $C_1 C_2$ no significance (m.s. = perp/base = 0).
Suppose it becomes noxious.

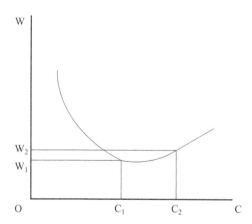

Then turns up. Meaning from C_1 C_2 involves $W_1 - W_2$ if combination to remain indifferent.

Thus far the individual. Now the Market with which he is confronted.

We have just seen that can represent subjective "price" by slopes. Same for actual prices. Thus:

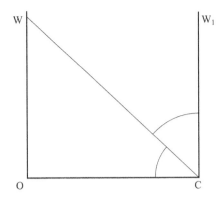

Corn can be turned into wine at rate of OW/OC = tan OCW

or wine into corn at OC/OW = tan OWC (which is the same as tan WCW_1).

If fixed prices in market individual can change if wishes.

Represent this by covering our map [with price lines]. Now let us draw complete picture tastes and obstacles.

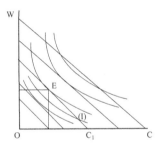

Suppose our buyer has OC_1 corn. Suppose he moves up to (1). Is he in equilibrium? No. Can travel ahead to E which touches higher indifference curve. Would not go beyond – on lower curve. Therefore in equilibrium where price line tangent to indifference curve, but tangent to indifference line gives m.s. Therefore there is equilibrium where m.s. equals price.

Now a step further. Clearly we may consider a number of points of equilibrium with different prices.

When value of corn in terms of wine OCP_1 offers M_1C for ON_1 wine.

When $P_2 M_2C$ for ON_2 etc. "Offer" curve. Equilibrium where cut by particular price. Now turn round clockwise. Or over.

What is this but a Marshall "international trade" curve showing:

(a) Demand for wine as function price of wine tan POW; or

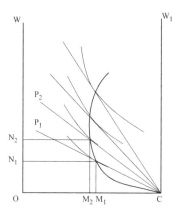

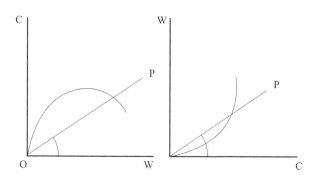

(b) Supply of corn as function price of corn tan POC?[3]

But now one step further. We can easily turn Marshall curve into our ordinary demand or supply curve.

Conditions of demand for wine. Conditions of supply of corn.

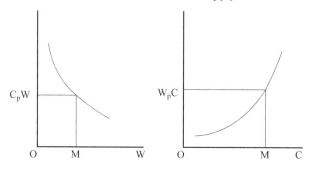

3 [A. Marshall, *The Pure Theory of Foreign Trade; the Pure Theory of Domestic Values* (1879) reprinted in the LSE Series of Scarce Works in Political Economy (1930)].

The exact derivation is not difficult. Given at length Sir H. Cunningham's Geometrical Political Economy p 108–111.[4]

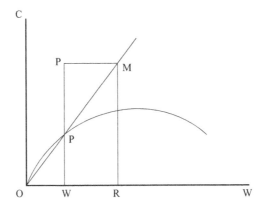

Given a Marshall curve. Demand for wine. Problem to derive unit curve.

X axis at right. But to represent corn price of wine Y axis unsatisfactory – too small – multiplier needed.

Measure OR [and] erect perp[endicular]

Project OP to cut perp at m.

Erect perp WPp. Draw Mp. Then pw = price multiplied by OR.

Demand curve a locus of such points.

Proof: pW = MR = OR.PW/OW. But PW/OW = price of wine in corn. OR is the multiplier.

Next in this connection notice elasticity of demand.

Conception familiar – I use Schultz's definition[5] – the proportion by which a given relative change in price alters the quantity demanded when the relative changes are small.

(The ratio of the relative change in the quantity to the corresponding relative change in price

$$n = (dx/x)/(dy/y)$$
$$= dx/dy.y/x$$

when x = quantity demanded and y price per unit)

n = 1 if given % change in price produces same % change in demand. Or a fall in price causes proportional increase in amount bought.

4 [H.H. Cunynghame, *Geometrical Political Economy* (Oxford: Clarendon Press, 1904)].

5 [H. Schultz, 'The statistical law of demand as illustrated by the demand for sugar' *Journal of Political Economy* Vol. 23 (October and December 1925) pp. 481–504 and 577–617].

Set this out geometrically. Marshall *Principles of Economics* 8th edition
p 102–3 and p 839. First unit curve (most familiar).

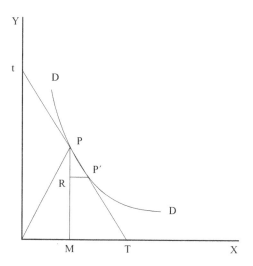

Draw PRM perp to OX and let PP' cut OX and OY.

P'R is the increment in commodity demanded which corresponds to diminution
PR in price.

Then elasticity = P'R/OM divided by PR/PM
(*proportionate change in amount demanded*)
proportionate change in price.

But this equals PR'/PR x PM/OM

= TM/PM x PM/OM
= TM/OM or PT/Pt.

In the limit PP' is tangent to PP.

Thus elasticity is PT/Pt or the tangent to the demand curve.

We can now see certain points regarding elasticity.

Suppose a straight line demand curve. Elasticity varies as you go along it.

Or a rectangular hyperbola: Elasticity same. Constant outlay curve.

Another way of judging elasticity: does curve cut rectangular hyperbola positively or negatively?

(By hypothesis $P_1A_1 = P_2A_2$ therefore P_2A_3 is obviously greater)

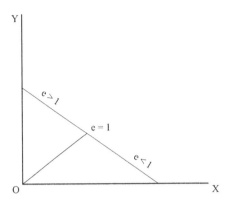

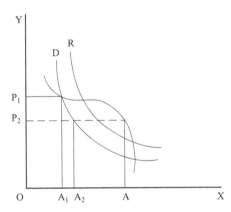

This notion of changes in the outlay leads to another idea of great importance –
marginal expenditure or outlay. What is this? When price changes outlay influenced by two things:

(i)   Increase (or decrease) due to increase (or decrease) in amount
(ii) Loss (or gain) due to change in price in infra marginal units.

Marginal expenditure resultant: if e = 1 balance; if e greater than 1 marginal
expenditure positive; if e less 1 negative. This can be exhibited by curve. M[arginal]
expenditure or outlay curve. (Same prop[erties] as M[arginal] Revenue.)
    If AD demand curve then P has rectangle BPEO outlay.
    If AD corresponding marginal outlay curve CE is marginal outlay at that point.
    Relation BPEO = AECO in area.
    Desirable to know how exactly to derive MO curve. Start with a straight line
demand curve.

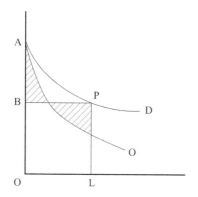

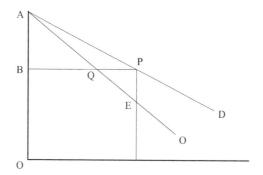

Area OP = area AC

Area BQECO is common. Therefore ABQ = QPE.
LB = LP (right angles)
LAQB = LPQE (opposite)
Therefore triangles are equal; therefore BQ = QP AB = PE.

Now to derive MO curve from D curve when not straight lines.

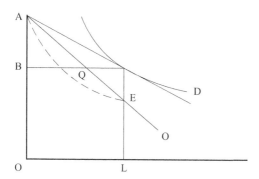

Draw tangent to curve at P.

Marginal value for tangent same as marginal value for curve here. We know that line which bisects BP gives marginal value for tangent.

PE = AB

EB is marginal value. Locus of points thus constructed is marginal curve.

Relation marginal outlay curve to demand curve depends on elasticity.

With the aid of the diagram this can be made very precise.

Elasticity = PE/PA

But (similar As) PE/PA = PC/AB

But AB = PE

Therefore ε = PC/AB = PC/PE = PC/(PC – EC)

= *Price (PC)*
Price – Marginal Outlay

This formula very important in monopoly theory. It also helps us to our final task here – to exhibit elasticity of demand on an integral curve.

Price = PB/OB

MO   = PR/TR = AT/OB

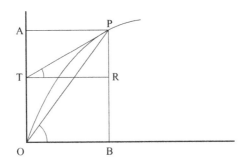

Therefore e = (PB/OB)/(PB/OB – AT/OB) = PB/(PB – AT) = OA/OT

This works out for e = 1 OA = OT.

A.P. Lerner, 'The diagrammatical representation of elasticity of demand' *Review of Economic Studies* (October 1933).

Another proof Alfred Marshall, *Money Credit and Commerce* (1923) p. 337.

7 Exchange continued

Barter between two individuals

So far individual vis-a-vis fixed prices. This enabled study of valuation.

Now study formation of prices. Start exchange two individuals. Encounter [of] peasant with wine and peasant with corn. Shall find our apparatus useful here. But let us commence with loose discussion – as before. May presume each has *some* use for both. Question whether any exchange takes place depends on relations relation between their valuations.

Suppose peasant with corn values one of corn as six of wine. Put this on scale apparatus.

Peasant with wine   Peasant with corn
value one unit of corn in terms of wine

No exchange possible for possessor of corn values it more highly than the possessor of wine.

But suppose a reverse case. The peasant with wine values corn as six wine and the peasant with corn values it as three wine.

Now an exchange is possible. At any rate between three of wine for one of corn and six both parties will gain. Suppose 1:4. Then P_c gives what values at 3 and gets 4. And P_w gives what values at 1/6 and gets 1/4.

These examples give us conditions of equilibrium. Will exchange if valuation lower than price. Will not if higher. Exchange therefore ceases when commodities occupy same place in relative scales of exchanges. E.g.

when relative utilities of commodities same to each party to exchange. Observations on this:

(1) Implies divisibility. If not then nearest position to this.
(2) No measuring of utilities implied.

Wicksell's formula.[1]
M.U. of wine to P_w = *M.U. of wine* to P_c
M.U. of corn M.U. of corn
Same as ours but implies utility independently measured.

(3) Nor personal comparisons of utility enjoyed. Only position on scale.
(4) No assumption relative utilities 1:1. Loose talk about equal marg[inal] Ut[ility] all commodities. Not so. Same to each party to exchange.

Equilibrium when for each corn = 4 wine. Not only when 1 corn = unit wine.

Thus far described conditions when exchange stops. But notice *no* determinate price. Look again at data: P_w 1:6 P_c 1:3.

Any intermediate rate possible. Therefore initial rate indeterminate. But if this [is] so final rate indeterminate too. For valuations are marginal relative to quantity possessed.

Suppose P_w makes very good terms – e.g. 1:3 1/2. Then gets at that rate much corn for small sacrifice wine. Valuation corn less probably that if better. Thus approaches more rapidly P_cs.

All this is more intelligible with diagrams.

Let us take persons separately.

1.   Peasant with corn. We may draw for him an indifference map.

Suppose he has OC_1 corn. I_1C_1 is indifference curve touching X axis at this point. Meaning of this:

Clear that tan V_1C_1O limiting rate at which will exchange few units.

1 [*Lectures on Political Economy* (1934) Vol. I p. 50].

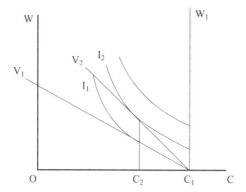

Why? Because V_1C_1 tangent to I_1C_1 and I_1C_1 is indifferent i.e. *no* advantage for him. Suppose exchanges a few at better rate C_1C_2 at V_2C_10. Then on new indifference curve I_2 and this curve now sets limit.

[2.] Now take peasant with wine.

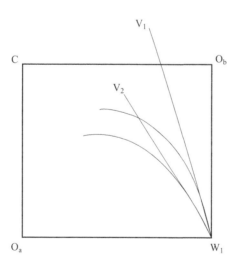

He possesses OW_1 wine. He will exchange if price of corn is less than tan $V_1W_10_a$ i.e. if price of wine is more than tan $V_1W_10_b$. Similarly with P_c: if he gets onto new indifference curve tangent to that it becomes limiting rate.

Now superimpose these two maps.

Any rate of exchange between I_{a1} and I_{b1} is possible.

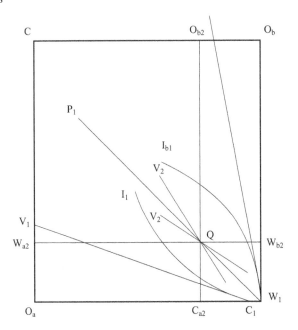

Note if P_c *compelled* to follow I_{a1} in successive bargains neither gain or lose. Similarly if $P_w I_{b1}$.

Suppose exchange at P_1 so that P_c sacrifices $C_1 C_2$ corn for $W_1 W_2$ wine (he then has $O_a C_{a2}$ corn and $O_a W_{a2}$ wine) and $P_w W_{b1} W_{b2}$ wine for $C_1 C_2$ corn?

Now no equilibrium. New range advantageous exchange rates $V_2 Q V_2$.

Eventually must reach point at which indifference curves touch i.e. have common tangent or the same relative utility of commodities exchanged.

Thus a point of equilibrium. No advantageous bargains afterwards (V_a above V_b). A continuous series of points of tangency between different individual indifference curves. Edgeworth's *contract curve*.

Edgeworth and Marshall always drew it turned round.

(See Math[ematical] Psychics p 28 Papers II pp 307 and 316. Marshall 8th Ed p 844–5 Math Ap[pendix] Note XII[2] *bis*).[3]

Now recollect *offer curves*.

Constructed on assumption any series exchanges all at one price.

Clear must intersect on contract curve.

2 [F.Y. Edgeworth, *Mathematical Psychics: An Essay on the Application of Mathematics to the Moral Sciences* (London: Kegan Paul, 1881) and 'Applications of mathematics to political economy' and 'On the determinateness of economic equilibrium' in *Papers Relating to Political Economy* (London: Macmillan, 1925) Vol. II pp. 273–312 and 313–19; A. Marshall, *Principles of Economics* 8th edition (1920) Mathematical Appendix].

3 Also Chapman p. 151 Outlines [S.J. Chapman, *Outlines of Political Economy* (London: Longmans, 1911)]

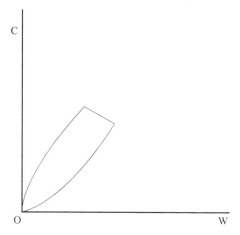

Why? Each point on offer curve marks point tangency indifference curve price slope.

Intersection therefore at price line tangent to two indifference curves. This lies on contract curve.

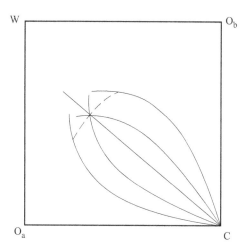

But no guarantee that this reached in barter between two individuals.

If hit on at first could go through at that rate till end. Marshall calls it true equilibrium rate. Why?

At that rate offers are equal.

Nothing brings this about.

Suppose they are proceeding by single bargains, as in the case of two monopolies. Bargaining as to price. Then if P_w were stronger bargainer will choose price at which P_c's offer curve tangent to his own indifference line. Why? Highest point possible.

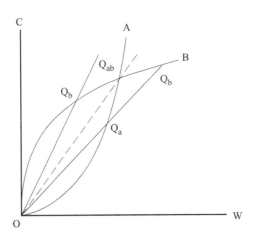

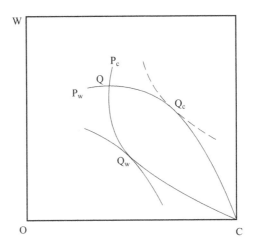

$Q_w Q Q_c$ bargaining locus.
Competition two commodities.
Now introduce many individuals.

Assume perfect knowledge. Therefore law of single price.

Assume trial bargains (Edgeworth's recontract). Then for each individual price and m.s equal. (And price will be such as to equalize amount demanded and supplied).

This expressed geometrically:

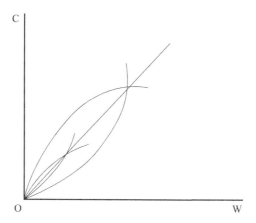

8   Valuation and exchange

Multiple exchange

The next task. Many individuals. Many commodities. Corn wine sheep – Multiple Exchange. This not only difference. Introduce Money. Indirect Exchange.

Definitions. Direct exchange: A B corn wine own consumption.

Indirect exchange: A gives corn for wine in order to get with wine someone else's wool. Money. General medium indirect exchange. Question of degree. No world money.

Justify transition money. When three commodities indirect exchange possible. Not inevitable. A has corn B wine C wool. A takes some wine and wool B some corn and wool C some corn and wine. But more probable A wants wool C wants wine B wants corn. Therefore indirect exchange.

Moreover suppose direct exchange separate markets

Corn against wine
Corn against wool
Wine against wool

   – Three rates of exchange

Will they be *consistent*?
E.g.

C.Wi	1–2	
C.Wo	1–4	
Wc.Wo	2–4	1–2

Is it not likely

1–2	Co. Wi
1–4	C.Wo
2–6 (1–3)	Wi.Wo

But in this case an *arbitrage* advantageous. I.e. if I want to get wool and I have corn. Instead of exchanging 1 corn for 4 wool, exchange 1 corn for 2 wine and with 2 wine get 6 wool. Thus an incentive to indirect exchange.

Thus in simplest cases indirect exchange arises.

When more commodities, indirect exchange with different media equally inconvenient. Money tends to emerge. Hence transition.

Implications of assumption. Community has two aspects: buyer and seller.

Barter buyers and sellers at once; part with corn to get wine.

Under money I buy in one market and sell in another. I buy with what I have obtained by selling.

In a sense distinction is linguistic. E.g. sale of hat. I buy hat, sell money, sell hat, buy money. But this is an unusual way of putting things.

Deeper significance of this. Use of Money means Say's Law no longer applicable. What is Say's Law? Demand for one commodity supply of others.

Demand for corn the offer of wine. Or demand for corn offer of wine and wool. No need for proof of this. Obvious.

But now if money exists the closed circle is broken. Exchange of goods is no longer Goods for Goods but Goods for Money for Goods.

Demand for money is amount of money offered for them. Not *directly* amount of goods other than money (Supplies)

This clearly gives opportunity for disharmony between total demand and total supply.

Either more money put in then total money demand more than total cost of production etc. Increase velocity.

Or some taken out or diminished velocity. Total demand less than total cost of production.

But so long as amount money unchanged and spent at same rate this disharmony not present. System *as if* Say's Law applicable. Neutral Money.

In what follows this assumption made.

(Note: *not* the same as assumption constant price level. Variations theory. Increase goods prices fall).

So much by way of preliminary. Our problem to describe conditions of equilibrium in market*s*. (Note markets. If disequilibrium in one place disequilibrium elsewhere).

But proceed by stages: (1) Individual (2) Markets.

A. To commence with Individual assume a certain amount money to spend in a certain period. System of ends etc. given. When examining barter idea of scale of relative valuations used. Have recourse to this here.

Given money and possessions – marginal valuations different things to be acquired. Notes on this:

1)   Expressed in terms of money

Diagrammatic apparatus of last lecture:

```
6    –    shirt
5    –
4    –    wine
3    –    theatre ticket
2    –
1    –
          Haircut
          Newspaper
0
```

What units. Minimum sensible. Different people.
(Expand in book).

2)   Scale expressed in terms of money. But implies valuation of money.

If I value 1 corn as 2 wine I value 2 wine as 1 corn.
Therefore

Wine	Corn
– (1 corn)	–
1 –	– 2 wine

So with more extensive scale.
This important for theory of money (Mises Marshall) later on.

3)   Note dealing with many commodities. Hitherto one or two. Position of each on scale dependent on quantity possessed *of others* as well as of it.

Recall relationships described in earlier lecture.
Substitutability. Bread and other food.
Complementarity. Some needs only active in conjunction with others. House and furniture.
Hence concept of dependent use very complex. Rearrangements. Rosenstein.[1]
Mathematicians.[2]

4)   Total valuations must not exceed resources.

So much for relative scale of individual. Individual confronted in markets with series of opportunities of exchange. Prices.
Prices also value goods in money terms. A 1/– B 2/– C 3/ – – – Note: Rates not amounts.
Now link up with what said in lecture on direct exchange.
Possibility of exchange when thing to be acquired higher on relative scale of individual than terms on which can be got. If I value wine as 2 of corn and I can get it for 1 of corn –
When our consumer goes out to buy he will certainly find that possessing relatively much money many things valued by market lower than by him.
An inducement to buy.
As he buys any good marginal significance of good falls – Each unit spent less of other things which might have bought – A approaches point occupied on market relative scale.

1   [P. Rosenstein-Rodan, 'Grenznutzen' in *Handwörterbuch der Staatswissenwschaften* Vol. IV (1927) pp. 1190–913].
2   Extend this in book.

Equilibrium reached when goods occupy same position on his relative scale as on markets.

Or when terms on which he buys goods correspond to his valuations of goods in money terms.

Put it yet another way. Money distributed in such a way that cannot be withdrawn from one use and spent on another without loss being greater than gain.

Here we come on celebrated generalization of utility theory. In a state of equilibrium marginal utilities of different commodities proportionate to price. (*Das Gesetz der Grenznutzen niveau*) This is much criticized. Way I have put it open to Mayer's strictures[3] or Rosenstein's.[4]

Notes on this description of equilibrium:

1) *Time*. As stated timeless. But implies time. Money distributed in such a way as to involve equivalent significance at all points in unit period.

This brings us to a point encountered in lecture on classification goods.

Easy enough to see in case of perishable goods.

But goods durable. Suit. House.

Remember yield use *through* time. Compare daily use with ephemeral goods. Suit costing £12 – £1 per month – 8d a day.

But this has to be bought in lump. This means much less available for other things at beginning. May be impossible. Whereas if available bit by bit possible.

Hence advantage of *hire*. Someone else advances money. Key to part of Interest theory.

2) Divisibility assumed. If not then as we have seen equilibrium incomplete. E.g. price of pair of shoes 30/-. Value one pair 40/-. Second pair 20/-.

Indivisibility of two kinds. (a) Timeless, and (b) In time.

(a) Timeless. Only sell by yard. Here very often qualitative differences help.
(b) House all year round. Car. Here device of hire useful.

B. But how are prices fixed? Market Equilibrium.
I. Single market first. (a) One seller.
Prices fixed by sellers. But this not all. Look closer. Assume single seller. Not able deal with buyers separately. Simple Monopoly.

Will try to imagine number bought at different prices. Will fix price where maximum gain. What is doing really trying to estimate valuations of buyers at different margins.

---

3 M. thinks if true elasticities equal. This wrong.
4 [H. Mayer, 'Untersuchungen zu dem Grundgesetz der wirthschaftlichen Wertrechnung' *Zeitschrift für Volkwirtschaft und Socialpolitik* Vol. I (1921) pp. 431–58 and Vol. II (1922) pp. 1–23; P. Rosenstein-Rodan, 'Grenznutzen' *Handwörterbuch der Staatswissenschaften* (1927) pp. 1190–223].

(b) Intermediate case

(a) Duopoly, Similar goods. (b) Competing goods.

(c) Now assume many sellers. Each anxious to sell whole stock. Competition.

Law of indifference. Single price. Buy cheapest. (Assumption here no attachment special dealers.)

Each seller try to fix price take off all goods. Again trying to read minds of all buyers and having regard to quantity in market to fix equilibrium price.

See how market works in more detail.

(1) Collective error. Assume fix price too high. Find stock being left on hand. Too low running out fast.

(11) But suppose *some* fix price too high. Suppose e.g. equilibrium price 6 and they ask 7. Transfer to others. These can raise price too and if keep below others, say 6 1/2, sell out at that price. This means curtailed market. The people who have made mistake have to lower price below 6. (Possible custom at 6 destroyed by forcing people to buy at 6 1/2 get substitutes.) Thus punished by failure to hit mark. Note at close of market no perfect equilibrium. Why. People who bought at high price buy from those who bought at low. But the new equilibrium not same as original ideal. Change of property distribution meantime.

(c) Now assume sellers only sell whole stock if price at some critical point. Does this complicate situation Supply schedule. No simply that valuations of sellers are operative. Reserve prices. People who go to market not knowing whether to buy or to sell.[5]

Now widen again. Markets interconnected. Amount bought in one market depends on amount bought in others. E.g. more market – e.g. mall.

Conditions of equilibrium:

(1) Individual relative scales coincide with communal relative scale.

I.e. marginal significances of different commodities same to different consumers.

(2) Demand = supply

Assumes constant stock of money held by different economic subjects.

Time again. Rates of supply and demand.[6]

---

5 [Here two very rough diagrams with the comment 'Errors in this explained later' were crossed through].

6 At this point the following was crossed through:

'Speculation (Production)

Function to bring about equilibrium through time.

Suppose error. Price too low stock throughout year. E.g. Price 50. Pay to buy until this price reached (Interest neglected here) If beyond it later on unload at lower price'.

9 Production

Factors fixed: simple

A. Start first with *Individual Economy* (Robinsoniad).

Factors fixed = in this case fixed working day.
(Assume equal reactions different productive activities.)
Clear situation not radically dissimilar from market situation.
Relative scales same.
No market scale. But series of technical opportunities. Environmental scale. Sacrifice time sacrifice money.

Therefore same fundamental generalizations apply. (1) Productive operations so arranged as to bring individual scale into harmony with objective scale; or (2) distribution of time such that no rearrangement without cost greater than gain.

Example of fish and oranges. Assumption equal attractiveness implied. Remove it. Fish debited with unpleasantness credit oranges. (Same as "buying for charity" in market). (Assumption equal effectiveness work hour by hour).

Note on costs. Time? But time not valued except product under our assumption. Cost of fish oranges value of.

B. Now introduce *society*. Competition.

(1) Preliminary assumption (a) Equal skill (b) Equal natures. (c) Assume further at first equal attractions.

Notice no separate income problem. Price problem and income problem are one. No employer. No apparatus of contract. Product market *is* factor market. (Compare value distribution approach).

Description of equilibrating process. Final equilibrium. Market equilibrium and Equal incomes because if not swap over.

Remove assumption equal attractions. Unequal prices and incomes. Equal net advantages. Each producer getting as much where he is as he could hope to get elsewhere.

(2) Introduce Employers. Normal Profits. Product markets and factor markets now different. But competition makes difference between incomes and sum of prices = normal profits.

Costs in this context. *Wieser's Law*.[1]

Relevance of this technical progress. If prices below costs anywhere factors need reshuffling.

Excursus on labour theory of value[2]

Point reached at which we can introduce L.Th.V.

Note that our discussion of production *includes* value. Price of products and price of factors determined simultaneously. Useful at this early stage look at old explanation in terms of production costs.

What was Labour Theory of Value?

Prevalent classics. Particular classics not. E.g Ricardo much more complex. Present idealized version. Two forms:

(1) Commodities have value because labour embedded in them.
(2) That exchange ratios determined by relationship quantity of labour.

> (1) Not true. Already studied valuation. Commodities have value when *no* production. Value and marginal utility. Puts cart before horse. Not valuable because labour; labour because valuable.

How then labour related value? M[arginal] U[tility] depends [on] supply. Labour modifies supply.

> (2) Much more respectable. In certain circumstances applicable. That is granted certain assumptions valid.

Suppose twice as long to kill beaver as deer? Suppose market? Is it not plausible that if ratio of exchange not 2 deer to 1 beaver tendencies set in motion which bring it about? Suppose 1:1? Then clearly better to get beaver by way of exchange than production (1 deer = 1 hour, 1 beaver = 2 hours). By exchange 2 beavers 2 hours. Therefore people "produce" only deer. Supply of beavers diminish. Deer increase. Change in exchange ratio until equivalent technical production ratio. (Labour cost ratio)

Note: cost *ratio*. Not absolute time on one thing determines *its* value. Comparison with others.

E.g. Beaver 2 hours

---

1 [As Robbins put it in his 'Remarks upon certain aspects of the theory of costs' *Economic Journal* Vol. 44 (March 1934) pp. 1–18 citing F. von Wieser, *Uber den Ursprung und die Hauptgesetz des Wirtschaftlichen Werthes* (Vienna, 1884) pp. 146–70 and *Natural Value* (London, 1893) pp. 171–214, the idea that costs of production reflect the value of alternative uses of productive factors].

2 [The student notes for 1939/40 include: 'Read Wicksteed's 'The Marxian Theory of Value' Shaw's comment and Wicksteed's rejoinder *Common Sense*, pp. 705–33; Robbins included '*Das Kapital*: A criticism', 'The Jevonian criticism of Marx (A comment on the Rev. P.H. Wicksteed's Article by Bernard Shaw)' and 'The Jevonian criticism of Marx: A rejoinder' in his edition of *The Common Sense of Political Economy* (1933)].

2 Days

2 months

True given assumptions. What are these?

1) Market mechanism explained by "utility theory". Equality of individual scales to communal scales etc. etc. (Diminishing demand price. Supply and demand.)
2) Constant cost. Labour time does not vary as production varies. More of this later.
3) Population "equal skilled". Mobility.
4) Population (a) equal natured; (b) attractions.
5) Simple production (production not *joint*).

Granted all these things the theory has validity. As Wicksteed emphasised, it still puts cart before horse. Value of Beaver [is] 2 deer not because [of] cost but because it pays to produce to that margin. But drop these assumptions and it ceases to be applicable. E.g. equal attractions. Swamp and grove. Equal skill. Expert beaver catchers. Joint production. Suppose wine and steel. That is joint production.

Suppose wine = 2x + 3y

steel = 3x + 2y

Which is greater?

Conclusion: Labour Theory only explains simple production in certain circumstances. Drop these and problem still unsolved.

Proceed to these.

B2. Drop assumption equal skill different members society. (Production still *simple*. Heterogeneity of factors as *between* different lines of production, not *within*).

(1) Assume first. Two groups people completely specialized two different jobs. Can't do anything else. In such circumstances if we assume fixed supply work theory of exchange exhausts subject.

 – Each has supply of what produced comes *via* labour not act providence. But supply determined by given conditions. No connection quantity labour.

Exchange determined by consideration already explained. Incomes sum of product prices – no presumption equal.[3]

---

3 [The brief notes for the rest of this lecture (which mentioned non-competing groups and gave the example which appears at the beginning of the next lecture) were crossed through].

10 Production

Non competing groups

Now an intermediate case.
  Mobility within noncompeting groups equal skilled etc. producers.
  Raises general question cooperation. Division of labour.
  Assume two commodities. Fish and Fruit. Possibilities:

(1) A better at fruit, B at fish.
(2) A better at both:

  (a) unequally
  (b) equally.

  Consider numerical example:

In One Day		Fruit	Fish
(1)	A 1	2	1
	B	1	2
(2)a$_1$	A	3	2
	B	1	1

[ADDED LATER:

a$_2$	A	3	2
	B	2	1]
(b)	A	2	2
	B	1	1

Same thing in cost terms. One unit.

		Fruit	Fish
	Days		
1	A	½	1
	B	1	½
2 (a$_1$)	A	1/3	1/2
	B	1	1

[ADDED LATER:

2 a$_2$	A		
	B]		
(b)	A	½	1/2
	B	1	1

One unit.

		Fruit	Fish
(1)	A	1/2(Fish)	2(Fruit)
		2(Fish)	½(Fruit)
2(a)	A	2/3(Fish))	½(Fruit)
	B	1(Fisht)	1(Fruit)

[ADDED LATER:

2 a$_2$	A	2/3	1½
	B½	1/2	2]
(b)	A	1(Fish)	1(Fruit)
	B	1(Fish)	1(Fruit)

Survey possibilities:

(1) A can only get fish at cost of time which involves surrender 2 fruit.

  B can get it at loss of 1/2 fruit. Suppose A concentrates fruit and B fish. A range of advantageous exchanges. 1:1. A gets for 1 what he would have to give 2 to produce. B gets for 1 what would have to give 2 to get.

(2) (a) In order to get 1 fish A surrenders 1½ fruit, while B surrenders only 1.

A range of exchange rates between 1:1½ and 1:1.
Suppose 1:1½. A would get for 1¼ what he would have to give 1½ for if he produced it. B would get 1¼ for what cost 1.
  (a$_2$) Suppose B's efficiency changes:

	Fruit	Fish
A	3	2
B	1	1

If A produces 1 fish he gives up 1½
If B produces 1 fish he gives up 2
If A concentrates on fish –

(2)(b) No advantageous exchange.

Result. Economic subjects concentrate on goods where opportunity cost less.
Classical economists compared ratio of labour costs.
E.g 2a,.

A	1/3	1/2
½		
B	1	1

A's comparative costs
1/3/1 less than ½/1
B's 1/1/3 greater than 1/½
Our conclusion foregone products
Clearly same thing when labour only factor of production in each group.
In other words, let a_1 and b_1 = A's costs and a_2 and b_2 B's costs.
It does not matter whether we compare a_1/a_2 and b_1/b_2 or a_1/b_1 and a_2/b_2.
For $a_1/a_2 : b_1/b_2 = a_1/a_2 b_1 . 1/b_2 = a_1/b_1 : a_2/b_2$.
This fundamental identity of two conceptions clearer when put into diagrams
(Barone).[1] OY Fruit OX Fish.
1 and 2a same case.

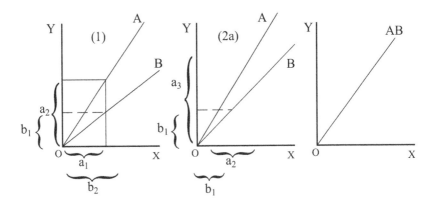

Economic subjects concentrate on products to whose axis slopes *relatively*
nearest.
Thus far division of labour, but only limiting price ratios. Full description equilibrium conditions needs more. Turn diagram round.

1 [E. Barone, *Grundzüge der theoretischen Nationalökonomie* trans. H. Staehle (Bonn: Schroder,
1927); for Robbins's enthusiasm for Barone's diagram see Robbins, *A History of Economic
Thought: the LSE Lectures* eds. S.G. Medema and W.J. Samuels (Princeton: Princeton University
Press, 1998) pp. 213–14].

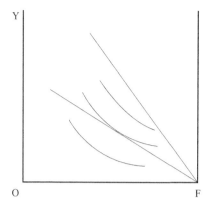

(OY Fish OX Fruit). Same as used already. Suppose no exchange. We know A would produce:

And B likewise. But they are specializing. Therefore A has OF_1 fruit and B – -

If they are monopolists then price indeterminate along a contract curve.

But if typically (equal natured) competitive market demand conditions make price determinate.

Draw offer curve assuming OF fruit.

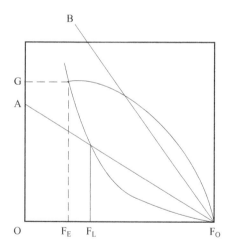

Note Will cut cost slope above F_1 because at that point tangent to indifference curve.

Similarly for B. Equilibrium at P. A retains OF_E and exchanges F_EF_O for OG fish. B –

This enables us to see gains of trade. With OF_E fruit and OG fish A on *higher* indifference curve. (Note: tangent triangle AFO = cost/price fruit in terms fish.) This is *terms of trade*. Bear in mind for I.T. [international trade] theory.

Translate into money terms.

Fake productivity figures 2a:

	Fruit	Fish
A	3	2
B	1	1

Suppose rate of wages £1 per day in both.
Then money costs:

	Fruit	Fish
A	1/3	½
B	1	1

No advantageous trade for A.
No advantageous production for B.
Therefore gold flow.
Suppose rate of wages £2 in A £1 in B.
Then costs:

	Fruit	Fish
A	2/3	1
B	1	1

A still lower fruit cost.
At any rate of wages just above will pay for A to specialize in fruit B in fish.
Suppose rates £3 in A £1 in B.
Then money costs:

	Fruit	Fish
A	1	1½
B	1	1

so that anything above £3 in A would lead to higher prices all around than in B, and therefore gold flow.

Now clearly it is not absolute height of wages which counts. If you multiply both rates by 10 the same follows. It is *relation*. If we look at our last two examples we see that they provide *limiting rates*. Wages in A must be at least 2 and not more than 3 times those in B. But this is same as ratio of least and highest comparative productivity figures. These therefore set limits.[2] Between these demand conditions determine he factorial terms of trade.

The fundamental proposition here is illustrated by Barone:

OY fruit OX fish. Relationship limit of wages follows from identity of price of fruit.

If fruit price same and productivity as 3:1 clearly wages in A 3 times in B. This the upper limit of trade. For lower limit assume price fish identical.

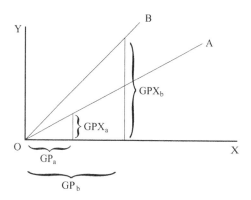

So far *two* commodities only.

Same condition equilibrium namely goods exported lower comparative cost than goods imported. Thus supposing five goods in question – a, b, c, d, e – whose comparative costs (labour):

a_1/a_2 less than b_1/b_2 less than c_1/c_2 less than d_1/d_2 less than e_1/e_2.
That is to say I's superiority greatest in a – least in e –
In equilibrium I's import goods from right. Export goods from left.
What goods actually imported and exported depend on wages. Which in turn
  depend on demand between limits of a_1/a_2 and e_1/e_2.

This can be worked out with numerical examples.
But Edgeworth's apparatus is best.[3]

E
| e'
|
| d'
D
C

---

2 This same with absolute cost differences
3 [F.Y. Edgeworth, 'The pure theory of international trade' *Papers Relating to Political Economy* (1925) Vol. II pp. 3–60].

```
                    |         e'
                    |         c'
      B             |
                    |         b'
      A             |
      A             |
                    |         a'
      0             |
```

Along log scale measure costs in I & II from O and O_1. Slide scale for that $OO_1 = \log W_{II}/W_1$. This brings it about that distance from O = log *money* costs (hence prices in different countries). (Absolute cost differences when OO_1 level and a lower e higher. Comp. when a b c d e lower).

Thus one can read off which "export" goods and which "import" goods.

(If wages equal log $W_{II}/W_1 = 0$).

Clear that if OO_1 changes there may be changes import and export goods.

Limits of wage – difference at a and e when log $W_{II}/W_1 = 0$.

This apparatus particularly important for case of more than two groups.

What said so far noncompeting groups in general. Particularly applicable I.T. geographically noncompeting groups. History classical to modern.

Two points especially applicable international trade theory:

(1) Exchange possible unequal incomes. Only if incomes equal competition fair. This is sheer folly. Barone's diagram final refutation.
(2) But notice competition works in such cases by eliminating areas. Not same in this case. Constant cost except exceptional case. Free trade fallacy.[4]

Read

J.A. Viner, 'The doctrine of comparative costs' *Weltwirtschaftliches Archiv* (1932) p. 356

F.W. Taussig, *International Trade* (1927)

4 [On these two points Urquidi's notes (30/11/38) read:
  '(1) An examination of international equilibrium has shown that it is fallacious to suppose that there will not be equilibrium if incomes are not equa. If incomes are equal it is sheer accident. There is no economic loss in trading with countries of lower incomes. What the theory of comparative costs does not say is that a country with a higher income might lose in competition with a low-income country. (2) The classical theory of International Trade shows that the mutually advantageous process of exchange and division of labour works by eliminating in each area the industries which are not suitable. If there are constant costs, the division of labour in unimpeded exchange results, for example, in all the x being produced in country A and all the y in country B. Therefore it is wrong to say that free trade will not result in the disappearance of some industries. Under increasing costs (as in agriculture), then under completely free trade you will find some wheat-growing in many industrial areas, as well as extractive industries'.

Gottfried Haberler, *Der International Handele* (1933) pp. 99–156[5]

Enrico Barone, *Grundzuge der theoretischen Nationalokonomie* (1927) p. 106

Alfred Marshall, *Money, Credit and Commerce* (1923) Appendix H

F.Y. Edgeworth, 'The pure theory of international trade' *Papers Relating to Political Economy* (1925) Vol. II p. 53

5 This was translated as *The Theory of International Trade* by A. Stonier and F. Benham (London: Hodge, 1936) but Robbins's page reference here is to the German edition.

11 Joint production
Fixed coefficients

So far simple production – one product one factor. Now joint – one product, more than one factor. Scarce "labour". Scarce "land". Scarce unskilled Labour. Scarce skilled Labour.

Problem to describe condition of equilibrium.

All old generalizations hold. Market relative utilities and prices supply and demand expenditure and receipts.

Production costs and prices.

But a new set of problems:

(a) How are factors combined – how much labour, how much land – per product? How to distribute between products?
(b) Pricing of factors. Price of products = cost = sum of incomes. But how are they divided?

A problem of production and a problem of distribution.

To discuss what classical economists called distribution, Austrian imputation. Contrast.

(1) Classical Economists different theories different factors. Rent. Wages. Ours uniform: talk simply of factors. Supply later.
(2) Imputation theory. Tended to take prices products for granted. General equilibrium approach emphasises simultaneity.

Division of theory to depend on technical coefficients.

Nature of these. In order to make 1 knife 1 blade 1 handle. Proportions in which factors need to be combined to make unit of product.

Clearly these can be of two kinds:

(a) fixed – as in case of knife
(b) variable – one hundred bushels of wheat many men little ground [or] few men much ground.

In practice given time most methods production variable. This therefore most important problem. Give most attention to it. Cost theory. Productivity theory.

But deal first with fixed.

Joint production: fixed coefficients

Suppose fixed coefficients. Outlines of problem.[1]

No problem of factor combination – optimal combination. Only one combination by hypothesis. But distribution problem remains (and problem of amounts of commodities produced). We know that product prices given supply = relative utilities. Given product prices demand deduced.

Therefore with given coefficients product prices at different factor prices can be calculated. Therefore given product demands at given factor prices. E.g. If at £2 100 units A demanded and technical coefficient 1:1 then at factor prices £1:£1 100 units A demanded. But if we know amount demanded and technical coefficient we know demand for factors. E.g. If 100 units product demanded at a price and technical coefficients 1:1 then 100 units X and 100 units Y demanded.

Thus demands for products and demands for factors can be written as functions of factor prices.

Not difficult to see that equilibrium solution determinate – Market conditions and –

Prices = costs.

Demand factors equal supply factors.

Easy to see how work out in practice.

Suppose price labour too high to equate supply and demand – unemployment.

Fall wages. Industries in which proportion labour high more profitable, extension demand labour. Extension supply this kind product.

Or suppose demand changes in favour of commodities high proportion labour. Relative wages tend to rise.

Good numerical example of all this in Taylor Chapter XXX.[2] But he takes product prices for granted. Note: solution fails if technical coefficients equal all around. (Analogy: Theory of noncompeting groups).

See

Leon Walras, *Elements d'Economie Politique* (1926) Lecons 20 and 21 [Production Equations and Solution of the Equations of Production]

J.R. Hicks, *The Theory of Wages* (1932)

---

1 No consideration firm etc.

2 [F.M. Taylor, *Principles of Economics* 9th edition (1924)].

12 Joint production

The laws of returns

Assume variability.
New Problems: (i) Equilibrium combination. Pricing
A digression necessary. Laws of Returns. The Production Function.
General statement. Average. Marginal.
Graphical representation:

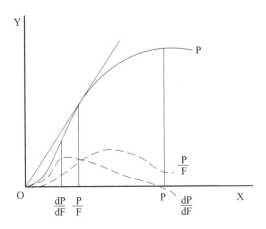

Note three concepts: P, P/F, dP/dF. Max P obvious. P/F clearly reaches maximum at point where a tangent. dP/dF reaches maximum before this at point of inflexion.

Draw derived curves. Note at point where P/F maximum P/F = dP/DF. Two curves cut. Before that point dP/dF above, after below P/F. At max P dP/dF = 0. Look closer find out range relevant. Beyond max P no activity. Not so clear but true no activity below P/F max.

Arithmetical Example. 1 acre.

[Labour]	[Productivity]	[P/L]
1	1	1
2	4	2

3	9	3	
4	16	4	- maximum
7	21	3	
20	40	2	
21	39		

Suppose 2 ap 2.

If land divisible 1/2 acre because 1/2:2 = 1:4 ap 4

Beyond land negatively productive. Similar to third stage.

This [is] clearer [in] three dimensions.

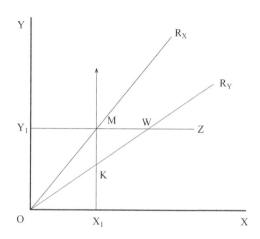

Along X mark off units of one factor along Y of the other (Adjust scales so as to get symmetry). Quantities of product on Z.

Looking down using fixed quantities of X and varying Y

KY_a is maximum average MHY_T maximum total.

A vertical section gives a Knightian curve. Repeat this for every value of X thus generating R_y and R_x. Ridge lines. Suppose however fixed OY – then M maximum average X N maximum total. Thus identity of Knight's stages shown.

At M proceeding parallel to OY we are at an absolute maximum. But proceeding parallel to X average returns to X are beginning to diminish. Between ridge lines activity expected.

Now a stage further. The three dimensional diagram permits us to take horizontal sections. A line at equal height from base will give combination of factors giving *equal product*. The equal product curve.

Looking down from above the isoquant II_1 is a locus of combinations which give equal products – OM.PM = 1.[1] (Analogy indifference curve equal satisfac-

---

1 Distinguish from production indifference curve – two commodities.

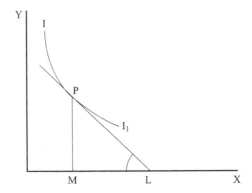

tions.) Clear then that slope at any point shows substitutability of factors. Thus MP/ML tan PLM = subs of X for Y.

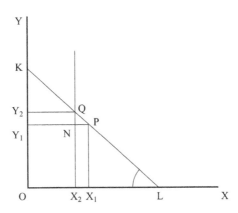

Thus diminish X by 1 X_1 to X_2. To get equal product Y must increase Y_1 to Y_2.

That is 1 X is substitutable for $Y_2 Y_1$ Y or NQ. That is substitutability of X = QN/NP = tan QPN = tan PLO. Conversely subs Y = tan PKO.

But now what determines substitutability? Surely marginal productivity.

If at a certain margin X has m.p. 1 and Y 2 then two units of X subst. for 1 Y so that substitutability in terms of units of other factor is inverse of ratio of marginal productivities.

Now notice certain properties of the curve.

1) Law [of] diminishing returns implies if you lose a unit of one factor you need a more than proportionate increase of other to make up – otherwise constant returns. Hence curve convex downwards. Law increasing rate substitution with diminishing quantities.

2) At point at which average returns of factors maximum becomes parallel to axis.

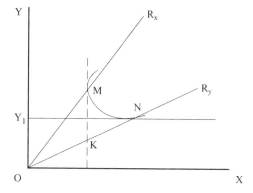

Why? Because total productivity a maximum there while other factor constant.

E.g. at N average productivity Y a maximum. And given OY_1 total product also a maximum. That is marginal productivity x is 0. Since YN is parallel to X axis substitutability X in terms of Y is 0.

That is after N X has negative productivity and more of Y is needed to keep product constant.

(Again note symmetry with indifference).

3) Finally, note just as considering changes demand we considered elasticity – proportionate change in demand/proportionate change in price – so we can consider *elasticity [of] substitution* proportionate change in substitution/proportionate change in ratio of factors.[2]

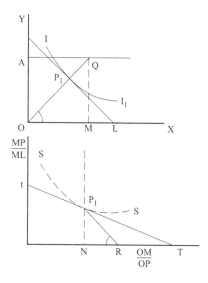

2 [V. Urquidi's notes for 1938/39 give two references on this: 'Notes on elasticity of substitution' *Review of Economic Studies* Vol. 1 no. 1 (October 1933) pp. 67–80 and O. Williams, 'Suggestions

Ratio factors OM/OP. Substitution ratio MP/ML.

To measure elasticity we need to have a curve showing OM/OP along X axis. And MP/ML along Y axis.

This constructed. Take any unit Y say OA. Draw parallel to OX from OP and project to Q.

Mark off ON = AG

Since OA = 1Y ON = AG = AG/OA = OM/MP.

Mark off NR = unit X

Draw RP^1 parallel LP.

Since NR = 1X NP^1 = NP^1/NR = MP/ML SS = locus of such points

Thus e of s at ON = TP^1/tP^1.

Suppose II_1 a straight line.

Then SS_1 horizontal = infinite e of s.

All this time assuming divisibility of factors. Should be clear enough that if one factor is indivisible then increasing returns possible. If on Knightian diagram Y not divisible then may be used in 1st stage (Fixed Plant). Clearly not a question of absolute divisibility, but divisibility in relation to other factor.[3]

---

for constructing a model of a production function' *Review of Economic Studies* Vol. 1 no. 3 (June 1934) pp. 231–5].

3 Pop. Theory. Difference L.D.R.
   1) Returns heterogeneous
      index number
      Population change.
   2) I.R. not ruled out.

13 Joint production

Now back to equilibrium problem.

Assume first very simple conditions. No firms. Landowners. Labourer.

Assume first Landowners hire labourers. Competition. Labourer gets v.m.p. [value of marginal product]. Landowner working D.R. [diminishing returns]. Hires labour constant price. Hiring will not go beyond point addition gross receipts less than addition gross expenses. Nor behind converse.

Diagram. Constant land. OY yield bushels *or* (constant price) value wage rate; OX labour.

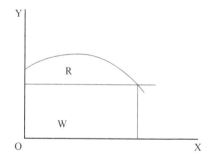

Easy to see how in market demand for labour determined in this way.

But what about landlords rent? Assume position as regards hiring reversed. Labourers hire land. Same process. D[iminishing] R[eturns] land. Same sort [of] diagram.

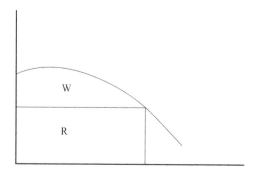

Equilibrium rate of rent = value [of] marginal product. Thus each factor tends to get value [of] marginal product.

Hired factors certainly do. If not demand expands. But if unhired factors don't then can hire themselves out.

Joint production (continued)

Now more realistic method of approach.

Assume entrepreneur (acapitalistic) hiring factors. Demand for factors to be considered. Assume first has decided upon output. Shall abandon this later. Investigate combination of factors at given prices. Object clearly to produce given output at *least cost*. Variation. Condition of equilibrium -

Marg[iginal] prod[uct] A/Price A = M.P.B./P.B.

Suppose it were not so. M.P.A./P.A. greater than M.P.B./P.B. E.g. 10/-/5/- greater than 3/-/2/6 (6/-/5/-) Clearly it would pay to substitute A for B. As A is substituted for B, M.P.A. falls, M.P.B. rises.

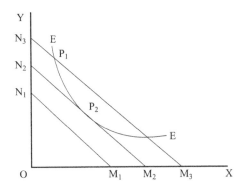

If we know prices of factors then we can represent total outlays by slopes $M_1 N_1$ etc. If a producer is going to produce E he will go to P_2.

Why. Lowest outlay. Notice properties. OM_2P_2 is substitutability X for Y and ratio of prices X and Y. Note substitutability X and Y determined Marginal productivity. So that in equilibrium prices of factors *proportionate* marginal productivity. Note symmetry theory of value.

But not yet proved equal marginal productivities. To do this examine output – hitherto assumed constant. To do this examine relation costs and price etc.

Two cost concepts:

(i) Average cost – cost per unit
(ii) Marginal cost – cost of last unit.

Relation of these: firm.

Suppose all factors variable.

Then variations of output at least cost combination.

Constant costs Av. C = M.C.

Size of firm indeterminate.

But suppose some fixed factor. Then average cost and marginal cost different. How?

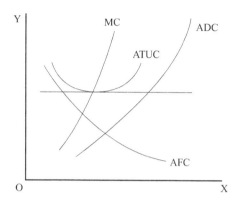

Meaning of curves. Relationship ATUC and ADC and AFC.

Note MC cuts average cost at lowest point. At that point equal to average cost. But can only be equal if average costs constant.

This can be better seen on integral diagram. OY total costs; OX quantity of output.

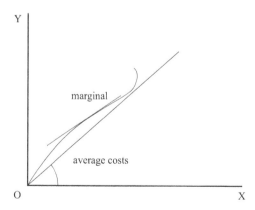

Now consider entrepreneur. He will try to make profits a maximum. How – producing to point where MC = MReceipts. We know marginal costs. What of marginal receipts. In competition equal price.

Hence will produce till MC = price.

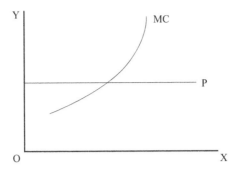

But now a second condition of equilibrium in line of production.

Average cost must equal price. Why? Average cost includes normal profits for entrepreneurs. If average cost less than price, profits more than normal.

Conversely. Hence in equilibrium average cost equals price.

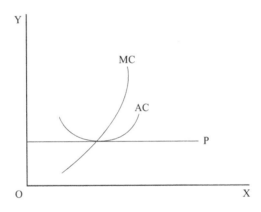

But if this case all along line then normal profits determined m.p. basis. And factors remuneration equal value of product. No abnormal profits. Therefore prices equal costs, equal prices factors.

Note all this depends on assumption some fixed factor to make firm determinate size.

Difficulty [of] conception if *perfect* foresight. Kaldor.[1]

The quasi static state.

Further note on costs values of factors value foregone products.

---

1 [N. Kaldor, 'The equilibrium of the firm' *Economic Journal* Vol. 44 (March 1934)]

See

Philip H. Wicksteed, *The Common Sense of Political Economy* (1910) Chapter XI

J.R. Hicks, *The Theory of Wages* (1932)

J.A. Viner, 'Cost curves and supply curves' *Zeitschrift für Nationalökonomie* Vol. 3 (1931)

Joan Robinson, *The Economics of Imperfect Competition* (1933) Book I Chapter 2 The Geometry Books II Chapter 7 Competitive Equilibrium[2]

2 [Robbins actually wrote 'Book II Chapter I Book III Chapter II' but Robinson's chapter numbers run from Chapter 1 to Chapter 27].

14 Monopoly

So far competition, now monopoly.

Definition – single sale – one seller clearly defined commodity – as distinct pure competition many sellers. Difficulties defining a commodity. Jam supplied by one firm and another actually always impurities of one sort or another present. Our job here abstract case. Patented article typical monopoly case.

Follows at once that will possess opportunity of influencing price. Price varies with supply. Supply is its supply. Therefore demand curve slopes downward. Contrast pure competition demand curve for separate producers a straight line. Problem to describe conditions of e.g. output and price, pricing factors, output.

Assume money is the only object. Therefore maximizing net receipts aim.

No difference here from competition difference consists in that may do this by restricting supply. Under pure competition this impossible.

Old method demonstrating this:

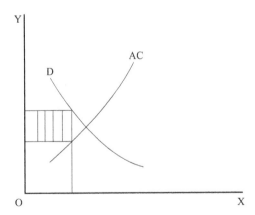

To make area a maximum. See Marshall.[1]

1 [*Principles of Economics* (1920) Chapter XIX].

New method – extension marginal analysis. Small changes. What small changes. Costs. Marginal costs. Difference between producing x and x + Ax.

Difference is between monopoly where others price policy negligible and monopoly where this is not the case. Duopoly problem is *the* problem of Monopolistic Competition. Further analysis possible. Stackelberg etc.[2]

My own opinion learn more here by going over to realistic studies.

[3]So long as the addition to receipts is greater than addition to costs it pays to expand output. If it is less it pays to contract. Therefore equilibrium position MR = MC. Price of output adjusted accordingly.

Diagrammatically:

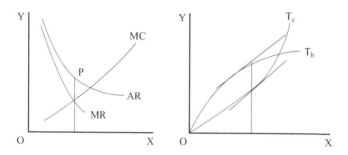

Same generalizations of course apply [to] competition. But here MR and AR are the same:

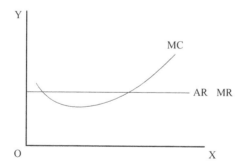

Hence under competition price = MC = MR. Whereas under monopoly since demand curve slopes down. P is greater than MR = MC.

Monopoly profit: the two ways are the area method and the marginal method.

---

2 [H. von Stackelberg, *Marktform und Gleichgewicht* (Vienna: Springer, 1934)].
3 [Here the order of the sheets is confusing; there may be one missing].

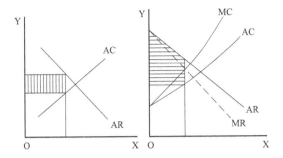

Multiple equilibrium.

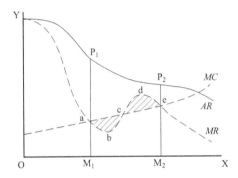

Discrimination. So far simple monopoly. Possibility separate markets.

(Dumping) Tariffs. Price which gives maximum receipts in one market not same as in other. Costs change with output. A complex problem which this appa-ratus clears up.

If e [elasticity of demand] same in both *no* discrimination. Why?

Condition of equilibrium clearly MR in each market = MC total output.

If e same in each and MR same, therefore in equilibrium price will bear same relation to MC. in each.

But if not – suppose *same* price charged. Then MR in less e. market *less* than MR in more. It will pay to contract sales here and extend there.

But this leads to *different* prices.

How conceive equilibrium now. Diagram.

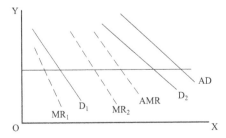

Draw two demand curves (price and quantity). And corresponding MR curves. Sum them. AD = aggregate demand assuming price same in both.

AMR = sales if MR same in each.

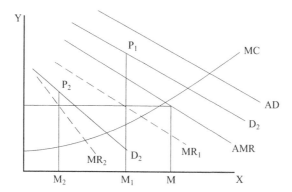

Equilibrium OM where MC cuts AMR. MR must be equal in each market.

So OM_1 equals amount sold in I where MR in that market equals MR in the whole. And OM_2 in II. P_1 in I where M_1P_1 cuts O_1. P_2 in II.

15 Monopoly and distribution

Programme.

(1) Monopoly product competitive factor prices.
(2) Monopsony. (Influence factor prices).

(1) Easy. Recollect Competition. Firm arranged factors so as proportionate to factor prices. Competition brought it about no abnormal profits – price = average cost – therefore equal factor prices. Able to assume physical productivity and value productivity moved together because of competition.

But now by definition competition absent. Will still arrange so that value of physical product proportionate to prices. But not equal – there will be profit. Will go on hiring till marginal cost = marginal revenue.

That is until marginal value product = marginal cost. But marginal value product not equal to value of marginal physical product – will be less.

Formula.

(2) Now monopsony. First general principle of buyer in market where price varies. Indifference curve apparatus.

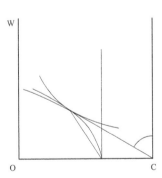

Price now a curve (price goes up as buys more) Position equilibrium where curves tangent – highest position. Marginal utility = marginal cost.

Price different – lower than marginal cost.

Clearly this applies to factors. Factors hired until marginal cost = marginal revenue derived from hiring. Thus under monopoly without monopsony factor prices proportional to value [of] marginal product. Under monopoly, with monopsony this is not so, unless elasticity of supply *same*.

See Mrs. Robinson.[1]

1 [J. Robinson, *The Economics of Imperfect Competition* (1933)].

16 Complex production (continued)
Joint supply

So far dealing with single product firms costs in respect of *one* product. This has expository convenience. But highly unrealistic. In practice exception rather than rule. Moreover definitely misleading in some respects. Adaptability of system greatly underestimated if suppose that for supply to be enhanced of any single product necessary for *new* firms to arrive. Extensions of existing firms. Hence demand for product of one firm more elastic.

Necessary to therefore discuss *joint supply*. Usual stages. Competition. Monopoly.

(1) Competition. $(MR = P)$

Two cases. Proportions (a) Fixed (b) Flexible.

(a) Fixed Proportions: Cotton and Cotton Seed.

Production of quantity of one involves production of other.
If this so *no* marginal cost of each product, only of output as a whole.
Equilibrium therefore when MC of output equals sum of prices of marginal output.

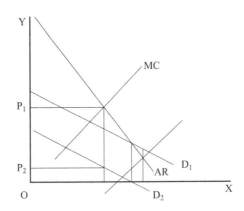

(Diagram constructed by adding separate curves. Note that after D_1 cuts X axis expenses are incurred by the byproduct and AR is less than the price of the other product by the difference between MC and price.)

(b) *Variable proportions.*

Fixed proportions the exception. Usually proportion capable of variation. Wool and Mutton. Metal products using common machinery etc. etc.

Then assignment costs possible. Difference to total costs by small variation of one product.

Each entrepreneur therefore will extend supplies until MC = P in each case.

(2) Monopoly.

(a) Fixed proportions.

Here problem is to make MR on sale of different products equal to cost of all.

But may not be desirable to sell all produced. MR may be negative for amount which for other items of joint supply maximizes receipts.

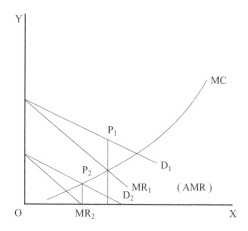

(b) Variable Proportions.

This easier. If variable as we have seen already marginal costs can be ascertained.

And marginal revenue on each equals marginal cost.

Only difficulty arises in interpretation marginal revenue.

If prices of commodities *independent* then straightforward.

$$d(p. x_1)/dx_1 = \delta p/\delta x_1 \; --$$

But if not independent then monopolist has to take account of effect on takings not only of product x_1 but x_2 x_3 etc.

$$p_1 + x_1.\delta p_1/\delta x_1 + x_2.\delta p_2/\delta x_1 = \delta\Theta/\delta x_1$$

Two cases conceivable – cross coefficients negative or positive. Negative when competitive. Positive when complementary.

Competitive lowering of price of first commodity leads to lowering price (demand) of others. Hence, restriction greater than if independent – MR less.

Complementary lowering of price of one leads to increase demand of the other. Hence, restriction less than if independent.

This leads to conclusion that may pay to sell product at price below cost if increase sale of others. Even to give it away.

The loss leader.

Advertising services.

17 Complex production

Oligopoly

So far dealing with cases in which monopolist regards price as function of what he does. Other things neglected. Island of monopoly in sea of competition. This not necessarily the case. Monopolist may have to take account of policy of other. Therefore a few words about this.

Best approached *theory of duopoly*. Theory of duopoly deals with case of two producers (linked no agreement) producing identical product. Clearly variations in output or price of either affects position of other.

First discussed by Cournot: Math[ematical] *Principles [of the] Theory of Wealth. 1838.*[1] 100 years ago; only recently solution. Cournot assumes that each producer assumes others output constant. Comes to conclusion a stable equilibrium. More sold than monopoly less competition.

Worthwhile looking at mode of proof. Take Chamberlain's [sic] example Mineral Springs (no costs).[2]

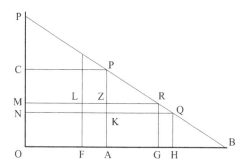

Demand DB. OA = OB rate of supply each spring. Therefore OA + AB = OB total supply. Price OB = 0. Monopoly point OA price AP.

1 [A.A. Cournot, *Researches into the Mathematical Principles of the Theory of Wealth* trans. N.T. Bacon (New York: Macmillan, 1927)].
2 [E. Chamberlin, *The Theory of Monopolistic Competition* (Harvard: Cambridge University Press, 1933)].

Suppose one producer only in action. Sales OA. Then producer II puts AH on market (best he can do). Price falls HQ. Producer I reduced to NKAO. Can increase by reducing to 1/2(0B – AH). Then producer II comes increasing again till each contributes equally.

Total output

$$OB(1 - \tfrac{1}{2} + \tfrac{1}{4} - 1/8 + 1/10 - 1/32 -) = 2/3\ OB = OG$$

Producer I

$$OB(1 - \tfrac{1}{2} - 1/8 - 1/32 - -) = 1/3\ OB = \tfrac{1}{2}\ OG$$

Producer II

$$OB(\tfrac{1}{4} + 1/16 + 1/64 -) = 1/3\ OB = \tfrac{1}{2}\ OG$$

For if either offers OF the best the other can do is ½(OB – OF) = FG.[3]

But now all this depends upon assumption that producer assumes others *output* constant. Suppose had assumed *price* constant. Then different result. Slight lowering of price takes all sales. Hence price competition until at competitive limit (Bertrand).[4] If make slightly different assumptions (divided market) price oscillation. Or (complete knowledge of everything) monopoly price.

Impasse!

Let us go back to fundamental proposition MR = MC. This still applies. *But estimates of MR now influences estimate of what effect of rivals behaviour* (conjectural variation). Now we can plot the output of each duopolist given his conjecture regarding output (and effect on price) of other.

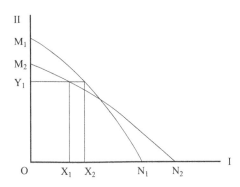

3 Generalizing this, Cournot gets when 100 producers 100/101 OB: unlimited numbers competitive price.

4 [Bertrand's review of Walras, *Theorie mathematique de la richesse sociale* and Cournot, 'Recherches sur les principes de la theorie des richesses' *Journal des Savants* (1883) pp. 499–508].

Which means, given Ox_1 for I, the output of II is Oy_1. *Reaction* curve. But if output of II Oy_1 output of I Ox_{ii}. Equilibrium at point of intersection of reaction curves.

Cournot's case is simply special example where conjectural variations.

Analysis of probable form of reaction curves can be pushed much further. Stackelberg etc. More important for us to realize that this solution is capable of extension to cases where products are not perfect substitutes. Always MR = MC. But MR includes estimate of price policy.

$$MR = d(px_1)/dx_1$$
$$= p_1 + x_1.9p_1/9x_1 + x_1.9p_1/9x_2(9x_2/9x_1)$$

(Hicks Econometrica 1935 p 16)[5]

Complementary and competitive cases. If complementary anticipated consequence expansion raises MR; if competitive lowers it.

Finally extension to oligopoly. *This* is the case of monopolistic competition. Sometimes said that Monopolistic Competition different from Monopoly or Competition. (e.g. Chamberlain [sic]). True but not for reasons alleged. Not product differentiation. Playing with words.

5 [J.R. Hicks, 'Annual survey of economic theory: The theory of monopoly' *Econometrica* Vol. 3 (January 1935) pp. 1–20].

18   Capitalist production
Conceptual

[Note: This lecture comprises two sets of notes, one apparently an earlier version of the other; both are here because the 1938/39 and 1939/40 student notes include material from both.]

Recapitulate.

Timeless production assumed. All factors production used directly.

Drop this. Labour to make bread. But also labour to plant corn, reap it etc. Drink water. Also to make pails etc. Some used *indirectly*. Some products not goods first order.

Clear notion what implies in equilibrium. Hayek's triangle.[1]

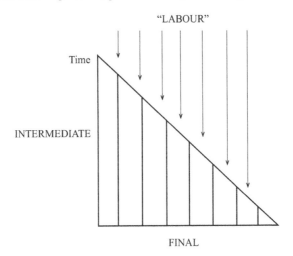

Double meaning of these diagrams. (1) Cross section. (2) History. In equilibrium these *same*. (Difficulties – durable goods. In equilibrium no additions durable goods.)

---

1 [From *Prices and Production* (1931) p. 39].

Monetary explanation. Contrast Money and Real.

1) Real. Employers have possession final product. Exchange it for labour services. (Integrated industry.)
2) Money. Employers have funds part spend on labour, part on intermediate products. Labour spends on final product.

Gross income. Net income.
[ADDED: Douglas. A + B.[2]]
Note conclusions immediately following on conception.

(1) Process involves waiting. If not why not done before – Abstinence
(2) Therefore payments to original factors essentially *advances*.

Confusions with regard to present wages. (a) Walker's examples of wage paid at end of period.[3] This merely accident institution – wage earners in such a case capitalists.[4]

_ _

Hitherto no time.
Now to take account various ways:

1) Production – (Income or Output) fixed.

    (a) Lending and Borrowing. Money now and later on.
    (b) Sale outright permit resources.

2 [The discussion of the 'A + B theorem' of Major Douglas's *Credit-Power and Democracy* (London: Cecil Palmer, 1921) follows Hayek's triangle in both 1938/39 and 1939/40 student notes. Robbins, who had in his youth been attracted by Douglas's ideas, had provided his criticism in 'Consumption and the trade cycle' *Economica* Vol. 12 (November 1932) pp. 413–30].
3 [F.A. Walker, *The Wages Question: A Treatise on Wages and the Wage System* (New York: Holt, 1906)].
4 [The rest of this set of notes was crossed through:
   '(b) Clark's thesis labour receives *present* product.
   This in light of A absurd (Taussig).
   Determinateness W.F.
   Not in sense that cannot have more.
   But sources
   (a) Rents etc. M.P. Theory Unemp.
   (b) Capital. Similar wages future'].

Gives rise to problem of interest *or* better said capitalization; ratio capital and income.

(2) Production capable of change by varying use of factors.

Time element twofold: (a) Making Period (b) Durability.
Two cases important:

i.   Continuous input point output. Fireworks
ii.   Point input continuous output. Walking stick.

Hayek's point (i) = joint demand over time (ii) joint supply.
How relate this to capital concept?
Separation Capital Land
Hayek
Kaldor[5]
But (i) land = capital value.
Moreover entrepreneurs spend money (capital) on wages rents – *all* factors.
Better use in ordinary sense.

(1) Capital values – all factors, even labour if sold.
(2) Proportionate claim.
(3) Sums of money – especially outlays of entrepreneurs.

This leads to structural analysis.
Take continuous input point output case.[6]
Distinction gross and net income or expenditure.
A + B.
Adam Smith on price of products. Veils capital complications. Marx.
That which is not wages rent etc. outlay goes on replacing stock.
Conclusions flowing from this:

(1) Involves waiting, not merely when net saving – can always invest for shorter periods.
(2) Payments for present resources essentially advances out of past output.

Confusions with regard to this:

(a) Walker – wages paid at end of period
(b) Clark synchronized production. See Taussig.

---

5 [The most likely candidates for these references would seem to be Hayek, 'On the relationship between investment and output' *Economic Journal* 44 (June 1934) pp. 207–31 and Kaldor, 'Annual survey of economic theory: The recent controversy on the theory of capital' *Econometrica* 5 (July 1937) pp. 201–33].
6 [Here Robbins drew an even rougher version of the Hayek triangle diagram (III.18.1 above)].

This is true in old wage fund theory.
But erred (4) (a) same for other factors.

(b) Rigid determination.

    –   Some flexibility – monopoly
    –   "Out of capital".

       Durable goods
       Complications
       Depreciation etc.

19 Time preference

So far no reference to exchange in time. This necessary interest theory etc.

Fundamental maxim. Goods of like technical qualities at different times [are] different goods. Eggs at different times. If they can be exchanged price relationship on lines with which familiar. Useful to generalize case for real incomes – bearing on interest theory.

The want structure through time. Constancy – I may have same need £100 now as year hence and so on. Or more or less. Clearly this a function of what I shall have then inter alia. If there exists market I can either borrow or lend and so get a more satisfactory distribution. Analytically this can be dealt with by our apparatus.[1]

Indifferent combinations.

Say £100 this year   95 this year
    110 next year   116 next

etc.

Rate of time preference.

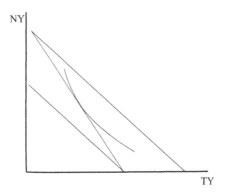

Confronted with opportunity to exchange income this year (OX) and income next year (OY). If equilibrium 45°. If a positive rate more – steeper.

Now combine:

---

1 [Here a very rough diagram is crossed through].

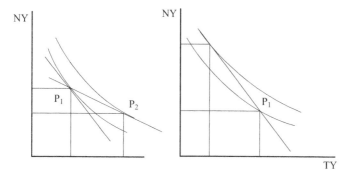

borrowing   lending

In each case rate of time preference equalized to market rate.

Extension market analysis competition shows how market rate itself a resultant of these adjustments.

Extend case buying and selling.

£100 now for £5 in perpetuity.

Buying and selling *includes* lending and borrowing. Lending £100 for year = buying £199 next year.

The ineradicability of interest. Prohibition of loans – doesn't drive it away – all sales have interest element.

20 Capitalistic production
Conditions of equilibrium

[Note: This lecture seems to be an earlier version of the next one and to have been replaced by the latter in 1938/39.]

Back to the main problem. Description [of the] conditions [of] equilibrium.
    Clearly interest essential feature.
    The interest problem stated.
    Interest a difference. Price paid factors. Price realized.[1]
    Why the difference?
    Apparent presumptions:

(a) Imputation
(b) Costs.

        Alternative solutions:
        Exploitation.

    Productivity. Abstinence use etc. all genus of right notion.

1.   Exploitation. Marx. Labour Theory of Value.

    Cost of Production. Labourers. (Not Malthus but monopoly)
    But labours produce more than cost of production. Surplus value.
    Criticism Labour Theory incorrect (unapplicable).
    Monopoly Theory wages incorrect (unapplicable).
    Inconsistency of final step with facts.
    Surplus value only on wage outlays. Therefore industries have larger profits.
Tendency profits equality.
    But of course actual original factors.
    No capital value of these – because capitalization rate (reciprocal time preference zero. (Time Preference infinite).

---

1 Non-durable. Corn bought and sold.
        Durable. Machine. Sums of rents greater than costs.

[By definition no actual value; no savings to buy them].

Provisional justification classical usage. But how meet difficulty. Business usage. Capital invested in land and "capital".

Answer *in equilibrium* this is not so.

All free funds spent *not* on outright purchase of output factors but on produced means of production – services of original factors.

Out of equilibrium from individual point of view this not so. Buying of "land". But buying of "land" not capital accumulation unless seller invests it in additional intermediate products. If consumes proceeds then no net saving in system – system not more capitalistic.

21 Equilibrium capitalist production

[Note: This lecture followed the lecture on time preference in the 1938/39 and 1939/40 student notes. There are two versions of it, which are both reproduced here, since the first version corresponds to the 1938/39 notes, the second to the 1939/40 notes.]

Recapitulate time preference.

Now however production.

Individual able not merely to vary distribution income but also volume by exploitation environment.

The proposition roundabout methods more productive.

In what senses to be understood (a) More same thing (b) more types products preferred.

Exemplified forestry – first one operation then another.

No difference. Time necessary combination with free goods (forestry) or combination of second unit period. Not possible unless combination of earlier period available. Stone breaking. Hammer.

Note:

(1) Not *all* roundabout methods.
(2) No indefinite increase.

Thus a law of diminishing returns of waiting.
Represented in case of forest:

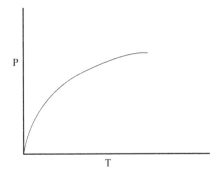

(Much more complex in case of continuous production).

(3) Different products, different functions.Thus two year investment one time say 10 another 9 etc.So that as it were diminishing returns in two dimensions – "backwards" in time and "sideways" given period.

Now turn to the equilibrium problem. Suppose first two year adjustment only.
As in time preference example. Individual now confronted not one position which vary by lending or borrowing. But range [of] options by producing.

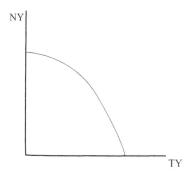

How it will move.

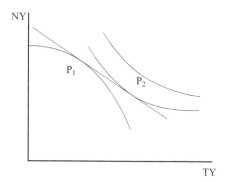

Clearly will maximize present value of opportunities.
(Note how this will change with changes in rate [of] interest).
But then may borrow to "maximize utility". Equilibrium marginal productivity of sacrifice this year's income next = rate of interest = rate of time preference.
Now look at matter vertically so to speak. Entrepreneur planting forest. Saplings may be assumed have value present labour. As we have seen will grow in value. How long to invest money? Not till maximum growth. But until maximum present value.

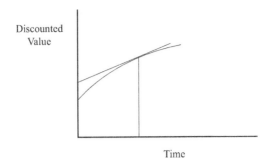

Generalize this. Great complexity of solution. But certain characteristics notable:

(1)   Factors invested at *different* time stages.

Not all processes of equal length.
But productivity of labour etc. at different points equal present value.

(2)   Differences of prices at different stages equal rate interest on capital invested.

But why interest not wiped out – why not processes extended until marginal productivity extensions zero. Answer: nothing analytically against zero interest. If people lived for ever. But if limited life then if rate falls below a certain amount probably tendency consume capital.
Why? Suppose have £1000. Rate 5% – £50 p.a. i.e. in 20 years get interest equal value capital (neglecting compound interest).
But suppose rate 1%. Then £10 p.a. i.e. 100 years to get value capital. Better consume some get higher income unless interested 100 years.
In stationary equilibrium therefore equilibrium rate of interest equal rate Time Preference equal marginal productivity of sacrifice.

See

I. Fisher, *The Theory of Interest* (1930)
K. Wicksell, *Lectures on Political Economy* (1934) Vol. I Part III Chapter 2 Capitalistic Production
G. Cassel, *The Theory of Social Economy* (1923)
Frank A. Fetter, 'The relations between rent and interest' *American Economic Association Papers and Proceedings* 5 (February 1904) pp. 176–98, 227–40
F.A. Hayek, *Prices and Production* 2nd edition (1935)
'On the relationship between investment and output' *Economic Journal* (June 1934)

Now production.
Individual not only able to vary distribution but *volume* of income. "*Dealing*" with environment. Problem Distributive Share.

Great complications here.

Error crude productivity – Capital instrument value £100 earns £5 therefore 5%. This circular – value of machine due to value of product and interest.

Start with simplest case 1 year investment. Range of options.[1]

How move. Maximize present value.[2] Note how changes [with] changes in interest rate. Higher – less for next year. But then borrow to maximize "utility". That is the general solution. But now examine in more detail.

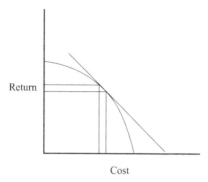

Rate of return over cost.

• Marginal productivity.

How to define? – rate at which all yields discounted to present = to all costs discounted.

How to identify? Two methods conceivable:

(a) variation of physical product variation input
(b) variation value product variation output.

Analogy – flexible and fixed proportions. Joint supply.

Full equilibrium. Factors distributed in space and time so as to equalize value discounted products. (a) Productivity factors. (b) Cost of output value output. No new *rentenguten*. Only replacements desirable and other intermediate products. Price differences equal cost services and interest compared.

Why is interest not wiped out?

Remember [*illegible*] diagram.

Nothing against zero interest save liquidity.

But assumes [*illegible*]

Neglect liquidity. If limited life low interest rates temptation live on capital. £1000 at 5% – in 20 years interest = cap (neglecting compound int.)

1 [Here the same diagram as III.21.2 was drawn].
2 [Here the same diagram as III.21.3 was drawn].

£1000 at 1% – in 100 years
Question interest due Time pref[erence]. Productivity:

(1) Productivity without T.P.
(2) Role of T.P.

Liquidity left for further consideration.
Put another way:

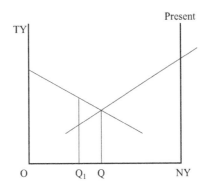

Rate of return [over] cost = difference direct and indirect investment.
Now diminishing returns in another dimension. Three year four year –
Superior productivity roundabout methods. In what sense to be understood
(a) More same thing (b) More preferred product. Forestry. Spectacles. Time necessary combination free goods – or uses of other. Note:

(1) Not *all* roundabout methods.
(2) No *indefinite* increase.Diminishing returns in time
(3) Different products different functions

Again investment rate return cost equal rate of interest or max present value.
Note compound interest – return two year period more than *two* one year
periods.
Discounted products equal.
Now *durable* goods.
Same principle – max[imize] present value or rate [of] return [over] cost = rate
[of] interest.

22 Production

Labour supply

[Note: These brief notes on this topic were followed in the 1939/40 notebook by the 1929/30 notes on 'Equilibrium of Production: Factors Flexible: Labour Supply' which are reproduced as Lecture 8. in Part I.]

Recapitulate.

Treatment capital carried from static to stationary state. Have dealt with capital supply. Now Labour.

Two sources flexibility:

(1) Population
(2) Hours etc.

(1) Population. Is labour supply a dependent variable.

The Slave State.
Equality M[arginal]P[roduct] and M[arginal] C[ost]
Whether large or small population depends on other things.
Cost of Production a technical quantity. Climate Death Rate etc.
Do similar relationships arise
Iron Law Wages
Adam Smith on stationary [state] Adv[ent of] Declining State
Differences. *Sex* not profit and *Death*.
Is this true. China and the East.
But not necessary. The story of Malthus.
Psychological and physiological subsistence.
Bottom out of M[althus]'s essay as regards Misery and Vice. Not as regards [illegible].
Is it convenient. Something in it. But the other things so important that a highly int[eresting] construction.
Heterogeneity of labour force.
(Family allowances)

[(2)] Hours. Why not treat this as independent variable too. Factory Acts etc.

But a difference. Here an active force snowed under. There something vague and weak.

Mode of dealing with equilibrium problem simple.

Isolated Man. A group.[1]

---

1 [At this point Robbins crossed through:

   'Concept of demand [for] income in terms [of] effort.

   Tax theory etc.' and three rough version of his diagrams in his 'On the elasticity of demand for income in terms of effort' article (1930b)].

23 The theory of rent

Meaning of term

(a) Normal
(b) Ricardian

Ricardian theory – fourfold implications:

(a) Why paid?
(b) Static Differences.
(c) Dynamic.
(d) Rent and cost.

Rent and cost. The classical. *Pons assinorum*. Marshall.
The surplus argument. Origin in Labour.

(a) Extensive margin.
(b) Intensive.

This important. Say. Henderson etc.
The Real Cost argument.
Senior –what truth in all this?
Surplus argument.
Individual entrepreneur.
Society. Universality of Diminishing Returns.
Another way of putting productivity analysis.

Real cost

Labour – alternative products.
But "land" also.
What then "truth"?
Labour supply price. "Land" not. (Park land? Not important).
Most important in regard to taxation.

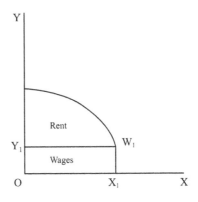

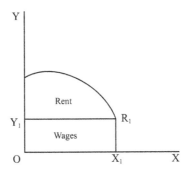

But costs –

Clearly transfer prices. Beet and Turnip. Margin of building.

But some kinds of "land" and other instruments – higher efficiency in one line than elsewhere. Hence payment not price determining.

More specific – the more pure rent.

Relevance of all this quasi rent theory later on.

Comparative Statics

24 Differences in demand for particular commodities

(a) commodity price[1]

1) First stage. Effects of differences with given stocks – or rate of supply.
2) But clearly the important thing differences assuming flexibility of supply.

The Cost curve to be investigated.

3) Does the Cost curve always slope upward.

At first sight if full employment – –
But hypothesis of equilibrium difference from hypothesis of variations.
Competitive Conditions
Traditional doctrine:

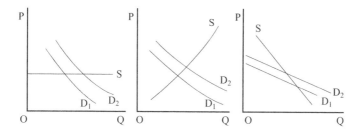

Constant costs   Increasing costs   Falling costs

Incidentally – elasticity of supply[2]

---

1 [The notebook also contains another, apparently earlier, shorter and probably incomplete version of this lecture, which is not reproduced here].
2 [The diagrams derive from R.F. Fowler, 'The diagrammatical representation of elasticity of supply' *Economica* (May 1938)].

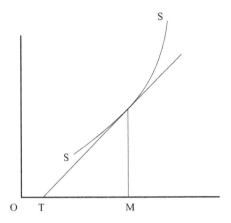

e_s less than 1

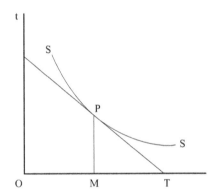

$e_d = PT/P_t = TM/OM$

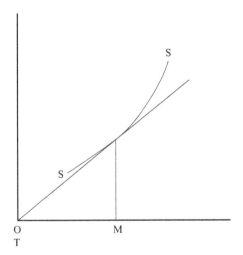

$e_s = 1$

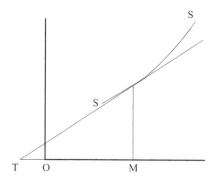

e_s greater than 1
The question is how does this happen?
Constant costs easy. Single factor production inevitable.
If Multifactor production and factor markets large.
Varying cost more difficult.

(1) *Differences*[3] *in value of factors.* Absence of indivisibility etc.

This case of increasing cost. Land more scarce. Worked in. Combinations giv-
ing less productivity. Price rises.
(Not *because* of D[iminishing] R[eturns] – in spite of it.)
Same possible in other direction. Not so much noticed. Probably not important.

(2) Differences assuming indivisibility. Reduction in price of materials etc.
(3) Differences[4] in external framework. road system. External Social Economies.

Technical Economies and Diseconomies.
This logical framework. History of Marshallian Internal and External
Economies.
Is downward sloping curve conceivable under competition.
Tendency to Monopoly – Cournot.[5]
Marshall's distinction.

3 [Here 'Changes' had been crossed out and replaced with 'Differences].
4 [Here 'Changes' had been crossed out and replaced with 'Differences].
5 [A.A. Cournot, *Researches into the Mathematical Principles of the Theory of Wealth* trans. N.T.
Bacon (1927)].

Critique. Shove.[6] Not independent. Dist[inction between] Economies due to changes in firm industry constant and changes industry changing.

What are latter.

Technical.

Value changes – due to indivisibility.

Now all this dealt with under comparative statics. Differences of Static Demand. But in fact more associated with changes of demand with growing population.

External Economies and Population theory.

But note here (1) Partial equilibrium analysis out of place. Disintegration of time and hence supply curve.

(2) Comparative Statics out of place. Irreversibility.

Monopoly

Under competition costs and demand the key.

Under monopoly elasticity of demand more significance. Not merely extent but direction of change.

See this simplest case. Constant cost.

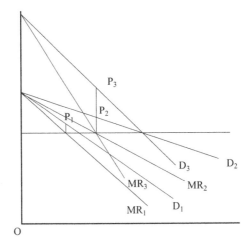

If e [elasticity of demand] same than MR same.

MR = MC.

Therefore no change in price.

But if e less then at same price MR less. Therefore for MR = MC price raised.

If costs vary then new effect.

But cannot say that with increase demand under I.C. price rises and D.C. falls.

6 [G.F. Shove, 'The representative firm and increasing returns' *Economic Journal* 40 (June 1930) pp. 99–116].

For if e increases may offset I.C.

Or if e diminishes may offset D.C.

For further refinements see Mrs Robinson.[7]

To make theory more applicable let us ask how elasticity affected by change of demand.

Four possibilities:

1) Increase due increase individuals. Probable e constant.
2) Increase due increase wealth. Probable e diminish.
3) Increase due increase price elsewhere. e diminishes.
4) Increase due Disappearance rivals.

    (a) Existing customers e diminishes.

    (b) Rivals customers indifferent between remaining e more.

7 [*The Economics of Imperfect Competition* (1933)].

25 Differences in demand for particular commodities

(b) factor prices

Fixed coefficients. Factor prices move in favour of factor proportionately most used.

Flexible coefficients. This offset to some extent substitution.

Diminishing returns makes price rise less.

Take example increase in food. If labour could not be used substituted for land higher rents.

Supply of factors to be taken into account.

Sometimes said analysis only holds full employment. To avoid confusion full employment assumed here. But as controversy has shown difficulties in defining full employment. Easy enough if all supply curves rigid. This Austrian model sometimes employed. But in fact this not case.

Equally case of underemployment – easy define if all supply curves infinitely elastic. But this not case either, some more than others. I conclude that employment controversy a matter of elasticity of supply.

All said above applicable to case of international trade.

Doctrine of causes changes in terms of trade falls under this heading. Increase of relative demand shifts:

(a) ratio between imports and exports
(b) ratio between factor prices at home and abroad.

a and b not same unless costs constant.

Such changes shown in money terms either (a) changes of rate of exchange under paper; or (b) Gold Flows. A favourable movement raises costs and prices of domestic goods. But imports cheaper and bought out of higher incomes.

Difficulties in conception involved by fact that many products imported and exported. Index number difficulties.

Note that favourable turn may hit export.

Diagram shows this:

A in second position gives more w for c. E gets better terms. But less c exported. Practical example.

Finally case of tariff may here be treated. Diminution of demand.

Edgeworth's assumption collective indifference curves.[1]

---

1 ['The pure theory of international values' *Papers Relating to Political Economy* (1925) pp. 3–60].

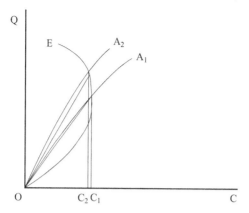

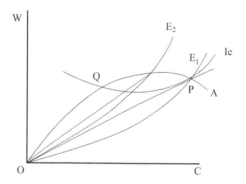

Easy to see that tariff shifts terms of trade in favour.
But if outside PQ then utility loss.
Unrealism of this:

(1) Indifference curves
(2) Single commodity and elasticity curves

(Marshall on his own curves).[2]

(3) Other things equal.

2 [*Principles of Economics* (1920) Chapter IV].

26 Differences[1] in conditions of supply

(a) differences[2] in commodity supply

Let us start with simplest case: purely arbitrary variation supply, X and X + c. Clearly here every[thing] depends on demand.

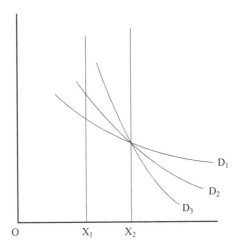

That is on elasticity [of demand]. Can we know this? Schultz and others.[3] Difficulties permanent coefficients.

But direction [of] movement. This is easier. Simple demand and supply formula. But not certain. Why? Necessary to go back elementary considerations demand curve. Remember [how] individual demand curves constructed.

---

1 [Here 'Changes' had been crossed out and replaced with 'Differences'].
2 [Here 'Changes' had been crossed out and replaced with 'Differences'].
3 [H. Schultz, *Statistical Laws of Demand and Supply, with Special Application to Sugar* (1928)].

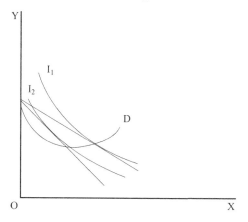

To study reasons [for] curvature. Demand curve refers [to] conditions [in] market. If prices change individual moves one indifference curve [to] another. To
know how changes need know

(a) shapes of curves
(b) relationship

(a) shape curve convex downwards. Law diminishing relative utility.
Increased substitution.
(b) Relations – This needs further study. New construction.

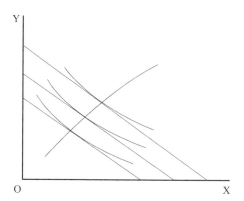

Problem how ind[ividual] dis[tributes] expenditure when *income* changes price
constant. This by representing him with more or less of x or y – price lines parallel. Join points tangency.
Possibilities

Positively inclined   Downward sloping   Backward sloping

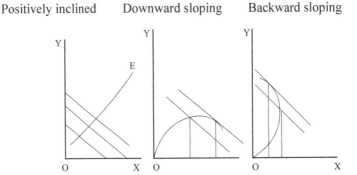

Increase income   Increase income   Increase income
increases X and Y   increases X   diminishes X not Y
                         diminishes Y

One commodity an inferior good consumed at low levels replaced by something else at higher levels. Examples. Margarine. Bread.

This gives rise to new conception [of] elasticity.

Income elasticity =

Relative increase in demand X

Relative increase in income

(prices constant).

Negative elasticity	=	backward sloping
Zero	=	vertical
Unity	=	straight line from origin
Less than 1	=	curving upward
Greater than 1	=	curving downward

Now back to demand curve.

Draw demand curve. P first point equilibrium.

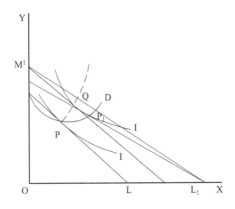

Price X falls L [to] L_1 P_1 new point equilibrium.

Supposing instead price change income change m^1 equilibrium Q. *Because I_1 is convex Q must be above P_1.* Or slope [of] demand curve less than slope [of] expenditure curve.

Moreover obvious that greater elasticity substitution – flatter curve – more difference demand curve and expenditure curve.

Can thus regard price elasticity [of] demand as resultant

(a) increase in income which fall in price [of] X causes?
(b) opportunity [of] substituting X for other goods which fall in relative price affords?

Clear if proportion spent on X large then given fall in price larger income effect than small.

Hence income elasticity larger part.

All this two goods. But same reasoning apply more than two if prices other goods fixed since Y, Z etc. perfect substitutes at fixed price – can be treated as composite commodity.

Clear elasticity [of] substitution X and Y greater more uses Y has. Therefore greater more commodities in Y.

Now should be clear that no a priori reason why individual demand curve [should] slope downward. If X is inferior good income elasticity negative and proportion spent large and elasticity [of] substitution and other goods small then might get demand curve with these qualities. Illustration. Giffen [goods]. Bread.

This is disquieting. *But* clearly not typical. Only possible low levels income and commodities for which no easy substitutes.

And less likely market demand curve in regime inequality. Fall of price brings new people in. Rise shuts out altogether.

Hence for most purposes assume downward curve and ordinary "supply and demand" formula.

27 Differences[4] in conditions of supply

(b) differences[5] in commodity supply continued

Now take into account costs.
This the case of taxes and bounties.
Assume (i) competitive conditions.

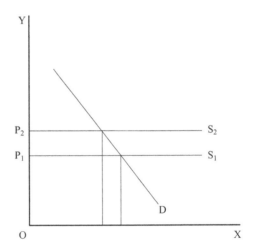

Constant costs.

4 [Here 'Changes' had been crossed out and replaced with 'Differences;'].
5 [Here 'Changes' had been crossed out and replaced with 'Differences;'].

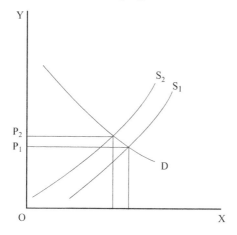

Increasing costs.
[Note here effect on Rents].

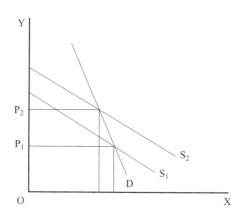

Diminishing costs.

Doubtful how far particular equilibrium analysis.

ii. *Monopoly*

Increase cost – Always raises price and reduces output.

• Contrast increases demand – difficult to be very precise. Two rules:

(i) If costs rising raised less rising

  – constant
  – falling more

(ii) More concave demand curve greater effect tax.

  – In general less than full amount.
  – Only when marginal cost falling faster than demand.
  – Or when demand curve sufficiently concave will rise in price = or greater than Tax.

(iii) Factor prices

Assume competition. At first sight taxes on commodities depress factor prices there. But must remember expenditure.

Therefore in end everything depends on way demand shifted *on the whole*.

Dr Benham[1] shows on assumption [of] diminishing returns: that if industry employing large proportion factor expands then factor prices rise. Why? more labour per unit land – diminishing return [to] labour increasing marginal productivity [of] land.

  Case agricultural.
  Taxes and subsidies.
  Specific and non-specific.
  No benefit non-specific.
  Tariffs.

1 ['Taxation and the relative prices of factors of production' *Economica* (May 1935)].

28 Comparative statics

Inventions

Meaning of term – change technical knowledge – actually adopted inventions treated in theory.

Broad economic effect – to release factors for other things or more things.

- Or to make new things possible.

Thus if willing to compare individuals can say raise social dividend. Move to preferred position. To be introduced must lower costs.

But position of factors?

Assume two factors only. Alternative classifications.

A. They may

(1) raise marginal product [of] A lower [that of] B
(2) raise marginal product A raise B *equally*
(3) raise marginal product A raise B unequally.

B. Better in terms *ratio* of marginal products

(1) Increase A to B
(2) Leave same
(3) Diminish.

Note (1) or (3) need not involve (1) of last classification, but may.

Suppose call A and B Capital and Labour. Then Labour Saving Capital Saving and Neutral Inventions.

If Mobility then probability against Labour Saving which actually diminishes marginal product of Labour. Though maybe a trend to Labour Saving in general (Pigou).

But absence of homogeneity makes more probable.

And absence of mobility still more.

But let us preserve sense of proportion. Employment and output during 19th century. Maybe increase capital.

Employment and Output recently.

Bearing of all this on monetary policy.

Neutral money two conceptions:

(1) Constant circulation
(2) Constant incomes.

If lat[t]er then change in relative share labour for worse – fall in money wages.

If rigid unemployment.

If not neutral.

This a dynamic question.

Again apply case international trade.

Invention which makes terms of trade adverse.

May not lower real incomes even if lowers money incomes. But absent mobility.

29 Comparative statics

Changes in factor supply: labour

A. Assume single factor production. Comp.

    i. Start single labourer.
      Increase *hours*. Increase income.

   ii. Now group. Depends on elasticity of demand for product.
      Note certainly a fall in rate (price).
      But only reduction income if elasticity less than 1.
      This quite possible. Industrial. Geographical.
      Reflections on incentive suggested by this.
      Reflections on mobility.
      The requirements of progress.

  iii. Working Population. Increase hours.

      (a) Assume mobility. Redistribution.
          Elastic and inelastic demand. New products.
          Incomes same. Prices lower. If costs constant relative prices same.

      (b) Assume immobility. Not possible speak of inelastic curve. For curve
          shifts. But still not expandable. Some incomes may fall, some rise
          (money and real).

      Hence importance again mobility.
      Population changes – not so likely.
      Extra demand same sort.

B. Now multi factor production.

Assume two factors. Now income problem more complex even if we assume mobility.

Assume general increase hours. Better go straight to real factors. The Law of Diminishing Returns.

The Clark diagram:

Marginal productivity lowered. Hence *rate* falls. But not necessarily incomes (real). That depends on rate of fall.

If e[lasticity] of d[emand] greater than [1] real incomes raised.

If less fall.

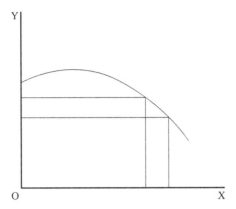

But how about division between factors – relative share. That depends on elasticity of substitution. If greater than 1 then rise; if less fall.

This has bearing on monetary position. If volume incomes constant then change in relative share shown by changes in relative money income.

Now note finally effect on product prices. Prices with high proportion labour lowered. Also proportions production.

30 Comparative statics

Differences in capital supply

Suppose increase capital.
More lengthy methods [of] production.
Not average period. This unnecessary.
General Distribution Theory applicable.
Rate of Interest falls. How much m[arginal] p[product of] capital.
But note especially relative price changes.
Diminution of margin intermediate product prices.
Increase prices durable goods. The more durable the greater the increase.

Dynamics

Final editorial note

In his notes on the 1938/39 lectures, Urquidi, under the heading PART IV DYNAMICS, covers 'The theory of profits' (16/5/39), 'The adaptation of the system to unexpected change: (1) Unexpected changes in relative demand and supply' (which discussed Marshall's period analysis and notion of quasi rents) (23/5/39 and 30/5/39), 'Equilibrating and disequilibrating tendencies' (30/5/39 and 6/6/39) and '(2) Unexpected changes in monetary circulation'. The material for the first two topics derives from Robbins's old notes on 'Profits' and 'Rent, quasi rent and costs'. The third topic, 'Equilibrating and disequilibrating tendencies', introduces the cobweb theorem.

Under the last topic, Urquidi has only the following:

'The real problem of dynamics begins to emerge when you waive the assumption that the money supply is managed so as to maintain the total money demand equal to the total supply prices.

'Money is to be regarded not only as a medium of exchange, as in the whole of the foregoing analysis, but as the most generalized form of wealth. Even if you assume a constant supply of money, fluctuations in the demand for money may be productive in the short period of disequilibrium. This can be conceived even in a country without banks and a banking system. With a banking system there are the most intricate possibilities of disequilibrium. Besides changes in the demand for money there are changes in saving.'

Ungphakorn, in his 1939/40 notes, helpfully began his notes for DYNAMICS with a comparison of the Outline set in the Calendar: Foreseen & Unforeseen Change; The Theory of Risk and Uncertainty; Profits; The Short Period & the Long; Quasi-Rents; Money & Interest; Industrial Fluctuations, and Subjects dealt with in the 1939/40 Course: 1) The Theory of Risk & Uncertainty – Profits 2) The Period Analysis: Quasi-Rents.

His subsequent, fairly full notes are on 'Theory of Profits' (9.5.40 and 15.5.40), 'Uncertainty & Risk' (16.5.40), 'Equilibrium and Disequilibrium Tendencies' (22.5.40) and 'Equilibrium of the system as a whole' (23.5.40).

The first outlined the history of the theory of profits. The second was based on Knight, Risk, Uncertainty and Profit Chapters XX, VII, VIII and IX and Hicks, 'The theory of uncertainty and profit' Economica 11 (May 1931). *The third discussed the possibility of attaining equilibrium, referring to Hicks,* Value and

Capital *(1939) as well as Marshall's* Principles *Chapter I and Appendix on Barter, and included the cobweb theorem, with references to Kaldor, 'A classificatory note on the determinateness of equilibrium',* Review of Economic Studies *1 (February 1934) pp. 122–36, Henry Schultz,* 'Der Sinn der Statischen Nachfragen' Veroffentlichen der Frankfurter Gesellschaft fur Konjunkturforschung *10 (1930), Umberto Ricci, 'Die Synthetische Okonomie von Henry Ludwell Moore'* Zeitschrift fur Nationalokonomie *1 (1930) and P.N. Rosenstein-Rodan, 'The role of time in economic theory'* Economica *ns 1 (February 1934) pp. 77–97. The fourth covered Marshallian period analysis and quasi-rent, with references to Marshall's* Principles *Book V Chapter V, Joan Robinson's* Economics of Imperfect Competition *and Marshall's letter to J.B. Clark of 11 September 1902 in* Memorials of Alfred Marshall *ed. A.C. Pigou (1925) page 414.*

References

Allen, R.G.D. and J.R. Hicks, 'A reconsideration of the theory of value' *Economica* 1 (February and May 1934) pp. 52–76 and 196–219

Allen, R.L., *Opening Doors: The Life and Work of Joseph Schumpeter Volume I: Europe* (New Brunswick, NJ: Transaction, 1991)

Ammon, A., *Objekt und Grundbegriffe der theoretisches Nationalökonomie* 2nd edition (Vienna: Deuticke, 1927)

Antonelli, G.B., *Sulla teoria matematica dell'economia politica* (Pisa: Edizioni Fochetto, 1886)

Barone, E., *Grundzuge der theoretischen Nationalökonomie* trans. H. Staehle (Bonn: Schroder, 1927) p. 106

Barone, E., *Principii di Economia Politica* 7th edition (Rome: Sampaolesi, 1929)

Benham, F., 'Taxation and the relative prices of factors of production' *Economica* 2 (May 1935) pp. 198–203

Bertrand, J., 'Review of Walras, "Theorie mathematique de la richesse sociale and of Cournot, Recherches sur les principes mathematiques de la theorie des richesses"' *Journal des Savants* (1883) pp. 499–508

Beveridge, W., *Unemployment: A Problem of Industry (1909 and 1930)* (London: Longmans, 1931)

Böhm-Bawerk, E. von, *Capital and Interest* trans. W. Smart (London: Macmillan, 1890)

Böhm-Bawerk, E. von, *Kapital und Kapitalzins Erste Abteilung: Geschichte und Kritik der Kapitalzins-Theorien* 4th edition (Jena: Fischer, 1921)

Böhm-Bawerk, E. von, *Kapital und Kapitalzins Zweite Abteilung: Positive Theorie des Kapitales* (Jena: Fischer, 1889)

Böhm-Bawerk, E. von, *Karl Marx and the Close of His System* trans. A.M. Macdonald (London: Unwin, 1898)

Böhm-Bawerk, E. von, *The Positive Theory of Capital* trans. W. Smart (London: Macmillan, 1891)

Boulding, K., *Economic Analysis* (New York: Harper, 1941)

Bowley, A.L., *The Division of the Product of Industry: An Analysis of National Income Before the War* (Oxford: Clarendon Press, 1919)

Bowley, A.L., *The Mathematical Groundwork of Economics* (Oxford: Clarendon Press, 1924)

Brentano, L., 'The doctrine of Malthus and the increase of population during the last decades' *Economic Journal* 20 (1910) pp. 371–393

Bullock, C.J., 'The variation of productive forces' *Quarterly Journal of Economics* 16 (August 1902) pp. 473–513

Cannan, E., *The Economic Outlook* (London: P.S. King, 1912)

Cannan, E., *A History of the Theories of Production and Distribution in English Political Economy* 3rd edition (London: P.S. King, 1917)

Cannan, E., 'Profit' in *Palgrave's Dictionary of Political Economy* 2nd edition ed. H. Higgs (London: Macmillan, 1926) Vol. III pp. 22–24

Cannan, E., *A Review of Economic Theory* (London: P.S. King, 1929)

Cannan, E., ' "Total utility" and "Consumer's surplus" ' *Economica* 10 (February 1924) pp. 21–26

Cannan, E., *Wealth: A Brief Explanation of the Causes of Economic Welfare* 3rd edition (London: P.S. King, 1928)

Cantillon, R., *Essai sur la nature du commerce en général* ed. H. Higgs (London: Macmillan, 1931)

Carr-Saunders, A.M., *The Population Problem: A Study in Human Evolution* (Oxford: Clarendon Press, 1922)

Carver, T.N., *The Distribution of Wealth* (New York: Macmillan, 1904)

Carver, T.N., 'The place of abstinence in the theory of interest' *Quarterly Journal of Economics* 8 (October 1893) pp. 40–61

Cassel, G., *Fundamental Thoughts in Economics* (London: Unwin, 1925)

Cassel, G., *The Nature and Necessity of Interest* (London: Macmillan, 1903)

Cassel, G., *A Theory of Social Economy* (London: Unwin, 1923)

Chamberlin, E., *The Theory of Monopolistic Competition* (Cambridge, MA: Harvard University Press, 1933)

Chapman, S.J., *Outlines of Political Economy* (London: Longmans, 1911)

Clark, J.B., *The Distribution of Wealth: A Theory of Wages, Interest, and Profits* (New York: Macmillan, 1899)

Clark, J.M., *Studies in the Economics of Overhead Costs* (Chicago: University of Chicago Press, 1923)

Committee on Higher Education, *Higher Education* (London: Her Majesty's Stationery Office, 1963)

Cournot, A.A., *Researches into the Mathematical Principles of the Theory of Wealth* trans. N.T. Bacon (New York: Macmillan, 1927)

Cuhel, F., *Zur Lehre von den Bedürfnissen* (Innsbruck: Wagner, 1907)

Cunynghame, H.H., *Geometrical Political Economy* (Oxford: Clarendon Press, 1904)

Dalton, H., 'The measurement of the inequality of incomes' *Economic Journal* 30 (September 1920) pp. 348–361

Dalton, H., *Public Finance* 5th edition (London: Routledge, 1929)

Davenport, H.J., *The Economics of Enterprise* (New York: Macmillan, 1913)

Davenport, H.J., *Value and Distribution* (Chicago: University of Chicago Press, 1908)

De Quincey,T. *Logic of Political Economy* (Edinburgh: Blackwoods, 1844)

Dobb, M.H., *Capitalist Enterprise and Social Progress* (London: Routledge, 1925)

Douglas, C.H., *Credit-Power and Democracy* (London: Cecil Palmer, 1921)

Edgeworth, F.Y., 'The application of the differential calculus to economics' in *Papers Relating to Political Economy* (London: Macmillan, 1925) Vol. II pp. 367–386

Edgeworth, F.Y., 'Laws of increasing and diminishing returns' in *Papers Relating to Political Economy* (London: Macmillan, 1925) Vol. I pp. 61–99

Edgeworth, F.Y., *Mathematical Psychics: An Essay on the Application of Mathematics to the Moral Sciences* (London: Kegan Paul, 1881)

Edgeworth, F.Y., 'On the determinateness of economic equilibrium' in *Papers Relating to Political Economy* (London: Macmillan, 1925) Vol. II pp. 313–319

Edgeworth, F.Y., 'The pure theory of international values' in *Papers Relating to Political Economy* (London: Macmillan, 1925) Vol. II pp. 3–60

Edgeworth, F.Y., 'The theory of distribution' in *Papers Relating to Political Economy* (London: Macmillan, 1925) Vol. I pp. 43–45

Eucken, W., *The Foundations of Economics* trans. T.W. Hutchison (London: Hodge, 1950)

Fetter, F.A., *Economic Principles* (New York: Century, 1915)

Fetter, F.A., 'Recent discussion of the capital concept' *Quarterly Journal of Economics* 15 (November 1900) pp. 1–45

Fetter, F.A., 'The relations between rent and interest' *American Economic Association Papers and Proceedings* 5 (February 1904) pp. 176–198, 227–240

Fisher, I., *Elementary Principles of Economics* (New York: Macmillan, 1911))

Fisher, I., *Mathematical Investigations in the Theory of Value and Prices* (New Haven: Connecticut Academy of Arts and Sciences, 1892)

Fisher, I., *The Nature of Capital and Income* (New York: Macmillan, 1906)

Fisher, I., *The Rate of Interest* (New York: Macmillan, 1907)

Fisher, I., *The Theory of Interest* (New York: Macmillan, 1930)

Fisher, I., 'What is capital?' *Economic Journal* 6 (December 1896) pp. 509–534

Fowler, R.F., 'The diagrammatical representation of elasticity of supply' *Economica* 5 (May 1938) pp. 213–229

Gossen, H.H., *Entwicklung der Gesetze des menschlichen Verkehrs und der daraus fliessenden Regeln fur meschliches Handeln* (Braunchsweig: F. Vieweg & Sohn, 1854)

Green, D.I., 'Pain-cost and opportunity-cost', *Quarterly Journal of Economics* 8 (1894) pp. 218–29

Haberler, G., *Der International Handele* (Berlin: Springer, 1933)

Haberler, G., *Der Sinn des Indexzahanlen* (Tubingen: J.C. Mohr, 1927)

Haberler, G., *The Theory of International Trade* trans. A. Stonier and F. Benham (London: Hodge, 1936)

Hayek, F.A., 'Das intemporale Gleichgewichtsystem der Preise und die Bewegungen des "Geldwertes"' *Weltwirtschaftliches Archiv* 28 (July 1928) pp. 33–76

Hayek, F.A., 'On the relationship between investment and output' *Economic Journal* 44 (June 1934) pp. 207–231

Hayek, F.A., *Prices and Production* (London: Routledge, 1931) 2nd edition (London: Routledge, 1935)

Hayek, F. von, *Geldtheorie und Konjunkturtheorie* (Vienna: Holder-Pichler-Tempsky, 1929)

Henderson, H., *Supply and Demand* (London: Nisbet, 1922)

Hicks, J.R., 'The theory of uncertainty and profit' *Economica* 11 (May 1931) pp. 170–189

Hicks, J.R., *The Theory of Wages* (London: Macmillan, 1932)

Hicks, J.R., *Value and Capital: An Inquiry into Some Fundamental Principles of Economic Theory* (Oxford: Clarendon Press, 1939)

Hicks, J.R., R.F. Kahn and A.P. Lerner, 'Notes on elasticity of substitution' *Review of Economic Studies* I (October 1933) pp. 67–80

Hobson, J.A., *The Economics of Distribution* (London: Macmillan, 1900)

Howson, S., *Lionel Robbins* (Cambridge: Cambridge University Press, 2011)

Howson, S., 'The origins of Lionel Robbins's "Essay on the Nature and Significance of Economic Science"' *History of Political Economy* 26 (Fall 2004) pp. 413–443

Hülsmann, J.G., *Mises: The Last Knight of Liberalism* (Auburn: Ludwig von Mises Institute, 2007)

Hume, D., 'Of interest' in *Essays Moral, Political and Literary* eds. T.H. Green and T.H. Grose (London: Longmans, 1931) Vol. I pp. 320–329

332   *References*

Jevons, W.S., *The Theory of Political Economy* (London: Macmillan, 1871)

Johnson, A.S., *Rent in Modern Economic Theory: An Essay in Distribution* (New York: Columbia University Press, 1903)

Kaldor, N., 'Annual survey of economic theory: The recent controversy on the theory of capital' *Econometrica* 5 (July 1937) pp. 201–233

Kaldor, N., 'A classificatory note on the determinateness of equilibrium' *Review of Economic Studies* 1 (February 1934) pp. 122–136

Kaldor, N., 'The equilibrium of the firm' *Economic Journal* 44 (March 1934) pp. 60–76

Kaldor, N., 'Recollections of an economist' *Banca Nazionale del Lavoro Quarterly Review* 156 (March 1986) pp. 3–30

Keynes, J.M., *The General Theory of Employment, Interest and Money* (London: Macmillan, 1936)

Keynes, J.M., *A Treatise on Money* 2 vols. (London: Macmillan, 1930)

Knight, F.H., 'Cost of production and price over long and short periods' *Journal of Political Economy* 29 (1921) pp. 304–335

Knight, F.H., 'The limitations of scientific method in economics' in *The Trend of Economics* ed. R.G. Tugwell (New York: Knopf, 1924) pp. 229–267

Knight, F.H., 'Neglected factors in the problem of normal interest' *Quarterly Journal of Economics* 30 (February 1916) pp. 279–310

Knight, F.H., *Risk, Uncertainty and Profit* (Boston: Houghton Mifflin, 1921)

Knight, F.H., 'A suggestion for simplifying the general theory of price' *Journal of Political Economy* 36 (June 1928) pp. 353–370

Komorzynski, J. von, *Der Wert in der isolierte Wirtschaft* (Vienna: Manz, 1889)

Landry, A., *L'Interet du Capital* (Paris: Giard, 1904)

Lavington, F., *The English Capital Market* (London: Methuen, 1921)

Lerner, A.P., 'The diagrammatical representation of elasticity of demand' *Review of Economic Studies* I (October 1933) pp. 39–40

Locke, J., *Some Considerations of the Consequences of the Lowering of Interest, and Raising the Value of Money* (London: printed for Awnsham and John Churchill,1692)

Longfield, M., *Lectures on Political Economy* (Dublin: Milliken, 1834)

Macgregor, D.H., 'Consumer's surplus: A reply' *Economica* 11 (June 1924) pp. 131–134

Macgregor, D.H., 'Family allowances' *Economic Journal* 36 (March 1926) pp. 1–10

Macvane, S.M., 'Analysis of cost of production' *Quarterly Journal of Economics* 2 (July 1887) pp. 481–487

Malthus, T.R., *An Essay on the Principle of Population* 1st edition [1798] reprinted (London: Macmillan, 1926)

Marshall, A., *Money, Credit and Commerce* (London: Macmillan, 1923)

Marshall, A., *Principles of Economics* 8th edition (London: Macmillan, 1920)

Marshall, A., *The Pure Theory of Foreign Trade; The Pure Theory of Domestic Values* (1879) reprinted in LSE Series of Scarce Works in Political Economy (London: London School of Economics,1930)

Mayer, H., 'Bedürfnis' in *Handwörterbuch der Staatswissenschaften* Vol. 2 (Jena: Fischer, 1924) pp. 450–456

Mayer, H., 'Gut' in *Handwörterbuch der Staatswissenschaften* Vol. 4 (Jena: Fischer, 1927) pp. 1272–1280

Mayer, H., 'Untersuchungen zu dem Grundgesetze der wirtschaftlichen Wertrechnung' *Zeitschrift fur Volkswirtschaft und Sozialpolitik* 1 (1921) pp. 431–458 and 2 (1922) pp. 1–23

Menger, C., *Grundsatze der Volkswirtschaftslehre* 2nd edition (Vienna: Holder-Pichler-Tempsky, 1923)

Mises, L. von, *Die Gemeinwirtschaft* (Jena: Fischer, 1922)

Mises, L. von, *Socialism* trans. J. Kahane (London: Jonathan Cape, 1936)

Mises, L. von, *Theorie des Geldes und der Umlaufsmittel* (Leipzig: Duncker & Humblot, 1924)

Mises, L. von, *The Theory of Money and Credit* trans. H. Batson (London: Jonathan Cape, 1934)

Morgenstern, O., 'Offene Probleme der Kosten- und Ertragstheorie' *Zeitschrift für Nationalökonomie* 2 (March 1931) pp. 481–522

Neubauer, J. 'Die Gossenschen Gesetze', *Zeitschrift fur Nationalokonomie* 2 (October 1931) pp 733–53

Pantaleoni, M., *Pure Economics* (London: Macmillan, 1898) Part II chap. I

Pareto, V., *Manuel d'economie politique* (Paris: Giard, 1927)

Pareto, V., *Manuele d'economia politica* (Milan: Societa Editrice Libraria, 1906)

Pigou, A.C., *The Economics of Welfare* 3rd edition (London: Macmillan, 1929)

Pigou, A.C., ed., *Memorials of Alfred Marshall* (London: Macmillan, 1925)

Pigou, A.C., 'Some remarks on utility' *Economic Journal* 13 (March 1903) pp. 58–68

Pigou, A.C., *Wealth and Welfare* (London: Macmillan, 1912)

Puey Ungphakorn, 'Temporary soldiers' [1953] in *Collected Articles by and about Puey Ungphakorn: A Siamese for All Seasons* 4th edition (Bangkok: Komol Keemthong Foundation, 1984) pp 248–94

Ramon Magsaysay Award Foundation, 'Puey Ungphakorn' [1965] in Collected Articles by and about Puey Ungphakorn: A Siamese for All Seasons 4th edition (Bangkok: Komol Keemthong Foundation, 1984) pp 29–53

Rathbone, E., *The Disinherited Family: A Plea for the Endowment of the Family* (London: E. Arnold, 1924)

Ricardo, D., *An Essay on the Influence of a Low Price of Corn on the Profits of Stock* (London: John Murray, 1815)

Ricardo, D., *Notes on Malthus' "Principles of Political Economy"* eds. J.H. Hollander and T.E. Gregory (Baltimore: Johns Hopkins Press, 1928)

Ricardo, D., *On the principles of political economy and taxation* ed. J.R. McCulloch (London: Murray, 1846)

Ricci, U., 'Die "Synthetische Okonomie" von Henry Ludwell Moore' *Zeitschrift für Nationalökonomie* 1 (October 1930), pp. 649–668

Robbins, L.C., *Autobiography of an Economist* (London: Macmillan, 1971)

Robbins, L.C., 'Consumption and the trade cycle' *Economica* 12 (November 1932) pp. 413–430

Robbins, L.C., 'The dynamics of capitalism' *Economica* 6 (March 1926) pp. 31–39

Robbins, L.C., 'The economic effects of variations of hours of labour' *Economic Journal* 39 (March 1929) pp. 25–40

Robbins, L.C., *The Economic Problem in Peace and War* (London: Macmillan, 1947)

Robbins, L.C., *An Essay on the Nature and Significance of Economic Science* (London: Macmillan, 1932)

Robbins, L.C., *The Great Depression* (London: Macmillan, 1934)

Robbins, L.C., *A History of Economic Thought: The LSE Lectures* eds. S.G. Medema and W.J. Samuels (Princeton, NJ: Princeton University Press, 1998)

Robbins, L.C., 'Notes on some probable consequences of the advent of a stationary population in Great Britain' *Economica* 9 (April 1929) pp. 71–82

Robbins, L.C., 'On a certain ambiguity in the conception of Stationary Equilibrium' *Economic Journal* 40 (June 1930) pp. 194–214

Robbins, L.C., 'On the elasticity of demand for income in terms of effort' *Economica* 10 (June 1930) pp. 123–129

Robbins, L.C., 'The optimum theory of population' in *London Essays in Economics: In Honour of Edwin Cannan* eds. T. Gregory and H. Dalton (London: Routledge, 1927) pp. 103–134

Robbins, L.C., 'The representative firm' *Economic Journal* 38 (September 1928) pp. 387–404

Robbins, L.C., *Wages: An Introductory Analysis of the Wage System Under Capitalism* (London: Jarrolds, 1936)

Robertson, D.H., *Banking Policy and the Price Level* (London: P.S. King, 1926)

Robertson, D.H., 'Increasing returns and the representative firm' *Economic Journal* 40 (March 1930) pp. 79–89 and 92–93

Robinson, J., *The Economics of Imperfect Competition* (London: Macmillan, 1933)

Rosenstein-Rodan, P.N., 'Grenznutzen' in *Handwörterbuch der Staatswissenschaften* Vol. 4 (Jena: Fischer, 1927) pp. 1190–1213.

Rosenstein-Rodan, P.N., 'The role of time in economic theory' *Economica* 1 (February 1934) pp. 77–97

Say, J.B., *Traité d'economie politique* (1803)

Schönfeld, L., *Grenznutzen und Wirtschaftsrechnung* (Vienna: Manz, 1924)

Schultz, H., 'Der Sinn der Statischen Nachfragen' *Veröffentlichen der Frankfurter Gesellschaft fur Konjunkturforschung* 10 (1930)

Schultz, H., 'Marginal productivity and the general pricing process' *Journal of Political Economy* 37 (1929) pp. 505–551

Schultz, H., *Statistical Laws of Demand and Supply, with Special Application to Sugar* (Chicago, IL: University of Chicago Press, 1928)

Schumpeter, J.A., *Das Wesen und Hauptinhalt der theoretischen Nationalokonomie* (Leipzig: Duncker & Humblot, 1908)

Schumpeter, J.A., *Die Theorie der wirtschaftslichten Entwicklung* (Leipzig: Duncker & Humblot, 1911)

Schumpeter, J.A., *Epochen der Dogmen- und Methodengeschichte* (Tubingen: J.C.B. Mohr, 1914)

Senior, N., *An Outline of the Science of Political Economy* (London: Clowes, 1836)

Shove, G.F., 'The representative firm and increasing returns' *Economic Journal* 40 (June 1930) pp. 99–116

Smith, A., *An Inquiry into the Nature and Causes of the Wealth of Nations* ed. E. Cannan (London: Methuen, 1904)

Sraffa, P., 'The laws of returns under competitive conditions' *Economic Journal* 36 (December 1926) pp. 535–550

Stackelberg, H. von, *Marktform und Gleichgewicht* (Vienna: Springer, 1934)

Stigler, G., *The Theory of Competitive Price* (New York: Macmillan, 1942)

Strigl, R., *Die ökonomischen Kategorien und die Organisation der Wirtschaft* (Jena: Fischer, 1923)

Taussig, F.W., *International Trade* (New York: Macmillan, 1927)

Taussig, F.W., *Principles of Economics* 3rd edition (New York: Macmillan, 1929)

Taussig, F.W., *Wages and Capital* (New York: Appleton, 1896)

Taylor, F.M., *Principles of Economics* 9th edition (New York: Ronald Press, 1924)

Thompson, H.M., *The Theory of Wages and Its Application to the Eight Hours Question and Other Labour Problems* (London: Macmillan, 1892)

Thunen, J.H. von, *Der Isolierte Staat in Beziehung auf Landswirtschaft und Nationakonomie* 3rd edition (Berlin: Weigandt, Hempel & Paren, 1875

Viner, J.A., 'Cost curves and supply curves' *Zeitschrift für Nationalökonomie* 3 (1931) pp. 23–46

Viner, J.A., 'The doctrine of comparative costs' *Weltwirtschaftliches Archiv* 36 (1932) pp. 356–414

Walker, F.A., *The Wages Question: A Treatise on Wages and the Wage System* (New York: Holt, 1906)

Walras, L., *Elements d'Economie Politique* Definitive edition (Lausanne: F. Rouge, 1926)

West, Sir E., *An Essay on the Application of Capital to Land, with Observations Shewing the Impolicy of Any Great Restriction of the Importation of Corn, and That the Bounty of 1868 Did Not Lower the Price of It* (London: T. Underwood, 1815)

Wicksell, K., *Lectures on Political Economy* 2 vols., trans. E. Classen ed. L. Robbins (London: Routledge, 1934–1935)

Wicksell, K., *Vorlesungen uber Nationalokonomie* (Jena: Fischer, 1913)

Wicksteed, P.H., *The Alphabet of Economic Science* (London: Macmillan, 1888)

Wicksteed, P.H., *The Common Sense of Political Economy* (London: Macmillan, 1910)

Wicksteed, P.H., *The Common Sense of Political Economy and Selected Papers and Reviews on Economic Theory* ed. L. Robbins (London: Routledge, 1933)

Wicksteed, P.H., '"Elementary mathematical economics", "Political economy and psychology" and "final utility"' in *Palgrave's Dictionary of Political Economy* 2nd edition ed. H. Higgs (London: Macmillan, 1926) Vol. I pp. 583–585, Vol. II pp. 140–142 and 857–859

Wieser, F., *Theorie des gesellschaftlichen Wirtschaft* 2nd edition (Tubingen: Mohr, 1923)

Wieser, F., *Social Economics* (New York: Greenberg, 1927)

Williams, O., 'Suggestions for constructing a model of a production function' *Review of Economic Studies* 1 (June 1934) pp. 231–235

Young, A.A., 'Increasing returns and economic progress' *Economic Journal* 38 (December 1928), pp. 527–542

Young, A.A., 'Jevons's theory of political economy' *American Economic Review* 2 (1912) pp. 576–589 (reprinted in *Economic Problems Old and New* (Boston: Houghton Mifflin, 1927))

Young, A.A., 'Marshall on consumers' surplus in international trade' *Quarterly Journal of Economics* 1 (November 1924) pp. 144–150

Young, A.A., 'Some limitations of the value concept' in *Economic Problems Old and New* (Boston: Houghton Mifflin, 1927) pp. 198–212

Index

For Product Safety Concerns and Information please contact our EU
representative GPSR@taylorandfrancis.com Taylor & Francis Verlag GmbH,
Kaufingerstraße 24, 80331 München, Germany

Printed and bound by CPI Group (UK) Ltd, Croydon, CR0 4YY
01/05/2025
01858438-0006